CAMBRIDGE LIBRARY COLLECTION

Books of enduring scholarly value

Classics

From the Renaissance to the nineteenth century, Latin and Greek were compulsory subjects in almost all European universities, and most early modern scholars published their research and conducted international correspondence in Latin. Latin had continued in use in Western Europe long after the fall of the Roman empire as the lingua franca of the educated classes and of law, diplomacy, religion and university teaching. The flight of Greek scholars to the West after the fall of Constantinople in 1453 gave impetus to the study of ancient Greek literature and the Greek New Testament. Eventually, just as nineteenth-century reforms of university curricula were beginning to erode this ascendancy, developments in textual criticism and linguistic analysis, and new ways of studying ancient societies, especially archaeology, led to renewed enthusiasm for the Classics. This collection offers works of criticism, interpretation and synthesis by the outstanding scholars of the nineteenth century.

An Elementary Latin Grammar

Henry John Roby (1830–1915) was a Cambridge-educated classicist whose influential career included periods as a schoolmaster, professor of Roman law, businessman, educational reformer and Member of Parliament. *An Elementary Latin Grammar* (1862) is a complete, concise introduction to the Latin language. Written for classroom use, it presents essential grammatical constructions in the clearest possible manner, using ample material from the classical authors as demonstrations of basic principles. The book guides the reader through noun and adjective declensions and the full array of verb conjugations before turning to prosody and syntax, where Roby's innovations in Latin instruction are most evident. Simple, direct, and based upon examples including texts by Livy and Cicero, the book shows students how to parse basic sentences while also introducing them to more subtle and complex constructions. It remains a useful resource for teachers of Latin, and a fascinating document in the history of education.

An Elementary Latin Grammar

HENRY JOHN ROBY

CAMBRIDGE
UNIVERSITY PRESS

CAMBRIDGE UNIVERSITY PRESS

Cambridge, New York, Melbourne, Madrid, Cape Town, Singapore,
São Paolo, Delhi, Dubai, Tokyo

Published in the United States of America by Cambridge University Press, New York

www.cambridge.org
Information on this title: www.cambridge.org/9781108011211

© in this compilation Cambridge University Press 2010

This edition first published 1862
This digitally printed version 2010

ISBN 978-1-108-01121-1 Paperback

ELEMENTARY

LATIN GRAMMAR.

AN

ELEMENTARY

LATIN GRAMMAR

BY

HENRY JOHN ROBY, M.A.

UNDER MASTER OF DULWICH COLLEGE UPPER SCHOOL,
LATE FELLOW AND CLASSICAL LECTURER OF
ST JOHN'S COLLEGE, CAMBRIDGE.

MACMILLAN AND CO.
Cambridge:
AND 23, HENRIETTA STREET, COVENT GARDEN
London.
1862.

PREFACE.

The following pages will be found to differ very considerably from the Eton Grammar and those formed more or less on its model—for instance, King Edward VIth's and Dr Kennedy's. On this account the Syntax at least may perhaps require one or two careful readings, before the mode in which it deals with grammatical difficulties be fully apprehended. My object has been in the Accidence to state, as accurately as I could within the limits of a book for learners, the inflexional forms in use among the Romans of the best period; and in the Syntax to explain briefly and precisely the use of them. The examples are chiefly from Cæsar, Cicero, or Livy, or such as they might have written; and have been so chosen and so translated as to give frequent subsidiary hints on Latin construction or English translation. Peculiarities, especially those of earlier or later writers and of the poets generally, have been usually left to be explained by the teacher on their occurrence. If the principles given be correct, such peculiarities will not cause much difficulty.

The leading principles and arrangement of the book, especially the Syntax, are chiefly my own, at least so far as direct help goes; but for details throughout I have made the amplest use of Madvig's Grammar. The facts of the Accidence have been almost entirely either derived from it, or corrected by its aid. In the Syntax I may particularly mention the treatment of objective propositions (§ 295. 4), of the tenses, and of the *oratio obliqua;* besides numerous examples. Where my use of his book has amounted almost to an abridgment of some length, his name has been added. I have not often deliberately differed from him. The edition which I have used is the first of the English translation: one correction (§ 81. 3) and some slight additions are from the last edition of the German (1857), to which no attention appears to have been paid in the last edition of the translation (1859).

My acknowledgments are also due to Morell's English Grammar for parts of the analysis (on Becker's system) of sentences; to Key's larger Grammar, 2nd ed. (a book well worth knowing, as it exhibits the results of a very fresh study of Latin) for some examples and useful hints; and to Donaldson's larger Grammar for similar occasional help, but in a less degree. Kennedy's School-grammar (almost always neat and ingenious) has been of some service, chiefly as indicating the amount of information usually required, but also in other ways. Many points of agreement with each of these writers will be found, where I am not conscious of any direct debt. Indeed Dr Kennedy's book I did not become acquainted with till I had written the first draught of the Syntax. My other obligations to books of this class are too slight to deserve separate mention.

There are some novelties in the Accidence which had perhaps better be noticed here. I have followed Madvig in his arrangement of the cases, which commends itself both by its propriety and simplicity: in omitting *mei, tui,* &c. as the direct genitive of the personal pronouns (see § 56); in distinguishing the imperative forms into a present and a future tense; and in omitting *amaminor,* &c. as being a form due only to a corruption of an old singular *amamino.* I have followed Donaldson in referring the gerundive to the active voice, and have given short reasons in a note to § 254. Madvig's view (see his *Bemerkungen*) and Key's appear to me substantially the same.

I have also confined the vocative case to those Latin nouns, substantive and adjective, of the 2nd declension which end in *us:* for in these alone is it different from the nominative. In pp. 12—23 no notice is taken of some rare words, which schoolboys are likely to have little or nothing to do with; and generally, but especially in the Prosody, Greek nouns have been banished to a note (p. 79) and Appendix A. No translation is given in the paradigms of the Subjunctive and Infinitive, but the matter is fully treated in the Syntax (especially §§ 238, 247). The usual translations correspond to but few of the uses of either, and, as I know by experience, constantly lead to blunders. *Prima facie* indeed they are wrong. *Amem* is not *I can love*, nor *I may love:* although the latter may serve in some sentences, the former is better avoided altogether. The term *potential* mood is, I think, product and cause of similar mistakes.

The treatment of much of the Accidence might be greatly improved, if it were the custom of schools to pay more attention to the principles of sounds and letter-changes. But it would not be easy to do this successfully for boys first learning Latin, and I have therefore acquiesced (e.g. in § 25) in an unscientific procedure.

The usual names for the cases, moods, tenses, &c. are retained and used without any reference to their etymological meaning. This appeared to me less objectionable than adding a new nomenclature or fresh selection of terms to those already existing. In the Syntax, the ordinary names of constructions, &c. will be often found appended even where I thought them very bad, e. g. Ablative *Absolute.* Such vague terms as a Genitive or Accusative of *respect* or *reference,* I have endeavoured to avoid. By Active or Passive *voice,* I have generally meant the form only, whether the meaning be transitive or intransitive.

The analysis of the sentence has been simplified from that given in Morell's Grammar; and the terms *secondary* and *oblique predicate* strictly defined (rather differently from Donaldson) and freely used. They will, I believe, be found valuable instruments in syntactical analysis. The logical *copula* is omitted altogether. Whatever may be said in logic, *Pastor est supinus* and *Pastor dormit supinus* are precisely the same grammatically, and *est* has as good a right to be considered the predicate as *dormit*. Moreover, it is very objectionable to treat an adverb as forming the predicate; and yet what is to be done with *bene est* if *est* be the copula?

In treating of the cases and moods, I have endeavoured to deduce *from their use* the proper meanings of each, considering their construction to be determined by this. Such a method is exactly the reverse of the Eton system, which treats the use of particular cases and moods as resulting from the arbitrary preferences of different classes of verbs and adjectives, or the several prepositions, or certain conjunctions. Upon this baseless theory rest the exhibition of the use of the genitive, dative, &c. after adjectives, as something quite separate from their use after verbs; the omission of any leading distinctions between the several cases (partially supplied in K. Edw. VIth's, and still more in Kennedy's Grammar); the separate treatment of their use to denote relations of space and time; perpetual dreams of an ellipse of this or that preposition (now, however, generally disclaimed); of *si*, of *ut*, of *o* with the vocative, of the '*participium existendi*' (a most gratuitous supposition when the language does not possess any participle of being, and *existere*, in good Latin, never denotes 'being'); and what is almost worst of all, rules to explain the moods based upon the frequency of their occurrence with particular conjunctions; in fact, a statistical statement, appealing, I presume, to some theory of probabilities, *substituted* for a rational explanation, even in so important a matter as the subjunctive mood.

But as such rules are often called safe practical guides, to be

used like a rule of thumb, it may be as well to examine one or
two of those most in use, to see how far this is the case. I give
Dr Kennedy's words, that the rules may wear the best face
possible.

1. "Cum duo substantiva diversarum rerum concurrunt,
alterum in genitivo ponitur, *When two substantives of different
things come together, one is put in the genitive case.*" Not to dwell
upon *diversarum rerum* and *concurrunt*, both of which contain
plenty of pitfalls, the rule actually does not state *which* substantive is to be put into the genitive, thus leaving the student to
adopt either the Latin or the Hebrew idiom. Other grammars
have *posterius* for *alterum;* and then we get a rule which has the
singular infelicity of flying in the face of the only case-inflexion
in English nouns. *Cæsar's friend,* Cæsaris amicus, are generally
better English and better Latin than *The friend of Cæsar,* Amicus Cæsaris (i.e. *friendly to Cæsar*), and probably more common.
But a boy does not really use these rules. In writing Latin he
is guided by the English inflexion or the preposition *of;* and in
translating from Latin he reverses the same process besides
thinking of the sense. The rule is carried in his mind as a
collateral piece of knowledge, and is recited as a mere incanta-
tion against the master's wrath with not so much meaning as
Cato's *Ista pista sista,* muttered over a sprain. Dr Kennedy
gives subsequently other rules respecting the genitive of a very
different character ; but what possible good can such a rule as
the above do at any time ?

2. "Dativum ferme regunt verba composita cum adver-
biis *bene satis* male, et cum præpositionibus præsertim his,
Ad ante ab, In inter de, Sub super ob, Con, post et præ." To
which, however, is wisely subjoined "Multa ex his variant
constructionem." But then what becomes of the rule of
thumb ?

The truth is, I believe, that verbs compounded with these
prepositions have other cases and constructions quite as often as
a dative. 2ndly, The rule (I do not speak of the examples

given) makes no distinction between the direct and indirect object, although many of these verbs are transitive, and therefore have both. 3rdly, The dative after such verbs, when it occurs, is only the ordinary dative of the indirect object.

3. " *Quum*, causali sensu, subjunctivum plerumque regit; sed interdum Indicativum:

" *Quod, quando, quia, quandoquidem, quoniam, siquidemque* causali sensu Indicativo gaudent: nisi opus sit subjunctivo.

" *Quum, quando, quoties, simul ut, simul atque, ubi, postquam* temporales Indicativo gaudent: *quum* sæpe subjunctivo, post et ante tempus Præteritum.

" *Dum, donec, quoad, antequam, priusquam* pro sententia loci, nunc Indicativum, nunc Subjunctivum capiunt."

What then should a boy do? first decide on his conjunction, and then put Indicative and Subjunctive alternately? or two Subjunctives for one Indicative? or *vice versâ?* There is not the slightest clue given to the real meanings of the moods in such sentences: all hinges on their comparative frequency after certain conjunctions. *Pro sententia loci* nowhere gets any explanation: *nisi opus sit subjunctivo* may refer to the Oratio obliqua, or to what Dr Kennedy mentions as the Potential and Optative uses, which however he distinguishes from the subjunctive 'as subjoined to particles:' but how, or to which it refers, is not said.

If the meaning of the cases and moods be well grasped, it is very interesting then to notice the natural or accidental attraction of particular verbs, &c. to particular constructions; but it does not appear to me possible to do this adequately within the limits of a boy's grammar. Madvig's does it well, but with much reduction it would lose its value.

If any should object that the treatment of the subjunctive mood in these pages is more difficult than that of the ordinary system, I would venture to ask whether, if so, this may not be due to the fact that the points of difficulty are really ignored in the ordinary system: and let a boy know the rules ever so per-

fectly, he would not be able to explain Latin authors, or know
when to use the subjunctive and when the indicative. But my
own belief is that boys get their first notions of grammar, not so
much from rules as from examples, and that in writing their
exercises they do not obey a precept but follow a precedent.
As they make progress, they will want the rule to fix their
nascent conceptions; and when they want it, they will begin to
understand it. Syntax is never interesting, except to an ad-
vanced or advancing scholar; the difficulty lies in the subject
itself, and cannot be conjured out of it by meaningless mesmeric
passes. If it could, Latin would lose its educational worth, and
the question might be fairly urged whether French or German
would not be more useful to English boys. A boy has no real
mental training unless some abstract thought be evoked, and
Latin syntax cannot be acquired without it. Of course a boy
need not go into the matter fully at first, but had better not get
into a wrong mode altogether.

The treatment of the Cases is more likely to be charged with
want of minute details. It will be found however that many of
the ordinary details are necessary only on the artificial system
adopted: and that others are only poetic, or rare. For boys
writing Latin prose, it is desirable to keep poetic usages in the
background: there will be little trouble with them if boys grasp
well the meaning of the cases. The Latin dative is, I fancy,
the very simplest oblique case in either Latin or Greek, and
seems to me adequately treated for school-boys in two or, at most,
four rules.* Now in Edward VIth's Grammar, the 'Dative after
the Adjective' contains 6 rules: and the 'Dative after the Verb'
22 more, all in large print; of these 5 do not belong to the dative,
but are due to some of the rules having overshot the mark: but,

---

* The list on pp. 88 and 89 might be rendered unnecessary by a boy's
learning from the first to connect an intransitive verb in English with
each of the words named. Appendix D has been added to obviate objections to the method adopted.

if they are deducted, their place is more than supplied by 7 other rules in other parts of the Syntax. A boy must have a good head to understand the use of a case which requires 30 rules to explain it, and 5 others to explain the rules. The Revised Eton Grammar reduces them to 14: Dr Kennedy's to 9 in the Syntaxis Minor. But all these grammars, by laying down arbitrary rules about verbs of *commanding* and *delighting*, make such a perfectly regular use as the accusative after the transitive verbs *lædo, delecto, juvo, rego, jubeo, guberno,* appear as an act of delinquency and violation of a general rule, or, as Dr Kennedy expresses it, 'they are joined to the accusative *contra regulam.*'

It must not be supposed that I regard the analysis of the cases, &c. as carried to its farthest point: I have stopped where I thought practical usage required it. Doubtless (in Latin) all genitives ultimately imply possession (or partition?): all datives, the person (or thing) *for whom.* The ablative has an obscure birth and is somewhat intractable: the accusative Madvig *may* be right in asserting to be the word used without any further grammatical definition than that it is not the subject, and that the notion of *place* is merely subordinate. But whether or not we can talk in such matters of actual historical priority, it seems to me more probable that in this case as in others, Space furnished the primary intuition and gave form and outness to the mental conception: and to this it is no objection that the general conception of *object* is far wider and includes in a sort that of *place towards which.* The genitive is hardly sufficiently appreciated in school-grammars, and its broad distinction from the other cases, as doing for substantives and partly for adjectives, what the nominative, accusative, and dative (and sometimes the ablative), do for verbs, is therefore frequently not caught. The genitive after verbs (§ 200. *b*) scarcely deviates from the proper conception (accuso = causam facio : indigeo = indigus sum, &c.) : certainly even so it is very different from any of the other cases.

The ultimate identity of many of the usages of each case is clearly indicated by their being equally referable to more than one head.

The Completed future is not free from difficulty. That the Latins treat it as a tense of the indicative mood is unquestionable: but could they have told whether *videris* (§ 235. 8) is an indicative or subjunctive? There is, it appears to me, much plausibility in Donaldson's identification of this tense with the perf. subj., as there is also in Madvig's deduction (see his *Opuscula*) of the perf. subj. from the compl. future: if the ground for such distinct subordination of the one to the other is not rather cut away from both by the common origin of *ero* and *sim*, of *amav-ero* and *amav-erim* (=*amav-esim*), which I believe is Curtius' view. Madvig goes the length of supposing a compl. future of the subjunctive as a different tense though the same in form with the perf. subj. This appears to me unnecessary, though his instances, in this case, as always, are very good. But when it is remembered how much more distinctly a completed future fixes events and circumstances which do not yet exist, than a simple future does, it may be doubted whether sufficient consideration has been given to the fact that the 1st pers. sing. which alone differs from the perf. subj., and differs by assuming an indicative termination, is the only one in which any positiveness of assertion respecting the future is natural. A man may speak positively of his own intentions, or may prophesy from knowledge of his own circumstances, but to do so of another must partake much more of the nature of a supposition, or a wish, or a command. *Sed hæc viderint doctiores: non equidem repugnavero.*

If any scholars should honour my little book with criticism either public or private, I shall be very grateful, as it will give me the best chance of improving it; and if objections be but specific, it will matter but little in this respect whether they be kindly or severely urged.

I have now only to thank warmly my kind friends, the Rev. J. E. B. Mayor, M.A., Rev. C. B. Hutchinson, M.A., and J. R. Seeley, Esq., M.A., for many valuable corrections and suggestions given amidst numerous engagements.

H. J. R.

Dulwich College,
October, 1862.

LATIN GRAMMAR.

ACCIDENCE *or*

STATEMENT OF INFLEXIONAL FORMS.

OF THE LETTERS.

§ 1. THE Latin Alphabet is the same as the English, with the omission of the letter *w*. The letters are also written and pronounced nearly the same as in English.

a, e, i, o, u, y, are called *vowels*, the rest are called *consonants*.

Of the consonants,

> •Some are pronounced in the throat, called *Guttural;* viz. *c* (hard), *g* (hard), *k*, *q* (both which have same sound as hard *c*).
> Some are pronounced at the teeth, called *Dental;* viz. *t, d*.
> Some are pronounced with the lips, called *Labial;* viz. *p, b, f*.

Of these *c, k, q, t, p* are called *sharp* consonants (tenues); *g, d, b, flat* consonants (mediæ).

l, r, m, n, are called liquids. Of these *m* is a *labial* liquid, *n* is a *dental* liquid.

s is a (sharp) *sibilant* (or *hissing* letter); *x* is a combination of *ks*.

h is a rough breathing or *aspirate*.

j and *v* are called *semi-vowels*.

R. G.

1

§ 2.   K was a letter but little used by the Romans: Y and Z only to write Greek Υ and Ζ.

C was probably always pronounced hard.

Q was always followed by *u*, and *qu* was pronounced as *kw* in English.

I and U, before a vowel at the beginning of words, or between two vowels, were pronounced like (English) *y* and *w* respectively. V was so pronounced also after *ng*, *l*, and *r*, unless the *v* belonged to the termination of inflexion, as *colui;* sometimes also after *s*, as in *suadeo*. (In this use they are generally written J and V). See § 7.

U (V) and H, when in the composition and inflexion of words they occur between two vowels were often omitted in pronunciation and the syllables coalesced : as *amavisse* (i.e. *amawisse*) is contracted into *amasse: præhibeo* into *præbeo. u* following *v* (*u*), and sometimes *e* following *v*, was changed into *o:* as *quom* for *quum, servos* for *servus, vorto* for *verto.*

M appears to have had at the end of words a faint pronunciation, on which account it was dropped in verse before a word beginning with a vowel.

R was perhaps originally like English *th* in *those:* at least words in the older period written with an *s* (as *arbos*) were afterwards written with *r* (as *arbor*), especially between two vowels, as *Papirius* for *Papisius*. Compare *meridie* for *media die* &c.

S final was at one time omitted in pronunciation. See § 21, 75, and App. F.

§ 3.   According to the mode of pronunciation the Latin consonants may be arranged as follows :

	Non-Continuous, Sharp. (tenues)	Flat. (mediæ)	Continuous, (aspiratæ) Sharp.	Flat.	Liquids.	Semi-vowels.
Guttural (*throat* letters)	C (*k, q*)	G (hard)	H			J
Dental (*tooth* letters)	T	D		R (?)	N	
Labial (*lip* letters)	P	B	F		M	V

§ 4. *Changes of Consonants.* (Madvig.)

When consonants of a different character are brought together, either by composition or by the addition of a termination of inflexion or derivation, one or other of the consonants is frequently changed so as to facilitate pronunciation : Thus sometimes—

(1) A sharp before a liquid is changed into the corresponding flat, as *neg-ligens* from *nec-lego.*

(2) A flat before a sharp, or before *s* is changed into the corresponding sharp (in pronunciation though not always in writing);

as *ac-tus* from *ag-o, scrip-tus, scrip-si*, from *scrib-o.*

(3) By *assimilation,* a consonant is completely changed into that which succeeds it : thus,

(a) *d, t, b* into *s,* as *ced-si* into *ces-si, pat-sus* into *pas-sus, jub-si* into *jus-si* (from *cedo, patior, jubeo*).

(b) *n, r* into *l*: as *corolla* (*coronula*) from *corona, agellus* (*agĕrŭlus*) from *ager.*

§ 5. *Changes of Vowels.* (Madvig.)

If the root-vowel be lengthened in inflection,

ă is generally changed into *e*; as, *ăgo, ēgi.*

If the root-vowel be weakened by an addition before the word,

ă is changed into ĭ if the syllable be open (i. e. ending in a vowel); as, *făcio, perfĭ-cio*: into ĕ if the syllable be close (i. e. ending in a consonant); as, *facio, perfec-tus.*

ĕ is often changed into ĭ (in an open syllable); as, *teneo, contineo; nomen, nomi-nis*; but remains in a close syllable, or before *r*; as, *teneo, conten-tus; fero, effero.*

Conversely, ĭ is changed into ĕ in a close syllable; thus the crude form *judĭc-* makes nom. *judex.*

ŏ in an open syllable often becomes ŭ in a close one; as, *adŏlesco, adultus; cŏlo, cultus*; so the nominative *corpŭs, ebŭr*, compared with *corpŏ-ris, ebŏ-ris.*

u often takes the place of these vowels before *l*; as, *pello, pepŭli; scalpo, exsculpo; famĭlia, famŭlus.*

1—2

§ 6.   Diphthongs are formed by the coalescence of two vowels rapidly pronounced into one vowel sound.   In Latin the diphthongs in ordinary use are

$\left.\begin{array}{l}æ \\ œ\end{array}\right\}$ sounded (in England) like *ee* in *feet,*

au .... *a* in *hall.*

eu=*ū, ei*=*ī, ui*=*ī* (e. g. *huic, cui*), are rarely found.

The Greek *αι, οι, ει* are usually expressed in Latin by *æ, œ,* and *ī.*

æ is changed into *ī* if the radical vowel be lengthened by an addition before the word; as, *lædo, illīdo.*

§ 7.   N.B.   In the rapid pronunciation of two vowels, if the first be a vowel sounded farther back in the mouth than the second, a diphthong is produced: if the contrary, the first becomes a semi-vowel.   Thus (sounding *a* as in *fāther,* o like *a* in *hall, i* as in *machine* and *u* as in *mute*) *ai* (=English *ī*), *au* (=English *ow*), *oi* (as in English) are compound vowel sounds; but *i* or *u* sounded before *a* or *e,* give *ya, ye, wa, we:* hence the consonant sound of *i* (*j*=*y* Engl.) and *u* (*v*=*w* Engl.) in Latin.

OF NOUNS.

§ 8.   Nouns are inflected, that is, have different terminations, in order to denote differences of number, gender, and case.

Nouns are either Substantive or Adjective.   (See the Syntax, § 140.)

1.   Substantives have inflexions of case and number, but each is only of one gender.   But see § 12.

2.   Adjectives have inflexions of number, gender, and case.

§ 9.   There are two *Numbers:*   Singular, used when speaking of one; Plural, used when speaking of more than one.

Three *Genders:* Masculine, Feminine, and Neuter.

Five *Cases,* called Nominative, Accusative, Genitive,

Dative, and Ablative. To which a *Vocative* is added in the singular of some nouns of the second declension (see § 21); and in Greek nouns (see App. A.).

N.B. The accusative, genitive, dative, and ablative are often called *Oblique cases.*

The genitive case often requires the preposition *of* to translate it into English; the dative *for*, sometimes *to;* the ablative *by* or *with.* The signification and use of these cases will be learnt from the Syntax; the forms will be found in the following examples, and are generally referred to five great types, called Declensions. The following general resemblances may be observed:

§ 10. SINGULAR. The accusative case always ends in *m* in masc. and fem. nouns, viz. 1st decl. *am;* 2nd, *um;* 3rd, *em* or *im;* 4th, *um;* 5th, *em.* In neuter nouns it is always like the nominative both in singular and plural.

PLURAL. Nom. and acc. of neuter nouns always end in *a.*

Gen. always ends in *um,* viz. in 1st decl. *ārum;* 2nd *ōrum;* 3rd, *um* or *ium;* 4th, *uum;* 5th, *ērum.*

Acc. of masc. and fem. nouns always ends in *s,* viz. in 1st decl. *ās;* 2nd, *ōs;* 3rd, *ēs* or *īs;* 4th, *ūs;* 5th, *ēs.*

Dat. and Abl. are always alike; and in 1st and 2nd decl. end in *īs;* in 3rd, 4th, 5th, in *bŭs;* viz. 3rd, in *ĭbŭs;* 4th in *ĭbŭs* or *ŭbŭs;* 5th in *ēbŭs.*

§ 10 *a.* The declensions of nouns substantive are (in dictionaries) distinguished by the endings of the genitive case singular; which

in the 1st declension ends in *ae,*

...	2nd	....	*i,*
...	3rd	....	*ĭs,*
...	4th	....	*ūs,*
...	5th	....	*ei.*

§ 11.

DECLENSION I.	DECLENSION II.	
Nom. ending in *a* (Fem.) e.g. mensa, *a table.*	in *us* and *er* (Masc.) e.g. dominus, *a lord*; puer, *a boy*.	*um* (Neut.) e.g. regnum, *a kingdom*.

Singular.

Nom.	mensă	Nom.	dŏmĭnŭs	puĕr	Nom. }	regnum
Acc.	mensam	Acc.	dŏmĭnum	puĕrum	Acc. }	
Gen.	mensæ	Gen.	dŏmĭnī	puĕrī	Gen.	regnī
Dat.	mensæ	Dat. }	dŏmĭnō	puĕrō	Dat. }	regnō
Abl.	mensă	Abl. }			Abl. }	
		Voc.	dŏmĭnĕ			

Plural.

Nom.	mensæ	Nom.	dŏmĭnī	puĕrī	Nom. }	regnă
Acc.	mensas	Acc.	dŏmĭnŏs	puĕrŏs	Acc. }	
Gen.	mensārum	Gen.	dŏmĭnōrum	puĕrōrum	Gen.	regnōrum
Dat. }	mensīs	Dat. }	dŏmĭnīs	puĕrīs	Dat. }	regnīs
Abl. }		Abl. }			Abl. }	

N.B. Most nouns in *er* omit *e* in the oblique cases: as ăger, agrum, agrī, &c. Nouns in *ius* have their vocative case ending in *i*, as fili*us*, Voc. fili.

DECLENSION III.

(On the terminations of the nominative see § 25 : on the gender, § 41—46.)

(a) Masc. or Fem. — Neut.

e.g. navis (fem.), *a ship*; mare, *the sea*.

Singular.

Masc. or Fem.		Neut.	
Nom.	nāvĭs	Nom. }	mărĕ
Acc.	nāvĕm	Acc. }	
Gen.	nāvĭs	Gen.	mărĭs
Dat.	nāvī	Dat.	mărī
Abl.	nāvī (or -ĕ)	Abl.	mărī

Plural.

Nom. }	nāvēs	Nom. }	mărĭă
Acc.		Acc. }	
Gen.	nāvĭum	Gen.	mărĭum
Dat. }	nāvĭbŭs	Dat. }	mărĭbŭs
Abl.		Abl. }	

(b) Masc. or Fem. — Neut.

e.g. labor (masc.), *labour*; e.g. corpus, *a body*.

Masc. or Fem.		Neut.	
Nom.	lăbŏr	Nom. }	corpŭs
Acc.	lăbōrem	Acc. }	
Gen.	lăbōrĭs	Gen.	corpŏrĭs
Dat.	lăbōrĭ	Dat.	corpŏrĭ
Abl.	lăbōrĕ	Abl.	corpŏrĕ

lăbōrēs		corpŏră
lăbōrum		corpŏrum
lăbōrĭbŭs		corpŏrĭbŭs

(c) Masc. Fem.	(d) Masc. Fem.
e. g. judex (masc. and fem.), *a judge.*	e. g. serpens (fem. usually), *a serpent.*

Singular.

Nom.	jūde*x*	serpen*s*
Acc.	jūdĭc*em*	serpent*em*
Gen.	jūdĭc*ĭs*	serpent*ĭs*
Dat.	jūdĭc*ī*	serpent*ī*
Abl.	jūdĭc*ĕ*	serpent*ĕ*

Plural.

Nom. Acc.	} jūdĭc*ēs*	serpent*ēs*
Gen.	jūdĭc*um*	serpent*ium*
Dat. Abl.	} jūdĭc*ĭbŭs*	serpent*ĭbŭs*

DECLENSION IV.	DECLENSION V.

Nom. in *us* (Masc. or Fem.)	*u* (Neut.)	in *es* (Fem. except *dies*, § 48.)
e. g. fructus, *fruit;*	e. g. cornu, *a horn;*	e. g. dies, *a day.*

Singular.

Nom.	fructŭ*s*	Nom.	} cornū	Nom.	diē*s*
Acc.	fructu*m*	Acc.		Acc.	diē*m*
Gen.	fructū*s*	Gen.	cornū*s*	Gen.	diē*ī*
Dat.	fructŭ*i*	Dat.	} cornū	Dat.	diē*ī*
Abl.	fructū	Abl.		Abl.	diē

Plural.

Nom. Acc.	} fructū*s*	cornu*ă*	diē*s*
Gen.	fructu*um*	cornu*um*	diē*rum*
Dat. Abl.	} fruct*ĭbŭs*	corn*ĭbŭs*	diē*bŭs*

§ 12. Some substantives have a different form for the masculine and feminine, and therefore are almost the same as adjectives, and are frequently (esp. class 3) used as such.

Ex. 1. ĕquus, *horse;* ĕqua, *mare:* so tībīcĕn (for tībīcĕnus), *flute-player;* tībīcĭna, *female flute-player.*

2. măgister, *master;* măgistra, *mistress.*

3. victor, *conqueror;* victrix, *conqueress.*

The forms victrīcia, *conquering,* ultrīcia, *avenging,* are used as neut. pl. adjectives.

4. Persă, *Persian man;* Persĭs, *Persian woman.*

5. Phœnix, *Phœnician man;* Phœnissă, *Phœnician woman.*

6. Tyndărĭdes, *son of Tyndărus;* Tyndărĭs, *daughter of Tyndarus.*

7. Thestĭădes, *son of Thestius;* Thestĭăs, *daughter of Thestius.*

N. B. The last two and similar forms are named *patronymics.* The last four are Greek forms.

DECLENSION OF NOUNS ADJECTIVE.

§ 13. Adjectives (in the positive degree) differ from substantives only in having inflexions to denote differences of gender. They may be divided into two classes.

1. Those which have a different form for all three genders.

2. Those which have one form for masculine and feminine, and either another form for the neuter or the same form.

The 1st class has a feminine termination (nom. in *a*) like the first declension; and masculine (nom. in *us* or *er*), neuter (nom. in *um*) like the second declension.

Thus Nom. bon*us,* bon*a,* bon*um;* just like domin*us,* mens*a,* regn*um.*

The 2nd class have terminations similar to the third declension.

(*a*) Those ending in *is,* neuter *e,* as trist*is,* trist*e,* like III. (*a*) nav*is,* mar*e.*

N.B. The ablative singular is always in *i.*

(*b*)　Those ending in *or*, neuter *us*, as meli*or*, meli*us*, like III. (*b*), lab*or*, corp*us*.

The penult however of adjectives of the comparative degree is always long; that of substantives like *corpus* always short.

(*c*)　Those ending in *x*, *as*, *es*, and *ans* or *ens*, (and some others), as feli*x*, nostr*ās*, am*ans*, &c. like III. (*c*) and (*d*); excepting that the neuter acc. sing. is the same as the nominative, and the neuter nom. and acc. plural end in *ia*, as felic*ia*, amant*ia*.

The formation of the cases from the genit. sing. is similar to that of substantives of the III. decl. (See § 25.)

N.B.　In (*b*) and (*c*) the ablative singular ends either in *e* or *i*, but in (*b*) *e* is more usual, and in (*c*) *i* is more usual: (but in ablatives absolute, § 184, always *e*).

§ 14.　1.　Ex. bŏnus, *good.*

	Singular.				*Plural.*		
	Masc.	Fem.	Neut.		Masc.	Fem.	Neut.
Nom.	bŏn*ŭs*	bŏn*ă*	bŏn*um*	Nom.	bŏn*ī*	bŏn*æ*	bŏn*ă*
Acc.	bŏn*um*	bŏn*am*	bŏn*um*	Acc.	bŏn*ōs*	bŏn*ās*	bŏn*ă*
Gen.	bŏn*ī*	bŏn*æ*	bŏn*ī*	Gen.	bŏn*ōrum*	bŏn*ārum*	bŏn*ōrum*
Dat.	bŏn*ō*	bŏn*æ*	bŏn*ō*	Dat.		bŏn*īs*	
Abl.	bŏn*ō*	bŏn*ā*	bŏn*ō*	Abl.			

N.B.　The Voc. Sing. Masc. is bŏn*ĕ*.

So also tĕner (for tĕn*ĕr*us), tĕn*ĕr*a, tĕn*ĕr*um, and other adjectives in *er*, the masculine being declined like *puer*.

2.　(*a*)　Ex. tristis, *sad.*

	Singular.			*Plural.*	
	Masc. and Fem.	Neut.		Masc. and Fem.	Neut.
Nom.	trist*ĭs*	trist*ĕ*	Nom.	trist*ēs*	trist*iă*
Acc.	trist*em*	trist*ĕ*	Acc.		
Gen.		trist*ĭs*	Gen.	trist*ium*	
Dat.		trist*ī*	Dat.	trist*ĭbŭs*	
Abl.			Abl.		

2. (*b*) Ex. mĕlior, *better.*

<table>
<tr><td colspan="2">*Singular.*</td><td colspan="2">*Plural.*</td></tr>
<tr><td colspan="2">Masc. and Fem.   Neut.</td><td colspan="2">Masc. and Fem.   Neut.</td></tr>
<tr><td>Nom.</td><td>mĕliŏr   mĕliŭs</td><td>Nom.⎫</td><td rowspan="2">mĕliōrēs   mĕliōră</td></tr>
<tr><td>Acc.</td><td>mĕliōrem   mĕliŭs</td><td>Acc.⎭</td></tr>
<tr><td>Gen.</td><td>mĕliōrĭs</td><td>Gen.</td><td>mĕliōrum</td></tr>
<tr><td>Dat.</td><td>mĕliōrī</td><td>Dat.⎫</td><td rowspan="2">mĕliōrĭbŭs</td></tr>
<tr><td>Abl.</td><td>mĕliōrĕ</td><td>Abl.⎭</td></tr>
<tr><td></td><td>(*or* mĕliōrī)</td><td></td><td></td></tr>
</table>

2. (*c*) Ex. ămans, *loving.*

<table>
<tr><td colspan="2">*Singular.*</td><td colspan="2">*Plural.*</td></tr>
<tr><td colspan="2">Masc. Fem. Neut.</td><td colspan="2">Masc. and Fem.   Neut.</td></tr>
<tr><td>Nom.</td><td>ămans</td><td>Nom.⎫</td><td rowspan="2">amantēs   amantiă</td></tr>
<tr><td>Acc.</td><td>amantem(*neut.*)amans</td><td>Acc.⎭</td></tr>
<tr><td>Gen.</td><td>amantĭs</td><td>Gen.</td><td>amantium</td></tr>
<tr><td>Dat.</td><td>amantī</td><td>Dat.⎫</td><td rowspan="2">amantĭbŭs</td></tr>
<tr><td>Abl.</td><td>amantĕ (*or* amantī)</td><td>Abl.⎭</td></tr>
</table>

§ 15. The following adjectives are declined like *tristis,* excepting that in the nom. sing. the masculine ends in *ĕr,* and only the feminine in *ris,* the neuter in *re,* as ac*er,* ac*ris,* ac*re.*

ācer, *keen.*	pĕdester, *of the infantry.*
ălăcer, *alert.*	pŭter, *putrid.*
campester, *of the field.*	sălūber, *healthy.*
cĕlĕber, *frequented.*	silvester, *of the wood.*
cĕler (gen. celĕris), *swift.*	terrester, *of the earth.*
ĕquester, *of the cavalry.*	vŏlŭcer, *winged.*
păluster, *of the marsh.*	

September, and other names of months.

The nom. masc. of these adjectives rarely ends in *is.*

§ 16. Some adjectives of the first class have the genitive and dative singular (ending in *īus* and *i* respectively) the same for all genders, as totus, *whole.*

	Singular.				*Plural.*		
	Masc.	Fem.	Neut.		Masc.	Fem.	Neut.
Nom.	tōt*us*	tōt*ă*	tōt*um*	Nom.	tōt*i*	tōt*œ*	tōt*ă*
Acc.	tōt*um*	tōt*am*	tōt*um*	Acc.	tōt*os*	tōt*as*	tōt*ă*
Gen.		tōt*īus*		Gen.	tōt*ōrum*	tōt*ārum*	tōt*ōrum*
Dat.		tōt*ī*		Dat.		tōt*īs*	
Abl.	tōto	tōt*ā*	tōto	Abl.			

Similarly are declined Sōlus, *alone,* ūnus, *one,* ullus (for ūnŭlus), *any,* nullus, *none,* alter (gen. alter*ius*), *the other* (of two), ŭter (gen. ŭtr*ius*), *which* of two (generally interrogative), and its compounds, neuter, *neither,* ŭterque, *each* (of two), &c.

§ 17. In the plural unus is only used with substantives whose plural *denotes* a singular; as, unæ litteræ, *one epistle,* uni Suevi, *the (nation of the) Suevi alone.* So utrique means *each set* of persons; neutri, *neither set,* &c.

§ 18. *Ullus* and *nullus* are the adjectives corresponding respectively to the substantives *quisquam* (§ 57) and *nemo* (of which *neminis* and *nemine* are not used in good authors). The gen. *ullius, nullius* and abl. *ullo, nullo* are also used of persons as *substantives:* so also (rarely) in the dat. *ulli, nulli.*

Peculiar forms of Cases in the several Declensions of Nouns.

§ 19. FIRST DECLENSION.

Genitive Singular.

   (a) Fămĭlia, *a household,* in old expressions has the genitive in *ăs;* as păter familiăs, *the head of the household.* In plural we find both patres familias and patres familiarum for *heads of households.*

   (b) In the older poets sometimes in *āī* as aulāī, *of the hall.*

Genitive Plural. arum is sometimes contracted into *um;* as cælĭcŏlum from cælĭcŏla, *a dweller in heaven.* So drachmum, amphorum.

Dative and *ablative Plural.* In *ābus* in some words; as *deābus, fĭliābus* (old form retained to distinguish them from the dative and ablative of *deus* and *fĭlius*).

§ 20. SECOND DECLENSION. To this declension belongs vĭr, vĭri, *a man.* The nouns in *er* which retain *e* in the oblique cases are sŏcer, *father-in-law*, gĕner, *son-in-law*, Līber, *Bacchus*, vesper, *evening*, and the adjectives asper, līber, lăcer, mĭser, tĕner, prosper, and those (of more than two syllables) ending in fer and ger.

(Probably all these words originally ended in *us:* e. g. *vĭrus, puerus.*)

§ 21. *Nominative.* When a person is spoken to, the *us* is shortened into *e*, thus domĭne audi, *hear, sir* (cf. *ipse* for *ipsus, ille* for *illus* or *ollus.* Compare *Willy* for *William*). In words ending in *ius* the *e* is absorbed by the *i*; thus fīlī (for fĭlie), audi, *hear, my son.* This form is called the *vocative* case. Most *Common* nouns in *ius* have no vocative; but meus, *mine*, makes mī, as mi fĭli, *my son.*

§ 22. *Genitive Singular.* Nouns (substantive, not adjective) whose nom. ends in *ius* or *ium* (except trisyllables with the first syllable short) in the best writers contract *ii* (of the genitive) into *i.* Thus ingĕnium, Gen. ingĕni.

§ 23. *Genitive Plural.* *orum* is sometimes contracted into *um;* as, *fabrum* for *fabrōrum.* So especially names of weights, measures, &c.; as, *nummum, sestertium, ducentum,* &c.

§ 24. Deus is thus declined :

Singular		*Plural*	
Nom.	Deus	Nom.	Di (sometimes Dĕi or Dii)
Acc.	Deum	Acc.	Deos
Gen.	Dei	Gen.	Deorum (or Deum)
Dat. } Abl. }	Deo	Dat. } Abl. }	Dīs (sometimes Dĕis or Diis)

The vocative does not differ from the nominative.

§ 25. THIRD DECLENSION. In this declension the terminations of the nominative are very various.

If, however, the genitive be known, the other cases may be easily formed. Nouns of this declension are divided into two classes, according as the genitive singular has the same number of syllables as the nominative (Parisyllabic nouns), or an increased number (Imparisyllabic nouns).

I. Parisyllabic nouns form their genitive by changing

1. *es, is, e* into *is;* as, nūbes, nūbis, *a cloud.*

2. *ter* into *tris;* as, pătĕr, patris, *a father* (except lătĕr, lătĕris, *a brick*); so also imber, imbris, *a shower.*

căro, *flesh,* makes carnis; sĕnex, *old man,* sĕnis; vīs, *force,* has no gen. or dat. sing., but acc. *vim;* plur. nom. vīres.

II. Imparisyllabic nouns form their genitive by

  1. adding *is* to *l, r, t, n* (*ĕn* is changed into *ĭnis.* cf. § 5).

  Except

fĕl, fellis, *gall.*	ĕbŭr, ĕbŏris, *ivory.*
mĕl, mellis, *honey.*	jĕcŭr, jĕcŏris (also jŏcĭnŏris), *a*
cŏr, cordis, *a heart.*	*liver.*
fār, farris, *corn.*	fĕmŭr, fĕmŏris, *a thigh.*
căpŭt, căpĭtis, *a head.*	ĭtĕr, ĭtĭnĕris, *a journey.*
rōbŭr, rōbŏris, *strength.*	Jūppĭter (=Jov-păter), gen.Jŏvĭs.

  2. adding *nis* to *o;* as, sermō, sermōnis, *discourse.*

  Except

  words ending in *do* or *go,* which change *o* into *ĭnis;* as, virgo, virgĭnis, *a virgin* (but prædo, prædōnis, *a robber;* lĭgo, lĭgōnis, *a hoe*);

  also hŏmo, hŏmĭnis, *a man.*
  turbo, turbĭnis, *a whirlwind.*

  3. changing *x* into *cis* (*ex* into *ĭcis.* cf. § 5).

  Except

nex, nĕcis, *death.*	lex, lēgis, *a law* or *statute.*
fæx, fæcis, *dregs.*	rex, rēgis, *a king.*
vervex, vervēcis, *a wether.*	grex, grĕgis, *a flock.*
sŭpellex, sŭpellectĭlis, *fur-*	rēmex, rēmĭgis, *a rower.*
niture.	strix, strĭgis, *a screech-owl.*
nox, noctis, *night.*	conjux, conjŭgis, *a mate* (i.e.
nix, nĭvis, *snow.*	husband or wife).

  4. changing *s* into *tis* (*ĕs* generally into *ĭtis:* sometimes into *ĕtis:* but quiēs, quiētis; also lŏcŭplēs, lŏcŭplētis (adj.), *wealthy*).

  Except

  (a) dissyllabic neuters in *us,* which make

  ĕris; as, pondŭs, pondĕris, *weight;* so also vĕtus, vĕtĕris (adj.), *old,* and others;

  or *ŏris;* as, pĕcŭs, pĕcŏris, *cattle,* and others;
  also lĕpus, lĕpŏris, *a hare* (masc.).

(*b*) the following, which change *s* into *ris:*

mōs, mōris, *custom, whim.*	tellūs, tellūris, *the earth.*
flōs, flōris, *a flower.*	æs, æris, *bronze.*
ōs, ōris, *mouth, face.*	glīs, glīris, *a dormouse.*
rūs, rūris, *the country.*	mās, măris, *a male.*
tūs, tūris, *incense.*	pulvĭs, pulvĕris, *dust.*
jūs, jūris, *law;* also a *sauce.*	cĭnĭs, cĭnĕris, *ashes.*
crūs, crūris, *a leg.*	sanguĭs, sanguĭnis, *blood.*
mūs, mūris, *a mouse.*	pūbĕs, pūbĕris (adj.), *grown up.*

(*c*) the following, which change *s* into *dis:*

vās, vădis, *a bail* (i.e. *surety*).	chlămȳs, chlămȳdis, *a cloak.*
pēs, pĕdis, *a foot,* and its compounds.	trĭpūs, trĭpŏdis, *a tripod.*
	custōs, custōdis, *a keeper.*
obsĕs, obsĭdis, *a hostage.*	laus, laudis, *praise.*
præsĕs, præsĭdis, *a protector.*	fraus, fraudis, *fraud.*
	incūs, incūdis, *an anvil.*
dēsĕs, dēsĭdis (adj.), *inactive.*	pălūs, pălūdis, *a marsh.*
	pĕcŭs, pĕcŭdis, *a beast* (i.e. cow, sheep, &c.)
rĕsĕs, rĕsĭdis (adj.), *sluggish.*	glans, glandis, *an acorn.*
	frons, frondis, *a leaf.*
tyrannĭs, tyrannĭdis, *tyranny.*	urbs, urbis, *a city.*
	præs, prædis, *a surety.*
lăpĭs, lăpĭdis, *a pebble.*	hērēs, hērēdis, *an heir.*
cassĭs, cassĭdis, *a helmet.*	mercēs, mercēdis, *hire.*

also excors, excordis, *senseless,* and other compounds of *cor.*

(*d*) and the following, which change *s* into *vis* or *is* or *sis:*

bōs, bŏvis, *an ox.*	cælebs, cælĭbis (adj.), *unmarried* (of males only).
grūs, grŭis, *a crane.*	
sūs, sŭis, *a sow.*	stirps, stirpis, *a root.*
hērōs, herōis, *a hero.*	ădeps, ădĭpis, *fat.*
ŏs, ossis, *a bone.*	forceps, forcĭpis, *pincers.*
ās, assis, *a pound.*	mūnĭceps, mūnĭcĭpis, *a freeman of a town,* from căpio;
vās, vāsis, *a vessel* (in plur. of the 2d declen.)	but the compounds of căpŭt
hiems, hiĕmis, *winter.*	change *s* into *ĭtis;* as, præceps, præcĭpĭtis (adj.), *headlong.*
trabs, trăbis, *a beam.*	

5. Nouns ending in *a* add *tis;* as, pŏēma, poēmătis, *a poem.* So lăc, lactis, *milk.*

§ 26. *Acc. Sing.* (*a*) The following make *im* in the accusative :

vis, *force.*   sĭtis, *thirst.*
tussis, *a cough.*   ămussis, *a* (*carpenter's*) *rule.*

So also names of rivers, towns, &c. ending in *is*, as Tibĕris, Hispălis.

(*b*) The following make both *im* and *em :*

turris, *a tower.*   puppis, *the stern of a ship.*
nāvis, *a ship.*   clāvis, *a key.*
restis, *a rope.*   febris, *a fever.*
pelvis, *a basin.*   sĕcūris, *an axe.*
messis, *harvest.*

§ 27. *Abl. Sing.* Those nouns make the ablative in *i* which make the accusative in *im.* Also *ignis*, and a few others.

Also neuters, which have nominative in *e, al, ar* (except *jŭbar, far, nectar*). In the poets we have also abl. *rete, mare.*

Those nouns make the ablative in *i* or *e* which make the accusative in *im* or *em;* but *reste, sĕcuri* always. (For adjectives, see § 13.)

§ 28. *Nom. Plur.* Neuter nouns make nom. in *ia*, which make ablative sing. in *i.* Also the neuters of all adjectives of the 2nd class, except the comparative degree, and *vĕtus.*

But of adjectives of one termination (§ 13, *c*) only those which end in *ans* or *ens*, in *as* (rarely), *rs, ax, ix* and *ox*, and numeral adjectives in *plex*, have any neuter plural. Also in later writers *hebes, teres, quadrupes, versicolor.* Add also some occasional datives and ablatives, e. g. *supplicibus* verbis, *discoloribus* signis.

§ 29. *Gen. Plur.* The following make their genitive in *ium :*

a. Neuter nouns ending in *e, al, ar* (gen. *āris*).

b. Parisyllabic nouns (including adjectives of the 2nd class), except *păter, māter, frāter, sĕnex, jŭvĕnis, vātes, cănis.*

c. Nouns (including adjectives and participles) ending in *x* or *s* preceded by a consonant (except *ps*, also cælebs). These sometimes have the genitive in *um* also : but this chiefly in the poets. It is very rare in parisyllabic adjectives.

d. Also the monosyllables: mās, *a male;* mūs, *a mouse;* nix, *snow;* nox, *night;* ŏs, *a bone;* pax, *peace;* lis, *lawsuit;* dōs, *a dowry*; glīs, *a dormouse;* vīs (gen. vīrium), *force.*

N.B. The genitives plural of cor, *heart;* cos, *whetstone;* rus, *country;* sal, *salt;* sol, *sun;* vas, *gen.* vădis, *surety,* do not occur. MADVIG.

§ 30. *Acc. Plur.* This is in many editions written *īs,* not *es;* as, cædes, *slaughter;* acc. plur. *cædīs.* Both forms are contractions of *eis.* And the same form sometimes occurs in the *nom.* plural also.

FOURTH DECLENSION.

§ 31. *Dat. Sing. Ui* is often contracted into *u,* as *ĕquĭtātu* for *equitatui;* and this appears to be universal in neuter nouns.

§ 32. *Dat.* ⎱ *Plur.* The following nouns have *ubus* instead
$\quad\quad$ *Abl.* ⎰ of *ibus:*

ăcus, *a needle.*	artus, *a limb.*
arcus, *a bow.*	portus, *a port.*
lăcus, *a lake.*	partus, *a birth.*
quercus, *an oak.*	trĭbus, *a tribe.*
spĕcus, *a cave.*	vĕru, *a spit.*

§ 33. Dŏmus, *a house,* is thus declined:

Singular.		Plural.	
Nom.	domŭs	Nom.	domūs.
Acc.	domum	Acc.	domos (rarely domūs).
Gen.	domūs	Gen.	domuum, or domōrum.
Dat.	domui	Dat.⎱	domĭbus.
Abl.	domo	Abl.⎰	

Domi, *at home,* is the locative case. See § 201.

§ 34. FIFTH DECLENSION.

Gen. ⎱ *Sing.* Sometimes *ei* is contracted into *ē;* as, *die, acie,*
Dat. ⎰ $\quad$ *fide.*

Plural. The genitive, dative, and ablative are not found in good authors, except in the words, *res, dies,* and *spĕcies.*

GENDER OF NOUNS SUBSTANTIVE.

§ 35. MASCULINE. All names of *males, peoples, winds, months, mountains,* and *rivers.*

The rivers Styx and Lethe are feminine.

The names of months are really adjectives, agreeing with *mensis.*

§ 36. FEMININE. All names of *females, countries, cities, islands, plants.*

Except rŭbus, *bramble;* dūmus, *thornbush;* călămus, *reed;* carduus, *thistle,* &c. which are masculine.

§ 37. NEUTER. All indeclinable nouns.

§ 38. COMMON to masculine and feminine. Names derived from offices, employments, &c. held by either men or women; as, judex, *a judge;* hostis, *an enemy;* dux, *a leader.*

The above general rules must be borne in mind throughout.

§ 39. *First Declension.*

FEMININE. All excepting a few names of men; as, nauta, *a sailor;* agrĭcŏla, *a tiller of the ground;* advĕna, *a new comer.*

§ 40. *Second Declension.*

MASCULINE. Words ending in *us* and *er,* except feminine, alvus, *stomach;* hŭmus, *ground;* cŏlus, *distaff;* and a few others.

NEUTER. Words ending in *um;* also vīrus, *poison;* vulgus, *common people;* pĕlăgus, *the high sea; plur.* pĕlăgē *or* pĕlăgă.

Third Declension.*

§ 41. A. Parisyllabic nouns

1. MASCULINE. Nouns ending in *er*.

Except linter, *a boat*, which is feminine.

§ 42. 2. FEMININE. All words ending in *is* and *es*.

Except MASCULINE:

amnis, *a river*.	ignis, *fire*.
anguis, *a snake* (also fem.).	mānes (plur.) *ghosts*.
axis, *an axle*.	mensis, *a month*.
callis, *a path*.	orbis, *a circle*.
cănālis, *a canal*.	fustis, *a cudgel*.
cănis, *dog* (also fem.).	pānis, *a loaf of bread*.
cassis, *a hunter's net*.	piscis, *a fish*.
caulis, *a stalk*.	postis, *a door-post*.
collis, *a hill*.	sentis, *a bramble*.
crīnis, *hair*.	torquis, *a collar* (rarely
ensis, *a sword*.	fem.).
fascis, *a bundle*.	sŏdālis, *a companion*.
fīnis, *an end* (rarely fem.	torris, *a firebrand*.
and only in sing.).	unguis, *a finger-nail*.
follis, *a leather bag*.	vectis, *a bar*.
fūnis, *a rope*.	vermis, *a worm*.

annālis (sc. līber), *year-book*.
nātālis (sc. dies), *birth-day*.
mŏlāris (sc. lapis *or* dens), *grindstone*, or *grinder-tooth*.
pŭgillāres (sc. libri), *writing-tablets*.

COMMON to masc. and fem.

corbis, *a basket*, and clūnis, *haunch*.

§ 43. 3. NEUTER. Nouns ending in *ĕ*.

* Nouns neuter all end in *a, e,*
ar, ur, ŭs, l, c, n, and *t :*
Nouns masculine will all prefer
or, os, o (*ōnis*), *es, ex, er :*
The rest and *io* feminine; to these
Add parisyllables in *is* and *es*.

§ 44. B. Nouns Imparisyllabic.

1. MASCULINE. Nouns ending in *o* (not *io*), gen. *ōnis*, *er*, *or*, *es*, *os*, and *ex*.

Except in *er*, NEUT. ăcer, *a maple.*
  cădāver, *a corpse.*
  ĭter, *a journey.*
  păpāver, *the poppy.*
  pĭper, *pepper.*
  tūber, *a hump* or *swelling* (also *a truffle*).
  ūber, *an udder.*
  vēr, *spring.*
  verber (only used in plur.), *a blow.*

in *or*, FEM. arbor (also arbōs), *a tree.*

NEUT. ădor, *wheat.*   cŏr, *the heart.*
  æquor, *a surface.*   marmor, *marble.*

in *es*, FEM. ăbiēs (gen. abjĕtis), *fir-tree.*
  mergĕs, *a sheaf.*
  mercēs, *hire.*
  quiēs, *rest.*
  sĕgĕs, *standing corn.*
  tĕgĕs, *a mat.*

in *os*, FEM. cōs, *a whetstone.*   dōs, *a dowry.*

NEUT. ōs, ōris, *the face.*   ŏs, ossis, *a bone.*

in *ex*, FEM. fæx, *lees* (of wine, &c.).
  forfex, *scissors.*
  forpex, *curling-tongs.*
  lex, *a law* or *statute.*
  nex, *death.*
  pellex, *a concubine.*
  sŭpellex, *household furniture.*

§ 45. 2. FEMININE. Nouns ending in *o* (gen. *ĭnis*), *io*, *aus*, *as*, *is*, *ūs* (gen. *ūtis*), or *s* (preceded by a consonant), *ax*, *ix*, *ox*, *ux*, or *x* (preceded by a consonant).

Except Masc. in *o*, gen. *ĭnis,*   cardo, *a hinge.*
                              hŏmo, *a man.*
                              margo, *a border, brink.*
                              ordo, *order.*
                              turbo, *a whirlwind.*

Except Masc. in *io,*   pŭgio, *a dagger.*
                      scīpio, *a staff.*
                      sēnio, *the number six.*
                      septentrio, *the Great Bear* or *north.*
                      ūnio, *a pearl.*
                      vespertĭlio, *a bat.*

in *as,*   ās (a bronze coin).
          mās (gen. mǎris), *a male.*
          vās (gen. vǎdis), *a bail.*

in *is,*   cĭnis, *ashes.*
         glīs, *dormouse.*
         lǎpis, *a pebble.*
         pulvis. *dust.*
         sanguis, *blood.*
         sēmis, *half an as.*

in *s,* preceded by a consonant,
         dens, *a tooth.*
         fons, *a fountain.*
         mons, *a mountain.*
         pons, *a bridge.*
         rŭdens, *a cable.*
         scrobs, *a ditch* (sometimes feminine).

         ǎdeps, *fat,* forceps, *pincers,* are both masc. and fem.

in *ax,*   thōrax, *a breastplate.*

in *ix,*   cǎlix, *a cup.*
         fornix, *a vault* or *arch.*

in *x,* preceded by a consonant,
         deunx, *eleven-twelfths* (of an *as*).
         quincunx, *five-twelfths,* &c.

Neut.   vās (gen. vāsis), *a vessel.*

§ 46. 3. NEUTER. Nouns ending in *a, ar, ur, us* (except *ūs*, gen. *ūtis*), *c, l, n,* and *t.*

Also *æs, bronze.*

Except in *ar,* MASC. lār (gen. lăris), *a household god.*
pār, *a comrade* (from pār, adj.), but pār, *a pair,* is neuter.

in *ur,* MASC. augur, *a soothsayer.*
fūr, *a thief.*
furfur, *bran.*
turtur, *a turtle-dove.*
vultur, *a vulture.*

in *us,* MASC. lĕpŭs, *a hare.*   mūs, *a mouse.*

FEM. incūs, *an anvil.*
pălūs, *a marsh.*
pĕcŭs, pĕcŭdis, *a beast* (i.e. *cow, sheep,* &c.).
tellūs, *the earth.*
sūs, *a swine,* grūs, *a crane.* (These two are rarely masculine.)

in *l,* MASC. sāl, *salt* (gen. sălis).   sōl, *the sun.*
And some names of persons, as Consul, &c.

in *n,* MASC. pectĕn, *a comb.*   rēn, *the kidney.*
splēn, *the spleen.*

And some names of persons; as, tībīcĕn, *a flute-player.*

§ 47. *Fourth Declension.*

MASCULINE. Nouns ending in *us.*

Except FEMININE, ăcus, *a needle.*   portĭcus, *a portico.*
cŏlus, *a distaff.*   quercus, *an oak;* and
dŏmus, *a house.*   other trees.
īdūs (plur.), *the ides.* trĭbus, *a tribe.*
mănus, *a hand.*   spĕcus, *a cave.*
pĕnus, *a store of provisions.*

NEUTER. Nouns ending in *u.*

§ 48. *Fifth Declension.*

FEMININE. All

> Except *dies*, which is *feminine* sometimes, but in the singular only, and then generally denotes *a period of time:* otherwise it is masculine.

DEGREES OF NOUNS ADJECTIVE.

§ 49. Adjectives are also inflected in order to denote the degree of the quality exprest by them. The simple form is called the *positive.* The *comparative* expresses a higher degree of the quality in a comparison of two things or persons. The *superlative* expresses a higher degree in a comparison of more than two things or persons; as, dūrus, *hard,* dūrior, *harder,* dūrissimus, *hardest.*

§ 50. The comparative expresses also that the quality is possessed in *too high* a degree.

The superlative expresses also that the quality is possessed in a *very high* degree.

Many (especially derivative) adjectives have no comparative or superlative, their meaning not admitting of them.

Formation of Comparative and Superlative.

§ 51. From the positive are formed

(1) The comparative, by changing *i* or *is* of the genitive into *ior;*

(2) The superlative, by changing *i* or *is* of the genitive into *issimus.* Thus,

dūrus, gen. durī, comp. durior, superl. durissimus.
tristis, gen. tristis, comp. tristior, superl. tristi simus.
felix, gen. felīcis, comp. felīcior, superl. felīcissimus.

§ 52.   Adjectives ending in *er* form their superlative by adding *rĭmus* to the nominative case :
pulcher, gen. pulchrī, comp. pulchrĭor, superl. pulcherrĭmus.

The following form the superlative by changing *s* into *ĭmus* and doubling the *l ;* făcĭlis, *easy ;* sĭmĭlis, *like ;* diffĭcĭlis, *difficult ;* dissĭmĭlis, *unlike ;* grăcĭlis, *thin, slender ;* hŭmĭlis, *low ;* as, facilis, făcillĭmus.

§ 53.   If a vowel comes before *us* in the nominative case the comparative and superlative are not formed by a change of the word, but by prefixing măgis, *more,* for the comparative, and maxĭme, *most,* for the superlative ; as, arduus, *steep,* măgis arduus, *more steep,* maxĭme arduus, *most steep ;* except words ending in *quus,* as, antīquus, antīquior, antīquissimus.

§ 54.   The following are irregular :

Positive.	Comp.	Superl.
bŏnus, *good*	mĕlior	optĭmus
mălus, *bad*	pejor	pessĭmus
magnus, *great*	major	maxĭmus
parvus, *small*	mĭnor	mĭnĭmus
multus, *much*	plūs* (neut.)	plūrĭmus
nēquam (indecl.), *wicked*	nēquior	nēquissĭmus
dīves, *rich* {	dīvĭtior / dītior	dīvĭtissĭmus / dītissĭmus
sĕnex, *old*	sĕnĭor	(nātu maxĭmus)
jŭvĕnis, *young*	jūnĭor (for jŭvĕnior)	(nātu mĭnĭmus)
extĕrus, *outside* (in plur. only) {	extĕrior	{ extrēmus / extĭmus
infĕrus, *low* (chiefly used in plur. *the beings, places,* &c. *below*)	infĕrior	{ infĭmus / īmus
sŭpĕrus, *high* (chiefly used in plural, *the beings, places,* &c. *above*)	sŭpĕrior	{ sŭprēmus / summus

* *plūs,* gen. *plūris* (neut.).   Plural, *plūres, plūra, plūrium, plūrĭbus.*

Positive.	Comp.	Superl.
pŏstĕrus, *next* (in time)	pŏstĕrior, *later, hinder*	postrēmus, *last*
cĭtra (adv.), *on this side*	cĭtĕrior	cĭtĭmus
intra (adv.), *within*	intĕrior	intĭmus
ultra (adv.), *beyond*	ultĕrior	ultĭmus
præ (prep.), *before*	prĭor	prīmus
prŏpe (adv.), *near*	prŏpĭor	proxĭmus
pŏtis, pŏtĕ (only in these forms), *able, possible*	pŏtĭor, *better*	pŏtissĭmus, *best*
	dētĕrior, *worse*	dēterrĭmus
	ōcĭor, *swifter*	ōcissĭmus

OF PRONOUNS.

§ 55. Pronouns are

(A) SUBSTANTIVE.

1. *Personal.*

First Person.

Singular.		Plural.	
Nom.	ĕgo, *I*	Nom.	nōs, *we*
Acc.	mē	Acc.	
Dat.	mĭhī	Dat.	nōbīs
Abl.	mē	Abl.	

Second Person.

Singular.		Plural.	
Nom.	tū, *thou*	Nom.	vos, *ye*
Acc.	tē	Acc.	
Dat.	tĭbī	Dat.	vōbīs
Abl.	tē	Abl.	

2. *Reflexive* Pronoun, referring to subject of sentence.

Singular and Plural.

Acc. sē (*or* sēsē), *himself, herself, themselves*
Dat. sĭbī
Abl. sē (*or* sēsē)

§ 56. The genitives of *ego* and *tu* were *mis* and *tis*, but these became obsolete after Plautus' time, and in place of the genitive of these pronouns and of *se,* the adjectives meus (voc. masc. *mi*), *mine;* noster, *ours;* tuus, *thine;* vester, *yours;* suus, *his, her,* or *their* are used *

For the (*a*) possessive genitive, they are used as adjectives; as, mea manus, *my hand.*

(*b*) partitive genitive, (and possessive genitive when *omnium* precedes) the gen. plur. *nostrûm, vestrûm* (for *nostrōrum, vestrōrum*) and *suorum* or *ex se* are used; as, omnium nostrum dignissimus, *worthiest of us all.*

(*c*) objective genitive, the gen. sing. neut. *mei, nostri, tui, vestri, sui*; as, mĭsĕrēre mei, *have pity on me.*

3. For *interrogatives* (*quis, ecquis,* &c.) see below, § 59; and for *quisquam* see § 57.

§ 57. (B) ADJECTIVE.

1. *Possessive* pronouns: meus, tuus, &c. as above, § 56. From these are formed nostrās, vestrās (gen. ātis), *of our, your, country.*

2. *Demonstrative*:

First person; hic, *this near me.*

Second person; iste, *that near you.*

Third person; ille (*for* ollus), *the man, &c. at a distance from either of us.*

To these add 'is,' *that, he,* and its compounds, ĭdem, *the same;*

ipse (*for* ipsus), *he himself.*

----

* It is due to this that we have constructions such as, Ut mea defunctæ molliter ossa cubent (Ovid), *That my bones when I have done with life may softly lie* (*mea* being equivalent to *mei*). Vestra consilia accusantur, qui mihĭ summum honorem imposuistis, *It is your plans that are really subject to the charge, for you have put me in the highest office* (where *vestra* is equivalent to the genitive of *vos*).

Hence moreover the adjective is sometimes used for the objective genitive; as, ob simultatem suam, *from hatred to him.*

3. *Relative:* qui, *who* or *which;* quisquis, quīcunque, *whoever,* or *whichever.*

Of quisquis only *quisquis, quidquid* or *quicquid* (subst.), *quoquo,* and gen. *cuicuimodi* are usual: and but few other forms are found at all.

4. *Interrogative:* quĭs or qui*? quisnam or quīnam? *who?* or *which?* ecquĭs or ecqui? *anyone?*

5. *Indefinite:*

quĭs, *any one* (after relative and interrogative particles ; *si,* &c.). Its compound *quispiam* has the same meaning.

quisquam, *any one at all* (in negative, interrogative, or conditional sentences, where *all* are *excluded).*

Always *used* as a substantive; unless it be considered an adjective when used with names of persons, as *quisquam scriptor, quisquam Gallus,* &c.

(Quisquam is not used in the feminine or plural.)

quīvīs } *any one you please;* where *all* are *in-*
quīlĭbĕt } *cluded.*

ălĭquĭs, *some one.*

quīdam, *a certain person* (known but not named).

quisque, *each one,* in *distributive* meaning.

§ 58. The adjective pronouns are thus declined:

| | *Singular.* | | | *Plural.* | |
	M.	F.	N.		M.	F.	N.
N.	hĭc	hæc	hōc	N.	hi	hæ	hæc
A.	hunc	hanc	hoc	A.	hos	has	hæc
G.		hujus		G.	hōrum	hārum	hōrum
D.		huic		D. }		hīs.	
Ab.	hōc	hāc	hōc	Ab. }			

* The interrogative pronoun is merely the relative pronoun in a particular use, as (*Tell me the man*) *who did it.* The relative again is originally a demonstrative, as is clearly seen in (especially the Homeric and Platonic usage of) the Greek ὅs, and is implied in the identity of the indefinite *quis, quidam,* &c., with *qui, quis?* Compare Shakespeare (*Cor.* v. 5): *Him I accuse, The city gates by this has entered,* i. e. Quem accuso, urbem ingressus est.

	Singular.				Plural.		
	M.	F.	N.		M.	F.	N.
N.	ill*e*	ill*ă*	ill*ud*	N.	ill*i*	ill*æ*	ill*ă*
A.	ill*um*	ill*am*	ill*ud*	A.	ill*os*	ill*as*	ill*ă*
G.		illī*us*		G.	ill*ōrum*	ill*ārum*	ill*ōrum*
D.		ill*i*		D.		ill*ī*s.	
Ab.	ill*o*	ill*ā*	ill*o*	Ab.			

In the same way as *ille* are declined iste, ista, istud;
alius, alia, aliud (Gen. alīus for ali*ius*, Dat. al*ī*i), *another;*
also ipse, ipsa, ipsum, only with *m* (not *d*) in the neuter
sing. See also § 16.

Istic (i. e. *iste ce*) and *illic* (i. e. *ille ce*) are declined like *hic* in
the nom. acc. and abl. sing. The neut. nom. and acc. is often
istuc. The other cases of *iste* and *ille* rarely have *ce* appended.

	Singular.				Plural.		
	M.	F.	N.		M.	F.	N.
N.	is	e*ă*	id	N.	ei *or* ī	e*æ*	e*ă*
A.	eum	eam	id	A.	eos	eas	e*ă*
G.		ejus		G.	eōrum	eārum	eōrum
D.		ei		D.	eis *or* īs.		
Ab.	eo	e*ā*	eo	Ab.			

The nom. masc. and abl. plur. are sometimes written *ii, iis.*

In the same way is declined īdem, *ea*dem, *ĭ*dem ; *dem*
being added to the cases of *is,* and *m* being changed into
n, as eu*n*dem, earu*n*dem.

	Singular.				Plural.		
	M.	F.	N.		M.	F.	N.
N.	qui	quæ	quod	N.	qui	quæ	quæ
A.	quem	quam	quod	A.	quos	quas	quæ
G.		cujus		G.	quōrum	quārum	quōrum
D.		cūī		D.	quĭbus *or* quîs		
Ab.	quo	quā	quo	Ab.	(sometimes written		
	(or quī, used only ad-				queis)		
	verbially : how? or						
	with the prep. *cum*)						

§ 59. The relative is also used as an interrogative, both substantively and adjectively. When used adjectively it preserves the same forms; as, qui homo, *what man?* when used substantively it has nom. sing. quis, quæ, quid.

And this distinction of *quid* for substantive, *quod* for adjective holds through the compounds; as, quiddam, *a certain thing;* quoddam os, *a certain bone;* alĭquid, *something;* alĭquod os, *some bone.*

§ 60. Alĭquis, and quis (indef.) make aliquă, quă in fem. sing. nom.

The compounds of quis and qui are declined like them; as, quivis, quævis, quidvis or quodvis, gen. cujusvis, &c.

The neut. sing. nom. and acc. of quisquam is quicquid.

§ 61. The following is a list of correlative (pronominal) adjectives. (Madvig.)

Demonstr.	Rel. and Interrog.	Indef. Rel.	Indef.
talis, *such*	qualis, {*of which quality, as,* {*of what quality?*	qualiscunque, *of what quality soever*	qualislibet, *of any quality you please*
tantus, *so great*	quantus, {*as great,* {*how great?*	quantuscunque, *how great soever*	aliquantus, *of some considerable size*; quantuslibet, quantusvis, {*of any size you please*
tantŭlus, *so small*	quantŭlus, *as small*	quantŭluscunque, *how small soever*	aliquantŭlum, *a little* (subst.)
tot (indecl.), *so many*; tŏtĭdem (indecl.), *just so many*	quŏt, {*as many,* {*how many?*	quotcunque, quotquot, {*how many* {*soever*	aliquot, *some*
tŏtus (rare) *such in numerical order*	quŏtus, {*what in numerical order?* {*which,* &c. (rare)		

Qualiscunque and quantuscunque are also used as simply indefinite (non-relative) pronouns; aliquantus is commonly only used in the neuter (aliquantum, aliquanto), and then as *substantive*, or *adverb*.

OF ADVERBS.

§ 62. Adverbs are indeclinable words, mostly oblique cases of nouns and pronouns.

I. Adverbs derived from *nouns* adjective (were probably originally oblique cases, and) end

1. In *ō*, as certō, *certainly;* citŏ, *quickly:* or (more frequently) in *ē**, as certē, *certainly;* dignē, *worthily;* from adjectives and participles in *us, a, um.*

2. In *ter,* as fēlīcĭter, *happily;* grăvĭtĕr, *heavily;* amanter, *lovingly;* from other adjectives and participles.

3. In *im,* chiefly from participles;
    as, sensim, *by degrees* (lit. *in perceived* parts).
    trĭbūtim, *tribe by tribe* (lit. *in distributed* parts).
    partim, *by parts, partly.*
    turmātim, *troop-wise, in troops.*
    prīvātim, *as a private person.*

4. In *ĭtus,* as cælĭtus, *from heaven,* chiefly from subst.

Sometimes the neuter of the adjective is used adverbially (cf. § 175); as, multum anxius, *very anxious;* făcĭlĕ primus, *easily first;* and the neuter of the comparative adjective always forms the comparative of the adverb; as, dignius, *more worthily;* plus, *more;* minus, *less.* The superlative is formed in *ē;* as, dignissimē, *most worthily.*

§ 63. II. A. The following are the chief *pronominal* adverbs of *manner, cause,* &c. :

Demonstr.	Rel. and Interrog.
sīc, ⎫ *so, thus.* ĭtă, ⎭	ŭt, *as* (for cut or quut). utcunque, *in whatsoever way.*
ălĭōquī, *in other respects, besides.*	quī, *how?*
tālĭtĕr (rare), *in such a way.*	quālĭtĕr, *in which way.*
tam, *so, so very.*	quam, *as.*
ĕō, *therefore.* (cf. § 194.)	quŏd, ⎫ quia, ⎬ *because.* cūr, *why?*

* *Macte* (in verse mactĕ : cf. *benĕ, malĕ*) is considered to be an adverb by Madvig, who says the word is invariable in form, the supposed instances of *macti* in Livy and Pliny not being supported by the manuscripts.

§ 64. B. The following are the chief *pronominal* adverbs of *place*:

ō (= om, accus.?)	dē = ðeɤ, gen. (or abl.)	ŭō or ĭ; dat. (cf. § 183, 201.)	ā, abl. fem. (cf. § 190.)
Quō, {whither? / whither.}	undĕ, {whence? / whence.}	tĭbĭ, {where? / where.}	Quā, {by what way? / by which way.}
hūc, hither.	hinc, hence.	hic, here.	hāc, by this way.
eō, thither.	indĕ, thence.	ĭbĭ, there.	eā, by that way.
istūc, to your place.	istinc, from your place.	istic, there (where you are).	istāc, by your way.
illūc, to that place.	illinc, from that place.	illīc, there (where he is).	illāc, by that way (near him).
eōdem, to the same place.	indĭdem, from the same place.	ĭbĭdem, in the same place.	eādem, by the same way.
utrōque, to both places.	utrinque, from both sides. / undĭque, from all sides.	utrōbique, in both places. / ŭbĭque, everywhere.	
ălĭquō, to some place or other.	ălĭcunde, from some place or other.	ălĭcŭbĭ, somewhere or other.	ălĭquā, by some way.
quōvis, / quōlĭbet, } to any place you please.	undĕvis, / undĕlĭbet, } whence you please.	tĭbĭvis, / tĭbĭlĭbet, } where you please.	quāvis, / quālĭbet, } by any way you please.
quōquam, anywhither (in negative, &c. sentences).	usquam, anywhere (in negative, &c. sentences).		
sĭquō, if anywhither.	sīcunde, if from any place.	sīcŭbĭ, if anywhere.	siquā, if by any way.
nequō, lest anywhither.	nēcunde, lest from anywhere.	nēcŭbĭ, lest anywhere.	nequā, lest by any way.
ălĭō, to another place.	ălĭunde, from another place.	ălĭbĭ, elsewhere.	ălĭā, by another way.
quōcunque, / quōquō, } whithersoever.	unăĕcunque, whencesoever.	ŭbĭcunque, wheresoever.	quācunque, / quāquā, } by whatsoever way.
quātĕnus? {how far? / as far as.}		nusquam, nowhere.	

hāctĕnus, *thus far.*
eātĕnus, *so far.*
ăllquātĕnus, *to some point.*
quādamtĕnus, *to a certain point.*
quorsum (i.e. }*whitherwards?*
quŏversum) }*whitherwards.*

R. G.

N.B. The *c* in *alicubi, sicubi, nēcubi,* &c. shows the original form of *ubi,* viz. *cubi,* the dative of *cuis*
or *quis,* contracted into *cui.* So *sicunde,* &c. shows the original form of *unde,* viz. *cunde.*

§ 65. C. The following **are** the chief *pronominal* adverbs *of time:*

Quando, { *when?*
{ *when.*

quum, *when.*
nunc, *now.*
tunc, } *then.*
tum, }
antehāc, *before this.*
posthāc, *after this.*
nondum, *not yet.*
ălĭās, *at another time.*
intĕrim, } *meanwhile.*
intĕreā, }
quondam, } *formerly,* or *hereafter* (*olim* is from
ōlim, } *ollus* (=*ille*) and so means *at that time*).

3

quamdiū, { *how long?*
{ *as long as.*
ălĭquandiū, *for some length of time.*
quousque, *till when?*
adhuc, *hitherto* (i.e. up to the time *now* present).

quŏtĭēs, { *how often?*
{ *as often as.*
tŏtĭēs, *so often.*
ălĭquŏtĭēs, *several times.*
ĭdentĭdem, *repeatedly.*
nonnunquam, } *sometimes* (i.e. *not unfrequently*).
ălĭquando, }
quandŏque, }
interdum, *sometimes* (i.e. *occasionally*).
sŭbinde, *one after the other.*
unquam, *ever* (after negatives, &c.).
usque, *ever* (of progressive continuance).

D. *Numeral* adverbs are given with the numeral adjectives on the following pages.

§ 66. Numerals (chiefly from Kennedy).

Arabic Signs.	Roman Signs.	Cardinal; answering the question Quot? how many? (Adjectives)	Ordinal; answering the question Quotus? which in numerical order? (All declinable adjectives)	Distributive; answering the question Quotēni? how many each? (All declinable adjectives)	Numeral Adverbs; answering the question Quotiēs? how many times?
1	I	ūnŭs, a, ŭm,	prīmŭs (prior, first of two)	singŭli	sēmĕl.
2	II	dŭŏ, ae, o	sĕcundŭs or alter	bini	bĭs.
3	III	trēs, trĭa	tertĭŭs	terni or trini	tĕr.
4	IIII or IV	quattŭŏr	quartŭs	quăterni	quătĕr.
5	V	quinquĕ	quintŭs	quini	quinquĭēs.
6	VI	sex	sextŭs	sēni	sexĭēs.
7	VII	septem	septĭmŭs	septēni	septĭēs.
8	VIII	octŏ	octāvŭs	octōni	octĭēs.
9	VIIII or IX	nŏvem	nōnŭs	nŏvēni	nŏvĭēs.
10	X	dĕcem	dĕcĭmŭs	dēni	dĕcĭēs.
11	XI	undĕcim	undĕcĭmŭs	undēni	undĕcĭēs.
12	XII	dŭŏdĕcim	dŭŏdĕcĭmŭs	dŭŏdēni	dŭŏdĕcĭēs.
13	XIII	trēdĕcim	tertĭŭs dĕcĭmŭs	terni dēni	trēdĕcĭēs.
14	XIIII or XIV	quattŭŏrdĕcim	quartŭs dĕcĭmŭs	quăterni dēni	quăttŭŏrdĕcĭēs.
15	XV	quindĕcim	quintŭs dĕcĭmŭs	quini dēni	quindĕcĭēs.
16	XVI	sēdĕcim	sextŭs dĕcĭmŭs	sēni dēni	sēdĕcĭēs.
17	XVII	septendĕcim	septĭmŭs dĕcĭmŭs	septēni dēni	septĭesdĕcĭēs.
18	XVIII or XIIX	dŭŏdēvĭginti	dŭŏdēvĭcēsĭmŭs	dŭŏdēvĭcēni	dŭŏdēvĭcĭēs.
19	XVIIII or XIX	undēvĭginti	undēvĭcēsĭmŭs	undēvĭcēni	undēvĭcĭēs.
20	XX	vĭginti (indeclinable)	vĭcēsĭmŭs	vĭcēni	vĭcĭēs.
21	XXI	ūnŭs ĕt vĭginti	ūnŭs ĕt vĭcēsĭmŭs	vĭcēni singŭli	sēmĕl ĕt vĭcĭēs.
28	XXVIII	dŭŏdētrigintā	dŭŏdētrigēsĭmŭs	dŭŏdētricēni	dŭŏdētricĭēs.
29	XXVIIII or XXIX	undētrigintā	undētrigēsĭmŭs	undētricēni	undētricĭēs.
30	XXX	trigintā	trigēsĭmŭs	tricēni	tricĭēs.
40	XXXX or XL	quădrāgintā	quădrāgēsĭmŭs	quădrāgēni	quădrāgĭēs.

50	L	quinquāgintā	quinquāgēsīmŭs	quīnquāgēnī	quinquāgīēs.
60	LX	sexāgintā	sexāgēsīmŭs	sexāgēnī	sexāgīēs.
70	LXX	septuāgintā	septuāgēsīmŭs	septuāgēnī	septuāgīēs.
80	LXXX	octōgintā	octōgēsīmŭs	octōgēnī	octōgīēs.
90	LXXXX or XXC	nōnāgintā	nōnāgēsīmŭs	nōnāgēnī	nōnāgīēs.
99	XCIX or IC	undēcentum	undēcentēsīmŭs	undēcentēnī	undēcentīēs.
100	C	centum	centēsīmŭs	centēnī	centīēs.
101	CI	centum ĕt ūnŭs	centēsīmŭs prīmŭs	centēnī singŭlī	centīēs sēmēl.
200	CC	dŭcentī, æ, ŏ	dŭcentēsīmŭs	dŭcēnī	dŭcentīēs.
300	CCC	trĕcentī, æ, a	trĕcentēsīmŭs	trĕcēnī	trĕcentīēs.
400	CCCC or CD	quādringentī, æ, a	quādringentēsīmŭs	quādringēnī	quādringentīēs.
500	D or IƆ	quingentī, æ, a	quingentēsīmŭs	quingēnī	quingentīēs.
600	DC	sexcentī, æ, a	sexcentēsīmŭs	sexcēnī	sexcentīēs.
700	DCC	septingentī, æ, a	septingentēsīmŭs	septingēnī	septingentīēs.
800	DCCC	octingentī, æ, a	octingentēsīmŭs	octingēnī	octingentīēs.
900	DCCCC	nongentī, æ, a	nongentēsīmŭs	nongēnī	nongentīēs.
1000	M or CIƆ	millĕ	millēsīmŭs	singŭlā millĭā	millīēs.
2000	MM or CIƆCIƆ	dŭŏ millĭā	bismillēsīmŭs	bīnā millĭā	bīs millīēs.
5000	VM or IƆƆ	quinquĕ millĭā	quinquīēs millēsīmŭs	quīnā millĭā	quinquīēs millīēs.
10,000	XM or CCIƆƆ	decem millĭā	dēcīēs millēsīmŭs	dēnā millĭā	dēcīēs millīēs.
50,000	LM or IƆƆƆ	quinquāgintā millĭā	quinquāgīēs millēsīmŭs	quinquāgēnā millĭā	quinquāgīēs millīēs.
100,000	CCCIƆƆƆ	centum millĭā	centīēs millēsīmŭs	centēnā millĭā	centīēs millīēs.
500,000	IƆƆƆƆ	quingentā millĭā	quingentīēs millēsīmŭs	quingēnā millĭā	quingentīēs millīēs.
1,000,000	CCCCIƆƆƆƆ	dēcēs centum millĭā	dēcīēs centēs millēsīmŭs	dēcēs centēnā millĭā	dēcīēs centīēs millīēs.

MULTIPLICATIVE, answering the question Quŏtŭplex? *how many fold?* are: sīmplēx, dŭplēx, trĭplēx, quādru-plēx, quincuplēx, &c. So sēptēmplēx, *sevenfold*; dēcemplēx, *tenfold*; centuplēx, *a hundredfold*.
PROPORTIONAL, answering the question Quŏtŭplŭs? *how many times more?* are: simplŭs, duplŭs, triplŭs, quădruplŭs, &c.
N.B. *Sexcenti* is used of an indefinitely large number, as we say *a hundred, a thousand.*

§ 67. Dŭŏ, *two*, Trēs, *three*, and Millĭă, *thousands*.

	M.	Plural. F.	N.		Plural. M. F.	N.	Plural. N.
N.	Dŭŏ	dŭǽ	dŭŏ	N. ⎱	Trēs	trĭă	Millĭă
A.	Dŭŏs	dŭăs	dŭŏ	A. ⎰			
G.	Dŭŏrum	dŭārum	dŭŏrum		Trĭum		Millĭum
D. ⎱ Ab. ⎰	Dŭŏbŭs	dŭābŭs	dŭŏbŭs	D. ⎱ Ab. ⎰	Trĭbŭs		Millĭbŭs

Ambō, *both*, is declined like Dŭŏ (acc. masc. *ambo* or *ambos*). The other Cardinal Numbers, from quattŭŏr to cēntum, are undeclined. Millĕ is also used as an undeclined Adjective. Thus, mille pedes, *a thousand feet*.

§ 68. From the ordinals are formed adverbs in *vm* (rarely *o*) to denote *for which time;* as, primum, *for the first time;* iterum, *for the second time;* tertium, quartum, &c., e. g. tertium consul, *for the third time consul*, &c. ; ultimum (postremum, extremum), *for the last time*.

§ 69. The distributives are used also as the cardinals of plural substantives ; as binæ litteræ, *two epistles* (duo litteræ, *two letters of the alphabet*).

§ 70. In compounding numbers, whether cardinal or ordinal, from 13 to 20, the units are prefixed to the ten *without et*, or the ten prefixed to the units *with et :* as *septemdecim*, or *decem et septem*.

In compounding numbers from 20 up to 100, either the ten *without et*, or the units *with et*, are placed first, as in English, thus, *viginti unus*, or *unus et viginti*. The hundreds (in prose) are always placed before the tens with or without *et ;* then the tens, then the units, as *centum sexaginta septem*, or *centum et sexaginta septem*.

§ 71. Fractions are exprest by the ordinal adjectives, agreeing with *pars* or *partes* exprest or understood: as $\frac{1}{3}$, tertia pars ; $\frac{3}{7}$, tres septumæ. But for $\frac{2}{3}$ and $\frac{3}{4}$ the Romans said quæ *partes*, tres *partes*.

For *twelfths*, the *as* (originally *pound of bronze*) was taken as the unit, and its parts (unciæ, *ounces*) denote the fractions. Thus

$\frac{1}{12}$ uncia, gen. *æ* (fem.).

$\frac{2}{12} = \frac{1}{6}$ sextans, gen. *tis* (masc).

$\frac{3}{12} = \frac{1}{4}$ quădrans.

$\frac{4}{12} = \frac{1}{3}$ triens.

$\frac{5}{12}$ quincunx, gen. *cis* (masc.).

$\frac{6}{12} = \frac{1}{2}$ sēmis, gen. semissis (masc.), (or pars dimidia, or dimidius, as adj., as dimidius modius, *a half bushel*). Semis is some-times used as indeclin-able.

$\frac{7}{12}$ septunx.

$\frac{8}{12} = \frac{2}{3}$ bes, gen. bessis (masc.).

$\frac{9}{12} = 1 - \frac{1}{4}$ dodrans (de-quadrans).

$\frac{10}{12} = 1 - \frac{1}{6}$ dextans (de-sex-tans).

$\frac{11}{12} = 1 - \frac{1}{12}$ deunx.

$1 = $ as.

§ 72. The following expressions should also be noticed, *quadrans quartus* (*a, um*) is $3\frac{1}{4}$: *semis sextus* is $5\frac{1}{2}$: *semis tertius* (contracted into *sestertius*) $2\frac{1}{2}$. The last quantity was represented in symbols by adding *s* (i.e. *semis*) to the symbol for two with a line running through the whole, as in our ℔ or £ pounds. Printers have substituted the letters HS*.

OF VERBS.

§ 73. Latin verbs have inflexions to denote differences of

1. NUMBER.

    (*a*) *Singular*, when one person is acting or suffer-ing.

    (*b*) *Plural*, when more than one person is acting or suffering.

2. PERSON.

    (*a*) *First person*, if the person acting or suffering be the *speaker*.

    (*b*) *Second person*, if the person acting or suffer-ing be *spoken to*.

    (*c*) *Third person*, if the person acting or suffering be *spoken of*, but is neither the speaker nor spoken to.

3. TENSE, i.e. the time when the action is performed.

    (*a*) *Present*: as, *I am loving*, or *I love*.

    (*b*) *Imperfect*: as, *I was loving*.

* Key, *Lat. Gr.* § 272.

(*c*) *Perfect:* as, *I loved;* also, *I have loved.*

(*d*) *Pluperfect:* as, *I had loved.*

(*e*) *Future:* as, *I shall love.*

(*f*) *Completed Future,* or 2*nd Future:* as, *I shall have loved.*

4. MOOD, i.e. the mode in which the action is conceived.

(*a*) *Indicative,* expresses a direct assertion.

(*b*) *Subjunctive,* expresses a supposition.

(*c*) *Imperative,* expresses a command.

To which are added certain verbal forms called the

(*d*) *Infinitive,* i.e. the verb used mainly as substantive.

(*e*) *Participle,* i. e. the verb used as an adjective.

(*f*) *Gerund* and *Gerundive,* i. e. a participle used as a substantive and adjective.

(*g*) *Supine,* i. e. certain cases of a verbal noun.

N.B.   The first three are called *Finite moods,* or the *Finite verb.* The rest are sometimes called the *Infinite verb.*

5. VOICE.

(*a*)   *Active:* used when the person spoken of *does* or *is* something.

(*b*)   *Passive:* used when the person spoken of has something *done to* him, whether by himself, or by others.

§ 74. Verbs are distinguished according to their meaning into

(1) *Transitive,* which express an action exercised *upon an object;* as, *I love a man.*

(2) *Intransitive,* which express either a *state* of being, or an *action not* exercised *upon an object;* as, *I stand, I faint.*

(A)   Verbs with active inflexions are either

   (*a*)   Transitive; as, amo, *I love.*

   (*b*)   Intransitive; as, sto, *I stand.*

N.B. These latter, called *neuter* verbs, have no passive voice, except when used impersonally in the 3rd pers. singular.

(B)   Verbs with passive inflexions are either

(1)   Verbs which have also an active voice:

   (*a*)   Passive; as, amor, *I am being loved.*

   (*b*)   Middle, or Reflexive; as, pascor, *I feed myself.*

(2)   Verbs which have no active voice, called *Deponents:*

   (*c*)   Transitive; as, hortor, *I exhort.*

   (*d*)   Intransitive; as, morior, *I die.*

§ 75. Sum, *I am*, is thus declined:

[It will be seen that some tenses are derived from a root *es* (whence *esum*, Greek εἰμί, originally ἐσμί), and some from a root *fu* (whence *fio*, cf. Greek φύω.)]

INDICATIVE MOOD.

	Present Tense.	Imperfect.	Perfect.	Pluperfect.	Future.	Completed Fut.
Sing. 1.	sŭm, I am	ĕram, I was	fŭi, I have been or I was	fuĕram, I had been	ĕro, I shall be	fuĕro, I shall have been
2.	ĕs, thou art	ĕrās	fŭistĭ	fuerās	ĕrĭs	fuĕrĭs
3.	est, he (she, it) is	ĕrăt	fŭĭt	fuĕrăt	ĕrĭt	fuĕrĭt
Plur. 1.	sŭmus, we are	ĕrāmus	fuĭmus	fuerāmus	ĕrĭmus	fuĕrĭmus
2.	estis, ye are	ĕrātis	fuĭstis	fuerātis	ĕrĭtis	fuĕrĭtis
3.	sŭnt, they are	ĕrant	fuĕrunt or fuēre	fuĕrant	ĕrunt	fuerint

SUBJUNCTIVE MOOD.

Sing. 1.	sim	essem *or* fŏrem	fuĕrim	fuissem
2.	sīs	essēs *or* fŏrēs	fuĕrĭs	fuissēs
3.	sĭt	essĕt *or* fŏrĕt	fuĕrĭt	fuissĕt
Plur. 1.	sīmus	essēmus *or* fŏrēmus	fuĕrĭmus	fuissēmus
2.	sītis	essētis *or* fŏrētis	fuĕrĭtis	fuissētis
3.	sint	essent *or* fŏrent	fuĕrĭnt	fuissent

IMPERATIVE MOOD.

Present.	*Future.*
Sing. 2. ĕs, be	estŏ, thou shalt be (or be thou)
3.	estŏ, he shall be
Plur. 2. estĕ, be ye	estōte, you shall be (or be ye)
3.	suntŏ, they shall be

INFINITIVE MOOD.

Present.	*Perfect.*	*Future.*
esse	fuisse	fŏre or fŭtūrus -a -um esse

PARTICIPLES.

Present.	*Future.*
(sens or ens only found in compounds)	fŭtūrus

N.B. When *est* came after a vowel or *m*, the *e* was omitted in the earlier period (so in Cicero) both in speaking and writing (*nata st*, *natum st*, *oratio st*). In the comic writers a short final syllable in *s* also coalesces with *est* (*factust*, *opust*, *similist*, for *factus est*, *opus est*, *similis est*); and both a final vowel and a final short syllable in *s* occasionally coalesce with *es* (*nactu's*, *nacta's*, *simili's*, for *nactus es*, *nacta es*, *similis es*). RITSCHL.

OF THE REGULAR VERBS.

Regular verbs are divided according to their form into four classes, called *Conjugations.*

§ 76. The differences of tense, mood, number, and person, are denoted mainly by the addition of certain syllables or letters to what is called the *crude form* (or *theme*) of each verb, and which in the following examples of the conjugations is printed in roman letters. The variable parts are printed in italics. It will be seen that if the first person singular of the present and perfect indicative, and the supine and present infinitive be known, all the other parts of the verb can be easily formed from them. The four conjugations are generally distinguished by the vowel preceding *re* in the infinitive mood ; which in the 1st conjugation is ā : in the 2nd ē : in the third ĕ (not belonging to the crude form): in the fourth ī. (N.B. ē and ī are shortened if they come before a vowel, and·ā, ē and ī are shortened before a final *t*.)

§ 77. The verbs are divided into *vowel* verbs, or *consonant* verbs, according as their crude form ends with a vowel or consonant.

I. First conjugation contains all vowel verbs, whose crude form ends in ā ; as ăm*o*, *I love*, perf. ămā*vi*, sup. ămā*tum*, infin. ămā*re.*

II. Second conjugation contains all vowel verbs whose crude form ends in ē ; as mone*o*, *I advise*, perf. mŏn*ui*, sup. mŏn*ĭtum*, infin. mŏnē*re.*

III. Third conjugation contains all verbs whose crude form ends in a consonant, or in the semivowel ŭ ; as lĕg*o*, *I pick* or *read*, perf. lēg*i*, sup. lec*tum*, infin. lĕgĕ*re:* ăcŭ*o*, *I sharpen*, perf. ăcu*i*, sup. (ăcŭ*ĭtum*, contracted into) acū*tum*, infin. ăcŭĕ*re.*

IV. Fourth conjugation contains all vowel verbs whose crude form ends in ī, as aud*ĭo*, *I hear*, perf. audī*vi*, sup. audī*tum*, infin. audī*re.*

§ 78. In the perfect tense additions are sometimes *prefixed* to the crude form, viz. the first consonant together with the root-vowel if it be *o* or *u*, otherwise with *e** ; as, mordeo, perf. *mo-mordi:* this is called a *reduplication.* Sometimes the vowel of the root † is lengthened; as, lĕgo, lēgi; and in reduplicated perfects changed according to § 5. The terminations also sometimes encroach upon or alter the final letter of the crude form; as, moneo, monui: and thus the characteristic vowel is shortened before another vowel in the 2nd and 4th conjugations, and the final consonant is frequently changed from a flat (i.e. *b, g, d*) into a sharp (i.e. *p, c, t*), as nūbo, perf. nupsi; or assimilated, as cēdo, perf. cessi; or omitted, as plaudo, perf. plausi. With these exceptions the crude form remains unaltered throughout. In the 3rd conjugation the short ĕ (preceding *re* in the infinitive) is merely a connecting vowel between the crude form and the termination, and is perhaps not part either of one or the other; it appears as *i* in regit, as *u* in regunt.

In the present tense we often find an insertion to strengthen a weak form, especially the letter *n;* as in *findo, pango,* &c. compared with the perfects, *fĭdi, pepĭgi.* So also the inchoatives in *-sco* (§ 109) exhibit a similar insertion.

---

* Originally the vowel of the prefix was always *e* (as in Greek). Both Cicero and Cæsar are said to have written *memordi, pepugi, spepondi.* In *spopondi* and *steti* the reduplication is inserted after the *s.*

† The *root* is the word itself without either formative or inflexional additions: e.g. *am* is the root of *amavi; ama-* is the crude form (i.e. the root with a formative addition); and *amavi* shows the inflexional addition for the 1st pers. sing. perf. indic. added to the crude form. In the 3rd conj. the crude form does not differ from the root (as the terms are here used).

REGULAR VERBS.

ACTIVE VOICE.

VOWEL CONJUGATIONS.

§ 79.

INDICATIVE MOOD. *Present Tense.*	I. in *a.*	II. in *e.*	IV. in *i.*	CONSONANT and in *u.* III.
Sing. 1. I *love*, &c. or I am *loving*, &c.	ămo	mŏnĕo	audĭo	lĕgo
2. Thou *lovest*, &c. or &c.	amās	monēs	audīs	legĭs
3. He *loves*, &c. or &c.	amăt	monĕt	audĭt	legĭt
Plur. 1. We *love*, &c. or &c.	amāmus	monēmus	audīmus	legĭmus
2. Ye *love*, &c. or &c.	amătis	monētis	audītis	legĭtis
3. They *love*, &c. or &c.	amant	monent	audĭunt	legunt
Imperfect.				
Sing. 1. I was *loving*, &c.	ămăbam	mŏnēbam	audiēbam	lĕgēbam
2. Thou wast *loving*, &c.	amăbās	monēbās	audiēbās	legēbās
3. He was *loving*, &c.	amăbăt	monēbăt	audiēbăt	legēbăt
Plur. 1. We were *loving*, &c.	amăbāmus	monēbāmus	audiēbāmus	legēbāmus
2. Ye were *loving*, &c.	amăbātis	monēbātis	audiēbātis	legēbātis
3. They were *loving*, &c.	amăbant	monēbant	audiēbant	legēbant

Perfect.

	amāvi	mŏnui	audīvi	lēgi
Sing. 1. I loved, &c. or I have loved, &c.	amāvi	mŏnui	audīvi	lēgi
2. Thou lovedst, &c. or &c.	amāvisti	monuisti	audīvisti	legisti
3. He loved, &c. or &c.	amāvĭt	monŭit	audīvĭt	legĭt
Plur. 1. We loved, &c. or &c.	amāvĭmus	monuĭmus	audivĭmus	legĭmus
2. Ye loved, &c. or &c.	amāvistis	monuistis	audivistis	legistis
3. They loved, &c. or &c.	amāvērunt *or* amāvēre	monuērunt *or* monuēre	audivērunt *or* audivēre	legērunt *or* legēre

Pluperfect.

	amāvĕram	mŏnuĕram	audivĕram	legĕram
Sing. 1. I had loved, &c.	amāvĕram	mŏnuĕram	audivĕram	legĕram
2. Thou hadst loved, &c.	amāvĕrās	monuĕrās	audivĕrās	legĕrās
3. He had loved, &c.	anivĕrāt	monuĕrāt	audivĕrāt	legĕrāt
Plur. 1. We had loved, &c.	amāvĕrāmus	monuĕrāmus	audivĕrāmus	legĕrāmus
2. Ye had loved, &c.	amāvĕrātis	monuĕrātis	audivĕrātis	legĕrātis
3. They had loved, &c.	amāvĕrant	monuĕrant	audivĕrant	legĕrant

Future.

Sing. 1. I shall love, &c. or I will love, &c.	amābo	mŏnēbo	audiam	lĕgam
2. Thou wilt love, &c.	amābis	monēbis	audiēs	legēs
3. He will love, &c.	amābit	monēbit	audiet	legĕt
Plur. 1. We shall love, &c. or &c.	amābĭmus	monēbĭmus	audiēmus	legēmus
2. Ye will love, &c.	amābĭtis	monēbĭtis	audiētis	legētis
3. They will love, &c.	amābunt	monēbunt	audient	legent

Completed Future.

	amo	moneo	audio	lego
Sing. 1. I shall have loved, &c.	ămāvero	mŏnŭĕro	audīvero	lēgĕro
2. Thou wilt have loved, &c.	amāvĕris	monuĕris	audīvĕris	legĕris
3. He will have loved, &c.	amāvĕrĭt	monuĕrĭt	audīvĕrĭt	legĕrĭt
Plur. 1. We shall have loved, &c.	amāvĕrĭmus	monuĕrĭmus	audīvĕrĭmus	legĕrĭmus
2. Ye will have loved, &c.	amāvĕrĭtis	monuĕrĭtis	audīvĕrĭtis	legĕrĭtis
3. They will have loved, &c.	amāvĕrint	monuĕrint	audīvĕrint	legĕrint

SUBJUNCTIVE MOOD.

Present.

Sing. 1.	ămem	mŏneam	audiam	lĕgam
2.	amēs	moneās	audiās	legās
3.	amĕt	moneăt	audiăt	legăt
Plur. 1.	amēmus	moneāmus	audiāmus	legāmus
2.	amētis	moneātis	audiātis	legātis
3.	ament	moneant	audiant	legant

Imperfect.

Sing. 1.	ămārem	mŏnērem	audīrem	lĕgĕrem
2.	amārēs	monērēs	audīres	legĕrēs
3.	amārēt	monērēt	audīrĕt	legĕrĕt
Plur. 1.	amārēmus	monērēmus	audīrēmus	legĕrēmus
2.	amārētis	monērētis	audīrētis	legĕrētis
3.	amārent	monērent	audīrent	legĕrent

Perfect.

Sing.	1.	amāverim	monuerim	audiverim	lēgerim
	2.	amāverīs	monuerīs	audiverīs	legerīs
	3.	amāverit	monuerit	audiverit	legerit
Plur.	1.	amāverīmus	monuerīmus	audiverīmus	legerīmus
	2.	amāverītis	monuerītis	audiverītis	legerītis
	3.	amāverint	monuerint	audiverint	legerint

Pluperfect.

Sing.	1.	amāvissem	monuissem	audivissem	lēgissem
	2.	amāvissēs	monuissēs	audivissēs	legissēs
	3.	amāvissēt	monuissēt	audivissēt	legissēt
Plur.	1.	amāvissēmus	monuissēmus	audivissēmus	legissēmus
	2.	amāvissētis	monuissētis	audivissētis	legissētis
	3.	amāvissent	monuissent	audivissent	legissent

IMPERATIVE MOOD.

Present.

Sing.	2.	Love (thou)	amā	monē	audī	lĕgĕ
Plur.	2.	Love (ye)	amāte	monēte	audīte	legĭte

Future.

Sing.	2.	Thou shalt love }	amāto	monēto	audīto	lĕgĭto
	3.	He shall love				
Plur.	2.	Ye shall love	amātōte	monētōte	audītōte	legitōte
	3.	They shall love	amanto	monento	audiunto	legunto

INFINITIVE MOOD.

Present.	ămāre	mŏnēre	audīre	lĕgĕre
Perfect.	ămāvisse	mŏnuisse	audivisse	lēgisse
Future.	ămātūrus (a, um) esse	mŏnĭtūrus (a, um) esse	audĭtūrus (a, um) esse	lectūrus (a, um) esse

(When a verb has no future participle the inf. fut. is formed by *fore ut*; as, Spero fore ut id contingat nobis, *I hope that will happen to us*.)

PARTICIPLES.

Present.	*Loving*	ămans	mŏnens	audĭens	lĕgens
Future.	*About to love*	ămātūrus	mŏnĭtūrus	audĭtūrus	lectūrus
GERUNDIVE.	ămandus	mŏnendus	audĭendus	lĕgendus
SUPINES.	ămātum	mŏnĭtum	audĭtum	lectum
	ămātu	mŏnĭtu	audĭtu	lectu

(N.B. There is no *perfect* participle in the active voice. (See § 259, 5.) The participles are declined like adjectives, viz. the present part. like adjectives of the second class; the future part. and gerundive like adjectives of the first class.)

§ 80. PASSIVE VOICE.

INDICATIVE MOOD.

Present Tense.

	amŏr	mŏnĕŏr	lĕgŏr	audĭŏr
Sing. 1. I am being loved, &c. (or I am loved, &c.)	ămŏr	mŏnĕŏr	lĕgŏr	audĭŏr
2. Thou art being loved, &c. or &c.	amārĭs	monērĭs	legĕrĭs	audīrĭs
3. He is being loved, &c. or &c.	amātŭr	monētŭr	legĭtŭr	audītŭr
Plur. 1. We are being loved, &c. or &c.	amāmŭr	monēmŭr	legĭmŭr	audīmŭr
2. Ye are being loved, &c. or &c.	amāmĭnĭ	monēmĭnĭ	legĭmĭnĭ	audīmĭnĭ
3. They are being loved, &c. or &c.	amantŭr	monentŭr	leguntŭr	audiuntŭr

Imperfect.

	Ămābăr	mŏnēbăr	lĕgēbăr	audiēbăr
Sing. 1. I was being loved, &c.	Ămābăr	mŏnēbăr	lĕgēbăr	audiēbăr
2. Thou wast being loved, &c.	amābārĭs	monēbārĭs	legēbārĭs	audiēbārĭs
3. He was being loved, &c.	amābātŭr	monēbātŭr	legēbātŭr	audiēbātŭr
Plur. 1. We were being loved, &c.	amābāmŭr	monēbāmŭr	legēbāmŭr	audiēbāmŭr
2. Ye were being loved, &c.	amābāmĭnĭ	monēbāmĭnĭ	legēbāmĭnĭ	audiēbāmĭnĭ
3. They were being loved, &c.	amābantŭr	monēbantŭr	legēbantŭr	audiēbantŭr

R. G.

4

Passive Voice.

Perfect.

	amātŭs (ă, um) / amāti (æ, ǎ)	mŏnĭtŭs (ă, um) / monĭti (æ, ǎ)	audītŭs (ă, um) / audĭti (æ, ǎ)	lectŭs (ă, um) / lecti (ĕ, ǎ)
Sing. 1. I am (or was) loved, &c.	sum	sum	sum	sum
2. Thou art (or wast) loved, &c.	es	es	es	es
3. He is (or was) loved, &c.	est	est	est	est
Plur. 1. We are (or were) loved, &c.	stĭmus	stĭmus	stĭmus	stĭmus
2. Ye are (or were) loved, &c.	estis	estis	estis	estis
3. They are (or were) loved, &c.	sunt	sunt	sunt	sunt

Pluperfect.

	amātus (a, um) / amāti (æ, a)	monĭtus (a, um) / monĭti (æ, a)	auditus (a, um) / audĭti (æ, a)	lectus (a, um) / lecti (æ, a)
Sing. 1. I had been loved, &c.	ĕram (or fŭĕram)	ĕram	ĕram	ĕram
2. Thou hadst been loved, &c.	ĕras	ĕras	ĕras	ĕras
3. He had been loved, &c.	ĕrat	ĕrat	ĕrat	ĕrat
Plur. 1. We had been loved, &c.	erāmus	erāmus	erāmus	erāmus
2. Ye had been loved, &c.	erātis	erātis	erātis	erātis
3. They had been loved, &c.	erant	erant	erant	erant

Future.

	amā	monē	audi	leg
Sing. 1. I shall be loved, &c.	ămābŏr	mònēbŏr	audiār	legăr
2. Thou wilt be loved, &c.	amāběrĭs	monēběrĭs	audiērĭs	legěrĭs
3. He will be loved, &c.	amābĭtŭr	monēbĭtŭr	audiētŭr	legētŭr
Plur. 1. We shall be loved, &c.	amābĭmŭr	monēbĭmŭr	audiēmŭr	legēmŭr
2. Ye will be loved, &c.	amābĭmĭnī	monēbĭmĭnī	audiēmĭnī	legēmĭnī
3. They will be loved, &c.	amābuntŭr	monēbuntŭr	audientŭr	legentŭr

Completed Future.

	amā	monē	audi	leg
Sing. 1. I shall have been loved, &c.	amātus (a, um) ero (or fuĕro)	monĭtus (a, um) ero (or fuĕro)	audītus (a, um) ero (or fuĕro)	lectus (a, um) ero (or fuĕro)
2. Thou wilt have been loved, &c.	,, eris	,, eris	,, eris	,, eris
3. He will have been loved, &c.	,, erit	,, erit	,, erit	,, erit
Plur. 1. We shall have been loved, &c.	amāti (æ, a) erĭmus	monĭti (æ, a) erĭmus	audīti (æ, a) erĭmus	lecti (æ, a) erĭmus
2. Ye will have been loved, &c.	,, erĭtis	,, erĭtis	,, erĭtis	,, erĭtis
3. They will have been loved, &c.	,, erunt	,, erunt	,, erunt	,, erunt

4—2

SUBJUNCTIVE MOOD.

Present Tense.

Sing. 1.	ămĕr	mŏnĕăr	lĕgăr	audĭăr
2.	amērĭs	monēărĭs	legārĭs	audĭārĭs
3.	amētŭr	monēātŭr	legātŭr	audĭātŭr
Plur. 1.	amēmŭr	monĕāmŭr	legāmŭr	audĭāmŭr
2.	amēmĭnī	monĕāmĭnī	legāmĭnī	audĭāmĭnī
3.	amentŭr	monĕāntŭr	legantŭr	audĭantŭr

Imperfect.

Sing. 1.	ămārĕr	mŏnērĕr	lĕgĕrĕr	audīrĕr
2.	amārērĭs	monērērĭs	legĕrērĭs	audĭrērĭs
3.	amārētŭr	monērētŭr	legĕrētŭr	audĭrētŭr
Plur. 1.	amārēmŭr	monērēmŭr	legĕrēmŭr	audĭrēmŭr
2.	amārēmĭnī	monērēmĭnī	legĕrēmĭnī	audĭrēmĭnī
3.	amārentŭr	monērentŭr	legĕrentŭr	audĭrentŭr

Perfect.

Sing. 1.	amātus (a, um) sim	mŏnĭtus (a, um) sim	audītus (a, um) sim	lectus (a, um) sim
2.	" sis	" sis	" sis	" sis
3.	" sit	" sit	" sit	" sit
Plur. 1.	amāti (æ, a) simus	mŏnĭti (æ, a) simus	audīti (æ, a) simus	lecti (æ, a) simus
2.	" sitis	" sitis	" sitis	" sitis
3.	" sint	" sint	" sint	" sint

Pluperfect.

Sing. 1.	amātus (a, um) essem (or fŏrem)	mŏnĭtus (a, um) essem (or fŏrem)	audītus (a, um) essem (or fŏrem)	lectus (a, um) essem (or fŏrem)
2.	" esses	" esses	" esses	" esses
3.	" esset	" esset	" esset	" esset
Plur. 1.	amāti (æ, a) essēmus	mŏnĭti (æ, a) essēmus	audīti (æ, a) essēmus	lecti (æ, a) essēmus
2.	" essētis	" essētis	" essētis	" essētis
3.	" essent	" essent	" essent	" essent

IMPERATIVE MOOD.

Present.

Sing. 2.	Be thou loved, &c.	ămāre	mŏnēre	audīre	lĕgĕre
Plur. 2.	Be ye loved, &c.	ămāmĭnī	mŏnēmĭnī	audimĭnī	lĕgimĭnī

Future.

Sing. 2.	Thou shalt be loved, &c.	ămātŏr	mŏnētŏr	audītŏr	lĕgitŏr
3.	He shall be loved, &c.				
Plur. 3.	They shall be loved, &c.	ămāntŏr	mŏnēntŏr	audiuntŏr	lĕguntŏr

INFINITIVE MOOD.

Present.	amāri	monēri	audīri	lĕgi
Perfect.	amātus (a, um) esse	mŏnĭtus (a, um) esse	audītus (a, um) esse	lectus (a, um) esse
Future.	amātum iri	mŏnĭtum iri	audītum iri	lectum iri

(N.B. This future infinitive is composed of the *supine* and the passive infin. of eo, *go*. Amatum ire in the active, means *to go to love, to be about to love*: hence in passive, amatum iri. When a verb has no supine the fut. infin. pass. is formed by *fore ut*: as spero fore ut urgeatur, *I hope he will be pushed.*

PARTICIPLES.

Perfect.

Having been (*or being*) loved, &c.	amātus	mŏnĭtus	audītus	lectus

(N.B. There are no *present* or *future* participles in the passive voice. The perfect participle is declined like an adjective of the first class.)

DEPONENTS have all the inflexions of the passive voice (except the future infinitive) with the significations of the active voice. Thus, e.g. hortor, *I exhort*; hortatus sum, *I exhorted*; hortabor, *I shall exhort*; hortatus ero, *I shall have exhorted*; hortatus, *having exhorted*, &c. They have also gerundive, gerunds, supines, and future infinitive and participle similarly to the active voice: e.g. hortandus, hortatum, hortaturus esse.

Varieties of form in the Conjugations. (Madvig.)

§ 81. 1. In active perfects ending in *āvi*, and *ēvi*, and tenses formed from them, the semivowel *v* (pronounced *w* by the Romans) is often omitted, if *r* or *s* follow *ve* or *vi*, and the two vowels thus brought together coalesce into a long *ā* or *ē*. Thus *amavisse, implēvĕrint,* &c. become *amāsse, implērint*.

In active perfects ending in *ivi*, and the tenses formed from them, *v* is often omitted before *e*, or *is*: in which latter case *ii* in prose is almost always contracted into *i*. More rarely (in the poets) *v* is left out before *it*. Thus we have *quæsiĕram, audissem, sisti, audiit,* &c. for *quæsīvĕram, audīvissem, sīvisti, audīvit,* &c.

Iit is not unfrequent in *petiit*, and is the only form used in the compounds of *eo;* e.g. *rediit.* So always *desiit.* In the compounds of *eo* the 1st person is always in *ii.* Sometimes *petii.*

2. We also in the older writers and poets meet with such contractions as *scripsti, dixe, consumpset,* &c. for *scripsisti, dixisse, consumpsisset.*

3. In the passive voice the 2nd person singular very often (in Cicero usually) ends in *re* for *ris;* except in the present indicative, in which it is more rare, and confined to deponents; and in the 4th conjugation very rare. Thus *amabāre* for *amabāris, legĕrēre* for *legĕrēris,* &c.

4. In some poets the old form of the passive present infinitive (in *ier*) is retained, as *amāriĕr* for *amāri.*

5. The fut. ind. act. and pass. of the 4th conjug. in the older style ended in *ibo, ibor;* as, *audībo, audībor,* for *audiam, audiar.*

6. In the language of the comic poets we meet with another (simple) future formed by adding *so* or *sso* to the crude form; and a subjunctive form in *sim* or *ssim,* as *lĕvasso, prohĭbesso, axo* (= *ag-so*); *levassim, prohibessim, axim.* The later language retained *faxo* (only in 1st per-

son), *I will make,* and the subjunctive form *faxim, ausim* (from *audeo*). Many consider these forms to be *completed futures,* and as such the indicative form was occasionally used, but not in a principal sentence.

7. An active participle with a present signification is formed from some verbs by adding to the crude form *bundus (a, um),* e.g. cunctābundus, *loitering* (cunctor); deliberābundus, *deliberating* (delibero); furïbundus, *raging* (furo); tremĕbundus, *trembling* (tremo). It is rarely transitive.

§ 82. Some verbs of the 3rd conjugation end in *io.* These are conjugated like verbs of the 4th conjugation in the imperf. and fut. indic. and pres. subj. both active and passive; they also retain the *i* in the 3rd pers. plur. of the pres. indic. and of the fut. imper. both active and passive, and in the gerundive. In the other parts of the verb they are conjugated as if they ended in *o* instead of *io.* Thus,

					Active.	*Passive*
Indic.	Pres.	Sing.	1.		căpio	căpior
			2.		căpĭs	căpĕris
			3.		căpĭt	căpĭtur
		Plur.	1.		căpĭmus	căpĭmur
			2.		căpĭtis	căpĭmĭni
			3.		căpiunt	căpiuntur
	Impf.				căpiēbam	căpiēbar
	Fut.				căpiam, că-pies, &c.	căpiar, ca-piēris, &c.
Subj.	Pres.				căpiam, că-piās, &c.	căpiar, că-piāris, &c.
	Impf.				căpĕrem	căpĕrer
Imper.	Pres.	Sing.	2.		căpĕ	căpĕrĕ
		Plur.	2.		căpĭtĕ	căpĭmĭnĭ
	Fut.	S. 2 & 3.			căpĭto	căpĭtor
		Plur.	2.		căpĭtōte	
			3.		căpiunto	căpiuntor
Infin.	Pres.				căpĕrĕ	căpī
Gerundive.					căpiendus	

The following verbs and their compounds are so conjugated:

căpio	(lăcio) only in comp. e. g. *allicio*.
cŭpio	părio
făcio	quătio (compounds *concŭtio*, &c.)
fŏdio	răpio
fŭgio	săpio
jăcio	(spĕcio) only in comp. e. g. *aspicio*.

Also the following deponents; the three last however having some forms of the fourth conjugation.

grădior	mŏrior (inf. mŏrī or mŏrīri, part. fut. morĭturus).
pătior	ŏrior (inf. ŏrīri, imp. subj. ŏrīrer or ŏrĕrer).
	pŏtior (inf. pŏtīri, imp. subj. pŏtĕrer or pŏtīrer, perf. pŏtītus sum).

§ 83. IRREGULAR VERBS.

Indicative Mood. Present Tense.	Possum (pŏtis, or pŏte, sum), *be able.*	Vŏlo, *be willing.*	Nōlo (Ne-volo), *be unwilling.*	Mālo (Ma-volo for mag-volo), *prefer.*
Sing. 1.	possum	vŏlo	nōlo	mālo
2.	pŏtĕs	vīs	nonvīs	māvīs
3.	pŏtest	vult	nonvult	māvult
Plur. 1.	possŭmus	vŏlŭmus	nōlŭmus	mālŭmus
2.	pŏtestis	vultis	nonvultis	māvultis
3.	possunt	vŏlunt	nōlunt	mālunt
Imperf. Sing. 1.	pŏtĕram*	vŏlēbam	nōlēbam	mālēbam
Perf. Sing. 1.	pŏtŭi	vŏlŭi	nōlŭi	mālui
Plupft. Sing. 1.	pŏtŭĕram	vŏlŭĕram	nōlŭĕram	mālŭĕram
Future Sing. 1.	pŏtĕro	vŏlam	nōlam	mālam
2.	pŏtĕris	vŏles	nōles	māles
Comp. Fut. Sing. 1.	pŏtuĕro	vŏluĕro	nōluĕro	māluĕro
Subjunctive Mood. Pres. Sing. 1.	possim	vĕlim	nōlim	mālim
Plur. 1.	possīmus	vĕlīmus	nōlīmus	mālīmus
Imperf. Sing. 1.	possem	vellem	nollem	mallem
Perf. Sing. 1.	pŏtŭĕrim	vŏlŭĕrim	nōlŭĕrim	mālŭĕrim
Plupft. Sing. 1.	pŏtŭissem	vŏlŭissem	nōlŭissem	mālŭissem
Imperative. Pres. Sing. 2.			nōlī	
Plur. 2.			nōlīte	
Future Sing. 2.			nōlīto	
Plur. 2.			nōlītōte	
3.			nōlunto	
Infinitive. Present.	posse	velle	nolle	malle
Perfect.	pŏtŭisse	vŏlŭisse	nōlŭisse	mālŭisse
Future.				
Participle. Present.	pŏtens (only used as	vŏlens	nōlens	mālens
Perfect.	adjective)			
Future.				
Gerund and *Gerundive.*		vŏlendi -do -dum	nōlendi -do -dum	mālendi -do -dum

* In these pages the italic letters are used only to distinguish the

Eo, go.	Fio (used as pas- sive of facio), become.	Edo, eat.	Fero, bear.	Feror, be borne.
ĕo	fīo	ĕdo	fĕro	fĕror
īs	fīs	ĕdĭs or ēs	fers	ferris
ĭt	fĭt	ĕdĭt or est	fert	fertur
īmus	fīmus	ĕdĭmus	fĕrĭmus	fĕrĭmur
ītis	fītis	ĕdĭtis or estis	fertis	fĕrĭmĭni
ĕunt	fīunt	ĕdunt	fĕrunt	fĕruntur
ībam	fīebam	ĕdēbam	fĕrēbam	fĕrēbar
īvi	factus sum	ēdĭ	tŭlĭ	lātus sum
īvĕram	factus eram	ēdĕram	tŭlĕram	lātus eram
ībo	fīam	ĕdam	fĕram	fĕrar
ībis	fīes	ĕdes	fĕres	fĕrēris
īvero	factus ero	ĕdĕro	tŭlĕro	latus ero
ĕam	fīam	ĕdam or ĕdim fĕram		fĕrar
ĕāmus	fīāmus	ĕdāmus or ĕdīmus	fĕramus	fĕrāmur
īrem	fĭĕrem	ĕdĕrem or essem	ferrem	ferrer
īvĕrim	factus sim	ēdĕrim	tŭlĕrim	lātus sim
īvissem	factus essem	ēdissem	tŭlissem	lātus essem
ī	fī	ĕde or ēs	fĕr	ferre
īte	fīte	ĕdĭte or este	ferte	fĕrĭmĭni
īto		ĕdĭto or esto	ferto	fertor
ītōte		ĕdĭtōte or estōte	fertōte	
ĕunto		ĕdunto	fĕrunto	fĕruntor
īre	fĭĕri	ĕdĕre or esse	ferre	ferri
īvisse	factus esse	ēdisse	tŭlisse	lātus esse
ĭtūrus esse	factum iri	ēsūrus esse	lātūrus esse	lātum iri
ĭens or ĕuns G. ĕuntis		ĕdens	fĕrens	
	factus			lātus
		ēsūrus	lātūrus	
ĕundum -di -do	făcĭendus	ĕdendus	fĕrendus	
(compounds have eundus.)				

part of the word which must be altered to form the other persons, &c.

DEFECTIVE VERBS.

§ 84. Quĕo, nĕquĕo, are declined like *eo*, but have no imperative, future participle, or gerund.

§ 85. Ajo, and inquam, both meaning *say, quoth*, have but few forms. Inquam is only used when a person's speech is given in his own words (i. e. not in the *oratio obliqua*), and is always inserted after one or more words of the speech cited.

	INDICATIVE.				SUBJUNCT.	IMPER.
	Present.	*Imperf.*	*Perfect.*	*Future.*	*Present.*	
Sing. 1.	inquam	inquĭēbam				
2.	inquis	inquĭēbas	inquisti	inquies	inquĭas	{inquĕ {inquĭto
3.	inquit	inquĭēbat	inquit	inquiet	inquĭat	
Plur.1.	inquĭmus	inquĭēbamus				
2.	inquĭtis	inquĭēbatis	inquistis		inquiātis	inquĭte
3.	inquĭunt	inquĭēbant			inquiant	
Sing. 1.	ājo	ājēbam				
2.	ăĭs	ājēbas			ājās	ājens
3.	ăĭt	ājēbat			ājāt	
Plur.1.		ājēbāmus				
2.		ājēbātis				
3.	ājūnt	ājēbant			ājānt	

§ 86. Cœpi, mĕmĭni, ōdi, are only used in the perfect and tenses derived from it: except that the imperative form *mĕmento*, *mĕmentōte*, and the perf. pass. participle *cœptus*, and future active participles *cœpturus* and *osūrus*, are also found. A present *cœpio* occurs in Plautus.

cœpi, *I began* or *begin;* cœpĕram, *I had begun* or *was beginning;* cœpero, *I shall have begun* or *shall begin;*

mĕmĭni, *I remember;* mĕmĭnĕram, *I was remembering;* mĕmĭnĕro, *I shall remember;*

ōdi, *I hate;* ōdĕram, *I was hating;* ōdĕro, *I shall hate.*

(Similarly, nōvi (from nosco, *I get knowledge of*) means, *I know;* nōvĕram, *I was knowing;* nōvĕro, *I shall know.* Proba-

bly cœpi *(in present signification) means, *I have taken in hand ;*
i.e. *I commence :* and memini, *I have noticed,* i.e. *I remember.*)

§ 87.   Infit, (*he,* &c.) *begins,* is only used in this one form.

§ 88.   Fari, *to speak,* with its compounds (affāri, præfāri,
prōfāri) is used only in the following forms (but those within
brackets are found only in the compounds):

	INDIC.	SUBJ.
Pres.	fātur (fāmur, fāmĭni)	
Imp.	fābar	(fārer, &c.)
Perf.	fātus sum, &c.	fātus sim, &c.
Plup.	fātus eram, &c.	fātus essem, &c.
Fut.	fābor (fābĕris) fābĭtur.	

	IMPER.	INFIN.	SUPINE.
Pres. Sing.	fāre	fāri	fātu

	PARTIC.	PERF.	GERUND.
Pres.	fantem fantis, &c. (no nom.)	fātus	fandus

§ 89.   The following imperatives of verbs otherwise defective
are also found:

Singular.	*Plural.*
salvē, *hail*	salvēte
salvēto	

(also *inf.* salvēre, *fut.* 2 *Sing.* salvēbis)

ăvē, *hail*	
avēto	avēte, *inf.* avēre
cĕdŏ, *give*	cette (for cĕdĭte).

* The derivation is supposed to be from co- apio, *join together ;*
whence *aptus, apiscor :* also *cōpula.*

IMPERSONAL VERBS.

§ 90. The following verbs (of the 2nd conjugation) are only used in the 3 pers. sing.

Pres.	*Perf.*
lĭbet, or, lŭbet (mihi), *it pleases*	lĭbuit, or, lĭbĭtum est
lĭcet (mihi), *it is permitted*	lĭcuit, or, lĭcĭtum est
mĭsĕret mĭsĕrētur } (me), *it pitieth (me)*	mĭsĕrĭtum est
ŏportet (me), *it behoves*	ŏportuit
pĭget (me), *it vexes*	pĭguit and pĭgĭtum est
pœnĭtet (me), *it repenteth*	pœnĭtuit
pŭdet (me), *it shames*	{ pŭduit { pŭdĭtum est
tædet (me), *it wearieth*	pertæsum est.

Many other verbs, e. g.

dĕcet (me), *it becomes*	dĕcuit
dēdĕcet (me), *it misbecomes*	dēdĕcuit

are used without a *personal* subject (see § 151), but have besides a regular personal use.

CLASSIFICATION OF PERFECTS AND SUPINES.

§ 91. There are four modes of forming the perfect active, which do not however differ in signification:

1. By reduplication (§ 78); as, *mordeo, mŏmordi.*

2. By lengthening the root-vowel; as, *lĕgo, lēgi.*

3. By adding *vi* or *ui* to the crude form or root, as *amā-, amāvi; mon-, monui.*

4. By adding *si* to the root (with occasional alteration of final consonant); as, *lūc-, luxi; reg-, rexi; plaud-, plausi* (cf. Greek aorist λύω, ἔλυ-σα).

Those verbs which form their perfect in *i* only, have probably either lost a reduplication, or absorbed the *v* (or *u*) of *vi*.

The supine is formed by adding *tum* or *sum* to the crude form or root.

(N.B. Where no perfect is mentioned, none is known to exist. The supine is not of common occurrence, but is here mentioned whenever a future part. act. or perfect pass. are known, as these are similarly formed. In the case of deponents, as the perfect gives the form, it is unnecessary to add the supine.)

FIRST CONJUGATION.

Regular perfect in *ā-vi*, supine in *ā-tum*.

§ 92. 1. PERFECT REDUPLICATED :

do, *give*   dědi   dătum

(Compounds are of 3rd conj. except *circumdo, satisdo,* &c. in which the preposition is almost a separate word.)

sto, *stand*   stěti   stătum (cf. § 120. 5. *b*)

§ 93. 2. PERFECT WITH ROOT-VOWEL LENGTHENED :

jŭvo, *help, delight*   jūvi   jūtum (fut. part. jŭvāturus)

lăvo, *wash*   lāvi   {lautum {lōtum

(Compounds are of 3 conj. ; as, *abluo*.)

§ 94. 3. PERFECT WITH *ui* ADDED :

applĭco, *apply, put in*   {applĭcui   applĭcĭtum
(to shore)   {applĭcāvi   applĭcātum

(So the compounds of *plico* generally; Cicero uses the forms in *avi, atum*.)

crěpo, *rattle*   crěpui   crěpĭtum
cŭbo, *lie, lie ill*   cŭbui   cŭbĭtum (cf. *cumbo*, § 106)
dŏmo, *tame*   dŏmui   dŏmĭtum
ēnĕco, *stifle completely*   {ēnĕcui   ēnectum
   {ēnĕcāvī
frĭco, *rub*   frĭcui   frictum (also frĭcā-tum)

mĭco, *vibrate, flash*   mĭcui

(But *emico* has sup. *emĭcātum*, and *dimico* is quite regular.)

sĕco, *cut*	sĕcui	sectum (fut. part. sĕcātūrus)
sŏno, *sound*	sŏnui	sŏnĭtum
tŏno, *thunder*	tŏnui	tŏnĭtum
vĕto, *forbid*	vĕtui	vĕtĭtum

4. PERFECT WITH *si* ADDED:

None.

SECOND CONJUGATION IN *e.*

Regular perfect in *ui;* supine in *ĭtum.*

§ 95. 1. PERFECT REDUPLICATED:

mordeo, *bite*	mŏmordi	morsum
pendeo, *hang,* intr.	pĕpendi	pensum
spondeo, *promise, pledge oneself*	spŏpondi	sponsum
tondeo, *shear*	tŏtondi	tonsum

§ 96. 2. PERFECT WITH ROOT-VOWEL LENGTHENED:

căveo, *beware, beware of*	cāvi	cautum (contracted for căvĭtum)
făveo, *favour*	fāvi	fautum (contracted for făvĭtum)
fŏveo, *keep warm, cherish*	fōvi	fōtum (contracted for fŏvĭtum)
mŏveo, *move,* trans.	mōvi	mōtum (contracted for mŏvĭtum)
păveo, *quake with fear*	pāvi	
sĕdeo, *sit*	sēdi	sessum
vĭdeo, *see*	vīdi	vīsum
vŏveo, *vow*	vōvi	vōtum (contracted for vŏvĭtum)

§ 97. PERFECT IN *i* SIMPLE:

connīveo, *wink*	{ connīvi { connixi	
ferveo, *boil, glow*	{ fervi { ferbui	(*ferbui* most generally in compounds)
langueo, *languish*	langui	

lĭqueo, *be clear*   { lĭqui
                           { lĭcui
prandeo, *dine*   prandi   pransum
strīdeo, *hiss, screech* strīdi

§ 98.   3. PERFECT WITH *vi* ADDED:

abŏleo, *destroy* (lit. *destroy growth*)	abŏlēvi	abŏlĭtum
cĭeo, *stir up*	cīvi	cĭtum (see *cio*, § 115)
dēlĕo, *blot out*	dēlēvi	dēlētum (contracted for *delevĭtum*), really a compound of *lăvo*
fleo, *weep*	flēvi	flētum (contracted for *flevĭtum*)
impleo, *fill*	implēvi	implētum
(So also the other compounds of *pleo*.)		
neo, *spin*	nēvi	nētum (contracted for *nevĭtum*)
vĭeo, *plait (twigs*, &c.)	viēvi	viētum

§ 99.   4. PERFECT WITH *si* (*xi* = *csi*) ADDED:

algeo, *be cold*	alsi	
ardeo, *be on fire*	arsi	arsum
augeo, *increase, endow*	auxi	auctum
frīgeo, *be cold*	frixi	frictum
fulgeo, *shine*	fulsi	
hæreo, *stick*	hæsi	hæsum
indulgeo, *be indulgent, yield*	indulsi	indultum
jŭbeo, *bid*	jussi	jussum
lūceo, *shine* } lūgeo, *mourn* }	luxi	
măneo, *remain, await*	mansi	mansum
mulceo, *soothe* } mulgeo, *milk* }	mulsi	mulsum
rīdeo, *laugh*	rīsi	rīsum
sorbeo, *sup up, swallow*	sorpsi (also sorbui)	sorptum
suādeo, *recommend*	suāsi	suasum
tergeo, *wipe*	tersi	tersum
torqueo, *twist, hurl*	torsi	tortum
turgeo, *swell*	tursi	
urgeo, *push, press*	ursi	

R. G.   5

§ 100. The following are regular in the perfect, but omit *i* in the supine :

censeo, *assess, think*	censui	censum (recenseo has also *recensi-tum*)
dŏceo, *teach*	dŏcui	doctum
misceo, *mix*	miscui	⎰mistum ⎱mixtum
tĕneo, *hold*	tĕnui	tentum (rarely used)
torreo, *roast*	torrui	tostum

§ 101. SEMIDEPONENTS (intransitive) :

audeo, *dare*	ausus sum
gaudeo, *be glad*	gāvīsus sum
sŏleo, *be wont*	sŏlĭtus sum

DEPONENTS :

făteor, *acknowledge*	fassus sum	
rĕor, *think*	rătus sum	(no pres. part.)
tuĕor, *look at, protect*	tuĭtus sum	

(The perf. is only found in compounds: *tutātus sum* is used for perf. of *tueor* in the sense of *protect*.)

N.B. Some of these verbs have another form belonging to the 3rd conjugation; as, *fervo, fulgo, tergo, strido. Cĭeo* has another form of the 4th conj. *cio.*

THIRD, OR CONSONANT CONJUGATION.

N.B. *All* the verbs (not compounds) of this conjugation that have any perfect or supine are here given.

§ 102. I. PERFECT REDUPLICATED :

(N.B. The compounds of these verbs rarely retain the reduplication; but the verbs with short penult. when compounded with *rĕ* (or *rĕd*) have the antepenult (of the perf. only) long : as, *rĕpulit*, or *reppulit*, as if for *repepulit*) :

cădo, *fall*	cĕcĭdi	cāsum
cædo, *fell, cut, slay*	cĕcīdi	cæsum
căno, *sing, play* (on a harp, &c.)	cĕcĭni	(*cantus*, subst.)

(The compounds *concĭno, occĭno, præcĭno*, have *concĭnui, concentum*, &c. ; other compounds have no perf.)

condo, *put by, hide,* build	condĭdi	condĭtum
crēdo, *entrust, believe*	crēdĭdi	crēdĭtum

(And other compounds of *do*. N.B. Accrēdo makes *accrēdĭdi*.)

curro, *run*	cŭcurri	cursum

(Accurro sometimes has *accucurri*.)

disco, *learn*	dĭdĭci (so addisco, *addidici*)	
fallo, *deceive, elude*	fĕfelli	falsum
păciscor, *bargain*	pĕpĭgi	pactum

(Pango (§ 108) not used in this sense.)

parco, *spare*	pĕperci	parsum
	(perf. *parsi* is rarely found)	
părio, *get, bring forth*	pĕpĕri	partum (but *părĭturus*)
pello, *push, drive back*	pĕpŭli	pulsum
pendo, *hang,* trans.	pĕpendi	pensum
posco, *demand*	pŏposci (so deposco, *depŏposci*)	
pungo, *prick*	pŭpŭgi	punctum

(But compounds have *punxi*.)

tango, *touch*	tĕtĭgi	tactum
tendo, *stretch, tend*	tĕtendi	{tensum / tentum}

(*Ostendo, ostensum;* but other compounds *-tentum*.)

tundo, *thump*	tŭtŭdi	{tūsum / tunsum}

§ 103. 2. Perfect with Root-vowel lengthened:

ăgo, *do, drive*	ēgi	actum

(So the compound *cōgo, coēgi, coactum.*)

căpio, *take*	cēpi	captum
ĕdo, *eat*	ēdi	ēsum (§ 83)
ĕmo, *buy* (cf. como, § 108)	ēmi	emptum*

* Such insertions as the *p* in *emptum, temptum,* and their compounds, are perhaps the only real *euphonic* additions. The *p* is naturally, but unintentionally, pronounced in passing from *m* to *t.*

făcio, *make, do*	fēci	factum
fŏdio, *dig*	fōdi	fossum
frango, *break in pieces*	frēgi	fractum
fŭgio, *flee, fly from*	fūgi	fŭgĭtum
fundo, *pour*	fūdi	fūsum
jăcio, *throw*	jēci	jactum
lĕgo, *pick up, choose, read*	lēgi	lectum

(So the compounds generally, but for *diligo, intelligo, negligo,* see § 108.)

linquo, *leave*	līqui	(rĕlictum, from compound *relinquo*)
rumpo, *burst, break*	rūpi	ruptum
scăbo, *scratch*	scăbi	
vinco, *conquer*	vīci	victum

§ 104. PERFECT IN *i* SIMPLE:

a. Verbs in *uo* (and *vo*):

ăcŭo, *sharpen*	ăcui	ăcūtum (for *ăcŭtum:* and so the others also)
argŭo, *charge* (with crimes, &c.)	argui	(argūtus, adj. *sharp*)
bātuo, *beat, fence*	bātui	
congruo, *agree*	congrui (so ingruo, *impend over*)	
exŭo, *put off* (clothes,&c.)	exŭi	exūtum
fervo, see *ferveo,* § 97.		
indŭo, *put on*	indui	indūtum
innŭo, *give a nod*	innui	

(So also other compounds of *nŭo.*)

imbŭo, *steep, imbue*	imbui	imbūtum
lŭo, *wash, expiate*	lŭi	

(Same word as *lăvo* of 1st conj.; compounds have supine, *ablūtum,* &c.)

mĕtŭo, *fear*	mĕtui	
mĭnŭo, *lessen*	mĭnui	mĭnūtum
plŭo, *rain*	{ plui / plūvi }	
rŭo, *tumble, dash*	rui	rŭtum (but *rŭĭtŭrus*)
solvo, *loosen, pay*	solvi	sŏlūtum
spŭo, *spit*	spui	spūtum

stătŭo, *set up, settle*   stătui   stătūtum
  with oneself
sternŭo, *sneeze*   sternui
sŭo, *sew*   sui   sūtum
trĭbŭo, *assign, grant*   trĭbui   trĭbūtum
volvo, *roll*   volvi   vŏlūtum

§ 105. *b.* Other Verbs:

accendo, *light up*   accendi   accensum

(So also the other compounds of *cando*.)

bĭbo, *drink*   bĭbi
cūdo, *hammer*   cūdi   cūsum
dēfendo, *ward off, guard* dēfendi   dēfensum

(So also offendo, *strike against,* from fendo (or fando ?),
  strike.)

dēgo, *dwell*   dēgi
findo, *cleave*   fĭdi   fissum
frendo, *gnash the teeth*   fressum
īco, *strike* (for the pres. īci   ictum
  fĕrĭo is generally used)
lambo, *lick*   lambi
mando, *chew*   mandi   mansum

pando, *open*   pandi   { passum
                                  { pansum

percello, *strike*   percŭli   perculsum
prĕhendo, *lay hold of* prĕhendi   prĕhensum
psallo, *play on a stringed* psalli
  instrument
scando, *climb*   scandi   scansum
scindo, *tear, cut*   scĭdi   scissum
sīdo, *settle* (intrans.) sīdi (*sēdi* and *sessum,* from sĕdeo,
                                    are more common)

(Strido, see *strideo* § 97.)

sisto, *set, stay*   stĭti (rare)   stătum
tollo, *lift up*   sustŭli   sublātum

(N.B. *tuli* (for *tĕtŭli*) and *latum* (properly *tlātum*) are taken
  by *fero;* so that *tollo* borrows *sustŭli, sublatum,* from
  its compound *sustollo.*)

vello, *pull, pluck*   { velli   vulsum
                            { vulsi (rare)

verro, *brush*   verri   versum
verto, *turn*   verti   versum

(Devertor, *put up* (at an inn), revertor, *return,* have usually active perf.: prævertor, *attend to first,* is deponent, but præverto, *be beforehand with,* act. trans.)

vīso, *visit*   vīsi

§ 106. 3. PERFECT WITH *ui* or *vi* ADDED.

a. With *ui* added.

ălo, *nourish*   ălui   {ălĭtum / altum

cŏlo, *till, pay attention to* cŏlui   cultum
compesco, *restrain* compescui (so *dispesco*)
concĭno, *sing in concert* concĭnui concentum

(So other compounds of *căno.*)

consŭlo *consult*   consŭlui   consultum
cumbo, *lie*   cŭbui   cŭbĭtum

(Only in compounds, cf. *cubo,* § 94.)

depso, *knead*   depsui   depstum
ēlĭcio, *lure forth* ēlĭcui   ēlĭcĭtum

(For *allicio* see § 108.)

excello, *excel*   excellui   (hence *excelsus*)
frĕmo, *roar, chafe at* frĕmui frĕmĭtum
gĕmo, *sigh, groan* gĕmui gĕmĭtum
gigno, *beget, produce* gĕnui gĕnĭtum
mĕto, *mow*   messui messum
mŏlo, *grind*   mŏlui mŏlĭtum
necto, *link together* {nexui / nexi} nexum
occŭlo, *conceal* occŭlui occultum
pinso, *pound* {pinsui / pinsi} pinsĭtum / pinsum
pōno, *place* pŏsui pŏsĭtum
răpio, *snatch, hurry away,* trans. răpui raptum
sĕro, *put in rows* sĕrui sertum

(This perfect and supine only in compounds.)

sterto, *snore* stertui
strĕpo, *make a din* strĕpui strĕpitum
texo, *weave* texui textum

trĕmo, *tremble*   trĕmui
vŏlo, *wish*   vŏlui

    (And so compounds of *volo ;* as, *mālo, nōlo.*)

vŏmo, *vomit*   vŏmui   vŏmĭtum

§ 107. *b.* With *vi* (some with *īvi*) added.

accerso, } *fetch, send for*   accersīvi   accersītum
arcesso, }   arcessīvi   arcessītum
căpĕsso, *undertake*   căpessīvi   căpessītum
cerno, *sift, distinguish,*   crēvi   crētum (hence adj.
    decide, see   *certus*)

    (N.B. The meaning *see* is not given to perfect or supine.)

cresco, *grow*   crēvi   crētum
cŭpio, *desire*   cŭpīvi   cŭpītum
făcesso, *cause*   făcessīvi   făcessītum
incesso, *attack*   incessīvi
lăcesso, *provoke*   lăcessīvi   lăcessītum
lĭno, *smear*   { līvi   lĭtum
     { lēvi
nosco, *get to know*   nōvi   nōtum

    (Agnosco, cognosco have *agnĭtum, cognĭtum ;* ignosco has
    ignōtum.)

pasco, *feed* (cattle), trans. pāvi   pastum
pĕto, *seek, aim at*   pĕtīvi   pĕtītum
quæro, *seek, inquire*   quæsīvi   quæsītum

    (Quæso, *prythee,* quæsumus, i.e. 1st sing. and plur. of
    pres. ind. are also found.)

quiesco, *rest*   quiēvi   quiētum
rŭdo, *roar, bray*   rŭdīvi (rare)
săpio, { *have a savour of,* săpīvi
     { *am wise*

    (Rĕsĭpisco has *resipui* or *resĭpīvi.*)

scisco, *enact*   scīvi   scītum
sĕro, *sow, plant*   sēvi   sătum
sĭno *, leave, suffer*   sīvi   sĭtum (hence sĭtus,
     situated)

* Sino in subj. pres. makes sīrim, sīris, sīrit, sīrint. Its
compound, desino, makes in *perf. &c. ind.* desīvi, desisti, desiit,
desieram, &c. *Pres. sub.* desierim.

sperno, *reject, despise*	sprēvi	sprētum
sterno, *throw on the ground, cover*	strāvi	strātum
suesco, *accustom oneself*	suēvi	suētum
tĕro, *rub*	trīvi	trītum

§ 108.   4.   PERFECT WITH *si* (*xi = csi*) ADDED.

afflīgo (trans.), *strike against, prostrate*	afflixi	afflictum

(And other compounds of *fligo*, except prōflīgo, which is of 1st conj.)

allĭcio, *entice*	allexi	allectum

(But for *ēlĭcio*, see § 106.)

ango, *throttle, vex*	anxi	anctum
carpo, *crop, pluck*	carpsi	carptum
cēdo, *go, yield*	cessi	cessum
cingo, *gird*	cinxi	cinctum
claudo, *shut*	clausi	clausum
cōmo, *put together, dress*	compsi	comptum

(So the other compounds of *ĕmo* (originally *take*), § 103, viz. dēmo, prōmo, sūmo.)

conspĭcio, *behold*	conspexi	conspectum

(So other compounds of *specio*.)

cŏquo, *cook*	coxi	coctum
dīco, *say*	dixi	dictum
dilĭgo, *love*	dīlexi	dīlectum

(So also intellĭgo, *understand*, and neglĭgo, *leave behind*.)

dīvĭdo, *divide*	dīvīsi	dīvīsum
dūco, *lead, account*	duxi	ductum
ēmungo, *wipe the nose*	ēmunxi	ēmunctum
ēvādo, *go out*	ēvāsi	ēvāsum

(And other compounds of *vado*.)

fĕro, *bring*	(festum, (?) compare *infestus, manifestus*: for perf. see *tollo*, § 105.)	
figo, *fix*	fixi	fixum
fingo, *form, invent*	finxi	fictum
flecto, *bend*	flexi	flexum

fluo, *flow*	fluxi	(fluxus, adj. *loose,* fluctus, subst. *wave*)
frīgo, *roast* (corn, &c.)	frixi	frictum
fulgo, see *fulgeo*, § 99.		
gĕro, *carry, perform*	gessi	gestum
glūbo, *peel*	glupsi	gluptum
jungo, *yoke, join*	junxi	junctum
lædo, *hurt*	læsi	læsum
lūdo, *sport*	lūsi	lūsum
lingo, *lick*	linxi	linctum
mergo, *sink*	mersi	mersum
mitto, *send*	mīsi	missum
ningo, *snow*	ninxi	
nūbo, *put on a veil (as a bride)*	nupsi	nuptum
pango, *fasten*	{panxi {pēgi	panctum pactum

(In sense of *make agreements*, *păciscor*, §102, is generally used.)

pecto, *comb*	{pexi {pexui	pexum
plecto, *plait*		part. *plexus*
pingo, *paint*	pinxi	pictum
plango, *beat* (esp. *the breast*)	planxi	planctum
plaudo, *clap the hands*	plausi	plausum
prĕmo, *press*	pressi	pressum
quătio, *shake*	(quassi not used)	quassum

(So its compounds, e.g. *concutio, concussi, concussum*, &c.)

rādo, *scrape*	rāsi	rāsum
rĕgo, *rule*	rexi	rectum
rēpo, *creep*	repsi	
rōdo, *gnaw*	rōsi	rōsum
scalpo, *scrape*	scalpsi	scalptum
scrībo, *write*	scripsi	scriptum
sculpo, *carve in stone*	sculpsi	sculptum
serpo, *crawl*	serpsi	serptum
spargo, *scatter, besprinkle*	sparsi	sparsum
stinguo, *exstinguish*	stinxi	stinctum

(Compounds chiefly used.)

stringo, *strip, graze, draw tight*	strinxi	strictum

struo, *heap up, build*	struxi	structum
sūgo, *suck*	suxi	suctum
tĕgo, *cover*	texi	tectum
temno, *despise*	tempsi	temptum
tergo, see *tergeo*, § 99.		
tingo, *dip, dye*	tinxi	tinctum
trăho, *draw*	traxi	tractum
trūdo, *thrust*	trūsi	trūsum
vĕho, *carry*	vexi	vectum
vīvo, *live*	vixi	victum
ungo, *anoint*	unxi	unctum
ūro, *burn*	ussi	ustum

§ 109. There are a great many verbs of this conjugation which end in *sco*, called *inchoatives*, because they express the beginning of an action; the perfect of course does not contain this addition. This strengthened form of the present has often superseded the regular form (of the 2nd conj.) in *eo*. Thus: horresco, *I begin to shudder;* horrui, *I shuddered.* Most have no supine, many no perfect.

§ 110. SEMIDEPONENT:

fīdo, *trust*   fīsus sum

DEPONENTS:

ădĭpiscor, *get for oneself,*	ădeptus sum
obtain	

(From ăpiscor, *to fasten to oneself,* hence aptus, *fitted.*)

amplector, *twine oneself*	amplexus
round, embrace	
commĭniscor, *devise*	commentus
defĕtiscor, *grow weary*	defessus

(From fătisco, fătiscor (rare), *gape, droop;* hence fessus, *wearied.*)

expergiscor, *awake one-*	experrectus
self	
frŭor, *enjoy*	{ fructus { fruitus
fungor, *discharge* (an	functus
office, &c.)	
grădĭor, *step*	gressus
īrascor, *grow angry*	īrātus

(iratus sum, *I am angry* ; succensui I *grew* angry.)

lābor, *slip, glide*	lapsus	
līquor, *melt away*	lĭquĕfactus	
lŏquor, *speak*	lŏcūtus	
mŏrĭor, *die*	mortuus	See § 82.
nanciscor, *obtain*	nactus	
nascor, *be born*	nātus	
nītor, *rest oneself on,*	⎰nīsus	
strain (intr.)	⎱nixus	

(Originally gnītor, *kneel*, from gĕnu, *knee*.)

oblīviscor, *forget*	oblītus	
ŏrĭor, *rise*	ortus	See § 82.
pătior, *suffer*	passus	
prŏfĭciscor, *set out*	prŏfectus	
quĕror, *complain*	questus	
sĕquor, *follow*	sĕcūtus	
ulciscor, *avenge oneself on, avenge*	ultus	
ūtor, *use*	ūsus	

FOURTH CONJUGATION.

Regular perfect in *ī-vi*. Regular supine in *ī-tum*.

§ 111. 1. PERFECT REDUPLICATED:
None.

2. PERFECT, WITH ROOT-VOWEL LENGTHENED:

vĕnio, *come*	vēni	ventum

§ 112. PERFECT IN *i* SIMPLE:

compĕrio, *discover*	compĕri	compertum
rĕpĕrio, *find*	reppĕri	rĕpertum

§ 113. 3. PERFECT WITH *ui* ADDED:

ăpĕrio, *open*	ăpĕrui	ăpertum

(From ab, părio, and so means *get off*: so ŏpĕrio for obperio, &c.)

ŏpĕrio, *cover*	ŏpĕrui	ŏpertum
sălio, *leap*	⎰sălui ⎱sălii	saltum

§ 114. 4. Perfect with *si* (*xi=csi*) added:

ămĭcio, *clothe*		ămictum
farcio, *stuff*	farsi	fartum
fulcio, *prop*	fulsi	fultum
haurio, *drain, draw (water)*	hausi	haustum (fut. part. *haustūrus* and *hausūrus*)
sæpio, *hedge in*	sæpsi	sæptum
sancio, *hallow, ordain*	sanxi	sanctum (also *sancīvi, sancītum*)
sarcio, *patch*	sarsi	sartum
sentio, *feel, think*	sensi	sensum
vincio, *bind*	vinxi	vinctum

§ 115. Irregular in Supine:

eo, *go*	īvi	ĭtum
cio, *stir up*	cīvi	cĭtum

(But accĭtus and sometimes excĭtus, see § 98.)

sĕpĕlio, *bury*	sĕpĕlīvi	sĕpultum

§ 116. Deponents:

expĕrior, *try*	expertus sum
mētior, *measure*	mensus
oppĕrior, *wait for*	oppertus
ordior, *commence*	orsus

PROSODY.

§ 117. PROSODY is that part of Grammar which treats of the Quantity of Syllables.

If the voice dwells upon a syllable in pronouncing it, it is called a *long* syllable: if it passes rapidly over it, it is called a *short* syllable.

Long syllables are marked by a straight line over the vowel: thus, *aūdī*.

Short syllables are marked by a curved line over the vowel: thus, *rĕgĕ*.

Two short syllables are considered to occupy the same time as one long syllable.

A syllable is long or short, (1) on account of the position of its vowel; (2) or because it contains a vowel naturally long or short.

§ 118. I. QUANTITY OF VOWELS BY POSITION.

1. A syllable containing a vowel immediately followed by two consonants*, or by *x, z,* or *j* is long; as, *regēnt, strīx, mājor.*

Except

If the two consonants so following a vowel be, the first a mute (*p, b, c, g, t, f*), the second *r* or *l*; in this case a syllable containing a vowel naturally short may either remain short or be lengthened; as, *pătris.*

(N.B. In prose these are pronounced as short syllables.)

But this does not hold if the combination of mute and liquid be due to composition only; as, *sŭbruo* (not *sūbruo*).

In the compounds of *jugum j* does not lengthen the preceding vowel, as *bĭjŭgus.*

§ 119. 2. A syllable containing a vowel (or diphthong) immediately followed by another vowel, or by *h* and a vowel, is short; as, *vĭa, prǣustus.*

* *h* is not reckoned a consonant in Prosody.

Except

(a) In the genitives of pronouns, &c. in *-ius;* as, *illĭus,* where *i* is common (but in *alterĭus* always short; in *alĭus* (gen. case) always long).

(b) The genitive of the 5th declension in *iēi;* as, *diēī* (but *rĕi, spĕi*).

(c) The old genitive of the 1st declension in *āi;* as, *aulāī.*

(d) In all the cases of proper names ending in *ius;* as, *Cāiŭs, Pompēiŭs.*

(e) In *fīo* (except before *er;* as, *fĭĕri*).

§ 120.　II. Quantity of vowels by nature, not in the last syllable of a word.

1. All diphthongs are long (except before another vowel); as, *aūrum.*

2. All vowels which have originated from contraction are long; as, *cōgo* for *cŏ-ăgo, mōmentum* for *mŏvĭmentum, tibīcen* for *tibĭĭ-cen.*

3. The quantity of the radical syllables of a word are *generally* preserved in composition or derivation, even when the vowel is changed; as, *māter, māternus; cădo, incĭdo; cædo, incīdo; ămo, ămor, ămīcus, inĭmīcus.*

4. Reduplicated perfects have the first syllable short; as, *mŏmordi.*

5. Dissyllabic perfects and supines have the penult long.

Except

(a) Perfects, *bĭbi, dĕdi, fĭdi, stĕti, stĭti, tŭli, scĭdi.*

(b) Supines, *dătum, ĭtum, lĭtum, cĭtum, rătum, rŭtum, sătum, stătum*, sĭtum.*

---

* Madvig gives *stātum;* in Lucan and Martial we have *stāturus, constāturus;* but all the derivatives have *ă:* e.g. *stătim, stătus* (adj. and subst.), *stătio, stătivus, stător, stătura, stătuo.*

6. The 3rd pers. plur. of the perf. act. in *erunt* has the penult short sometimes in poetry; as, *stetĕrunt*.

For the quantity of other vowels no rule can be given: they must be learnt from the dictionary.

§ 121.   III. QUANTITY OF VOWELS BY NATURE, IN THE LAST SYLLABLE OF A WORD.

(A) *Monosyllables* are long.

Except

(*a*) The enclitics *quĕ, nĕ, vĕ*.

(*b*) Words ending with *b, d, t*.

(*c*) *ĕs* (from *sum*), *făc, lăc, nĕc, fĕl, mĕl, ăn, ĭn, fĕr, pĕr, tĕr, vĭr, cŏr, quĭs, ĭs, bĭs, cĭs, ŏs* (a bone). The pronoun *hīc* is common.

§ 122.   (B) In *polysyllables*, being true Latin words *

1. *a* and *e* final are short.

* Greek words retain their proper quantity in Latin. Of these the most noticeable deviations from the above rules are *exemplified* by the following words. See also the declensions, App. A.

    I. 1. Tĕcmessa, Dăphne, Cŷcnus.

        2. āĕra (acc. sing.), herōas, Ænēas.

    III. B. 1. Æneā (voc.), Tempē (neut. pl.), crambē (fem. sing.).

           2. Parĭ (voc.).

           3. Æneān (acc.), Sirēn, Epigrammatōn (gen.). aēr, æthēr, cratēr.

           4. Iliăs, craterăs (acc.). Arcadĕs, craterĕs.

           5. Simoīs, Eleusīs. Delŏs, Erinnyŏs (gen.). Sapphūs (gen.), Panthūs.

Also *y* and *ys* are short, as molŷ, Cotŷs.

§ 123. Except *a* in

    (*a*) Abl. sing. of 1st declension; as, *musā.*

    (*b*) Imperative of verbs of 1st conjugation; as, *amā.*

    (*c*) Indeclinable words; as, *intrā, quadragintā;* but *pută, ită, quiă, ejă.*

§ 124. Except *e* in

    (*a*) Abl. sing. of 5th declension; as, *faciē;* so also *hŏdiē.*

    (*b*) Imperative of 2nd conjugation; as, *monē.*

    (*c*) Adverbs from adjectives in *us, a, um;* as, *doctē,* to which add *fĕrē, fermē;* but *benĕ, malĕ, infernĕ, supernĕ* (*mactĕ,* § 62).

§ 125.   2. *i, o, u* final are long.

§ 126. Except *i* in

    mihĭ̄, tibĭ̄, sibĭ̄, ubĭ̄, ibĭ̄, in which *i* is common, and *quăsĭ, nĭsĭ.*

§ 127. Except *o* in

    citŏ, immŏ, modŏ (and compounds), *duŏ, octŏ, egŏ, cĕdŏ* (§ 89).

§ 128.   3. Final syllables ending in any other single consonant than *s* are short.

    But the final syllable is long in

    (*a*) all cases of *illic, istic,* except the nom. masc.

    (*b*) all compounds of *pār,* as *dispār.*

    (*c*) *ĭit, petĭit,* and their compounds. (So Lachmann.)

§ 129.   4. Of the final syllables in *s,*

    ās, ēs, ōs, are long.

§ 130. Except

    (*a*) *ănăs, compŏs, impŏs, pĕnĕs.*

(*b*)   nom. sing. in *ĕs* of nouns of 3rd declension, which have *ĕtis, ĭtis, ĭdis,* in genitive, as *sĕgĕs, mīlĕs, obsĕs :* but *pariēs, abiēs, ariēs.*

(*c*)   compounds of *es* (from *sum*), as *abĕs.*

§ 131.   5.   *ĭs* and *ŭs* are short.

Except *īs* in

(*a*)   dat. and abl. plural, as *mensīs, vobīs ;* so *gratīs, forīs.* (Also *īs* for *ēs* or *eis,* § 30.)

(*b*)   2nd pers. sing. pres. ind. of 4th conj. *audīs :* also *possīs* and other compounds of *sīs, velīs, nolīs, malīs.*

(*c*)   in 2nd pers. sing. of perf. subj. and compl. fut. in which *ĭs* is common.

(*d*)   *Samnīs, Quirīs.*

§ 132.   Except *ūs* in

(*a*)   gen. sing. and nom. and acc. plu. of 4th declension.

(*b*)   nom. of 3rd declension, when genitive singular has long penultimate, as *tellūs, tellūris.*

§ 133.   IV. In verse notice is taken of the way in which the last syllable of a word is affected by the following word.

1.   A final vowel (or diphthong), or a final syllable in *m*, is omitted in pronunciation if the next word commence with a vowel (or diphthong), or with *h.*

Thus *vita est, vive hodie, monstrum ingens,* are read (in verse) *vit-est, viv-hodie, monstr-ingens.*

A long vowel or diphthong is rarely shortened instead of being elided, as

Insŭlæ̆ Īŏnĭo.   Virg. *Æn.* iii. 211.

§ 134.   2. A final syllable ending in a consonant is always long, if the next word begin with a consonant, as *regit ventos :* here *it* though naturally short is lengthened by its position if the words occur in verse.

3. A final syllable ending in a vowel is generally lengthened if the next word begin with *sc, sp, sq, st,* or *x.*

N.B. These rules hold only when the words are in the same line or verse.

§ 135. A foot is a particular number and order of long and short syllables:

Spondee is two long syllables; as, mūsās.

Dactyl is one long followed by two short; as, pēctŏrĕ.

Anapæst is two short followed by one long; as, tĕnĕrōs.

Iambus is one short followed by one long; as, rĕgūnt.

Trochee is one long followed by one short; as, lēgĕ.

Pyrrhich is two short syllables; as, rĕgĕ.

Tribrach is three short syllables; as, rĕlĕgĕ.

§ 136. An *Hexameter* line is a verse containing six feet, of which the first four may be either dactyls or spondees: the fifth must be a dactyl, and the sixth must be a spondee or trochee.

In some few verses we find a spondee for the fifth foot. If this be the case the fourth foot is generally a dactyl.

A *Pentameter* line is a verse containing two parts (called Penthemimers), of which the first contains two feet, either dactyls or spondees, followed by a long syllable: and the second contains two feet which must both be dactyls, followed by a syllable either long or short (rarely ending with a short vowel).

§ 137. Heroic metre consists entirely of Hexameter verses, in which the sentences are continued, irrespectively of the division into verses.

Elegiac metre consists of hexameter and pentameter lines alternately: and the sentence is rarely (in Ovid at least) carried *on from a pentameter* to the following lines.

Heroic metre is like the following:

Armă vī|rūmquĕ că|nō, Trō|jǣ quī | prīmŭs ăb | ōrīs
Ītălīǣ fā|tō prŏfŭ|gūs Lā|vīnăquĕ | vēnĭt
līttŏră | mūlt(ūm) īl|l(e) ēt tēr|rīs jāc|tātŭs ĕt | āltō.
  &c.

Elegiac metre:

Nūllŭs ăn|hēlā|bāt sŭb ăd|ūncō | vōmĕrĕ | taūrŭs:
   nūllă sŭb | īmpĕrĭ|ō || tērră cŏ|lēntĭs ĕr|ăt:
nūllŭs ăd|hūc ĕrăt | ūsŭs ĕ|quī: se | quīsquĕ fĕr|ēbăt:
   ībăt ŏ|vīs lā|nā || cōrpŭs ă|mīctă sŭ|ā.
  &c.

SYNTAX, *or*

USE OF INFLEXIONAL FORMS.

§ 138. SYNTAX teaches the right use of the different parts of speech (*i.e.* classes of words), and of their different inflexions.

§ 139. Words may be divided into three classes:

I. Words which *name*.
II. Words which *declare* (or *predicate*).
III. Words which *connect*.

§ 140. I. Words which *name*.

1. *Substantives* name persons and things and abstract notions.

    (*a*) *Personal Pronouns* (in Latin) are names to denote the person speaking and the person spoken to. Ex. *I, thou.*

    (*b*) *Proper* nouns are names of individual persons or places. Ex. *John, Rome.*

    (*c*) *Common* nouns are names of classes of persons or things. Ex. *conqueror, table.*

    (*d*) *Abstract* nouns are names of qualities, actions, and states, considered apart from the persons or things possessing or performing them. Ex. *greatness, health, departure.*

    (*e*) *Infinitive* mood of verbs and *gerunds* are verbs used as substantives.

2. *Adjectives* name relations and qualities considered as inhering in persons and things. They are used as attributes to substantives.

   (a) *Pronominal* adjectives are names of relations, chiefly derived from local nearness to the person speaking, spoken to, or spoken of. They are often used instead of nouns. Ex. *mine, this, that, which.*

   (b) *Noun* adjectives are names of qualities in general. Ex. *great, healthy.*

   (c) *Participles* (including *gerundive*) are verbs with adjective inflexions.

3. *Adverbs* name relations and qualities considered as qualifying qualities and actions. They are used as attributes to verbs and adjectives (and other adverbs).

   (a) *Pronominal* adverbs. Ex. *here, then.*

   (b) *Prepositions.* Especially used to give precision to the cases of nouns. Ex. *in, out, of.*

   (c) *Nominal* adverbs (of *quality* and *manner*). Ex. *well, brightly.*

II. Words which *declare.*

Finite Verbs (viz. in indicative, subjunctive and imperative moods). Ex. *say, do.*

III. Words which *connect.*

Conjunctions (are those adverbs which) connect names with names, assertions with assertions, or sentences with sentences. Ex. Henry *and* I walk *and* talk together. I am going, *but* he is coming.

§ 141. To these three classes may be added

Interjections; which are either natural vocal sounds, expressive of sudden emotions, or abbreviated sentences. Ex. *oh! mercy!*

PARTS OF A SIMPLE SENTENCE AND USE OF THE PARTS OF SPEECH.

§ 142. When we speak we (A) either *name* a person or thing,

(B) or we *declare* something of a person or thing.

(A) The name of a person or thing is expressed by a *substantive* (pronoun or noun).

(B) A complete thought always contains more than the name, for it *declares* something of the person or thing named. Every complete thought (called in Grammar a *sentence*) contains at least two ideas, viz.

1. The person or thing of which we speak, called the *Subject.*

2. Our declaration respecting it, called the *Predicate.*

§ 143. The subject (strictly speaking) is always a *substantive* in the nominative case, or something used as such.

The predicate (strictly speaking) is always a *finite verb**.

Thus in the sentence, equus currit, *the horse runs,* equus, *horse,* is the subject ; currit, *runs,* is the predicate.

§ 144. (A) If a single substantive does not name or define a person or thing sufficiently, additions are made to it, and these are either *adjectives* or of the nature of adjectives. They are called *attributes,* or sometimes *epithets.*

---

* If authority be needed for the omission of the *copula* in grammar, I may refer to Madvig, *Lat. Gr.* § 209 b, Obs. 1. It is convenient sometimes to divide the whole of a sentence into two parts only : in this view the grammatical subject with all its attributes &c. is the (logical) subject: the rest of the sentence is the (logical) predicate.

The principal kinds of simple attributes are

(*a*) Adjectives. Ex. Equus *albus, White* horse.

(*b*) Other substantives used *in apposition,* i. e. as additional names of the same person or thing. Ex. Equus albus *Victor,* The white horse *Conqueror.*

(*c*) Genitive case of substantives. Ex. *Cæsaris* equus albus, *Cæsar's* white horse.

(B) If a single verb does not express all that we wish to declare of a person or thing, additions are made of various kinds, viz.:

(*a*) If the verb express an *action upon* some person or thing, a substantive in the accusative case is added to denote the person or thing acted on. This is called the *object* (or *direct* or *immediate object*). Ex. Cæsar ferit equum, *Cæsar strikes the horse.*

(*b*) If the verb express an action or fact *indirectly* or *remotely affecting* a person or thing, a substantive (in the dative case in Latin) is added to express such an *indirect* (or *remote*) *object.* Intransitive verbs have this indirect object only: many transitive verbs have both a direct and an indirect object; this direct object being generally a thing, the indirect object being generally a person. Ex. Vulnus nocet puero, *The wound hurts (is hurtful for) the boy;* Puer dat librum fratri, *The boy gives the book to his brother.*

(*c*) If the verb express *being* or *state,* a noun is often added (and sometimes when it expresses *action*) to complete its meaning. Ex. Canis est rabidus, *The dog is mad.* The verb *est* expresses that the dog is in some state or other; *rabidus* expresses what that state is. So ·Canis manet rabidus, Canis vocatur rabidus, *The dog remains, is called, mad.* This construction is very common with verbs in the passive voice. The noun is called the *secondary predicate.*

N.B. In Latin, when there is a secondary predicate, the primary predicate, if it be some part of the verb *sum* (especially if in the indicative mood), is often omitted. If a sentence be short and have no verb exprest, the word *est* or *sunt* is frequently the right word to supply.

(*d*) Actions or states of being may be further qualified by adding the *place, time, manner, cause,* &c., at, in, or by which the action is done, or the state exists. These are most simply exprest by oblique cases of nouns (with or without prepositions) or by adverbs.

> Ex.   Cæsar ferit caput gladio, *Cæsar strikes the head with a sword.*
>
> Cicero habitabat ibi, *Cicero was dwelling there.*
>
> Sextâ horâ Julius moritur placide, *At the sixth hour Julius dies calmly.*

§ 145.   Sometimes an infinitive mood or noun (adjective or substantive) is added to an oblique case, especially the object, not as a part of its name but to convey an assertion respecting it.   This is called an *oblique predicate*, and the object is, with reference to this predicate, called its *subject.*

Ex.   Fabius consul Papirium inimicum suum dixit tacitus dictatorem, *The consul Fabius nominated in silence Papirius his enemy dictator.*   Here *consul* is an epithet of *Fabius* forming part of his name: *dixit* is the (primary) predicate: *tacitus* is the secondary predicate: *inimicum suum* is an epithet of *Papirium: Papirium* is object of *dixit,* and subject to *dictatorem: dictatorem* is an oblique predicate of *Papirium.*

> Sub Hasdrubale imperatore militavit, *He served under Hasdrubal as commander.*
>
> Jubet Cicero Rullum tacere, *Cicero bids Rullus be silent.*
>
> So   Hoc primum Cæsar fecit, *This was the first thing Cæsar did.*
>
> Hoc primus Cæsar fecit, *Cæsar was the first person to do this.*
>
> (But   Primo hoc Cæsar fecit, *In the first place* [i. e. *firstly*] *Cæsar did this.*)

See also the examples in §§ 155, 156.

§ 146. Thus a (primary) predicate is always a finite verb: a secondary predicate is a substantive or adjective used predicatively of the subject of the sentence : an oblique predicate is a substantive, adjective, or infinitive mood used predicatively of some substantive, which is in an oblique case.

§ 147. Besides their use to qualify verbs, adverbs and oblique cases of nouns with or without prepositions are used also to qualify adjectives, and oblique cases with prepositions sometimes qualify substantives*.

Ex. Valde utilis, *Very useful.*

Utilis ad hoc, *Useful for this purpose.*

Tuum in me odium, *Your hatred towards me.*

Plus (*or* plusquam) trecenti cadunt, *More than three hundred men fall.*

§ 148. Conjunctions unite those words only which occupy the same part of the sentence. (See also §§ 212, 260.)

Ex. Romani ac socii veniunt, *The Romans and allies come.*

Nec regem nec reginam ea res delectavit, *That thing pleased neither the king nor queen.*

Sunt multæ et graves causæ, *There are many (and) weighty reasons.*

Cui potius credam quam tibi ? *Whom should I believe rather than you?*

Bella fortius quam felicius geris, *You carry on wars more bravely than (more) happily.*

* N.B. A substantive in an oblique case (except the genitive) with or without a preposition, generally qualifies a verb or participle. If intended to qualify a substantive it should be placed close to the substantive and away from the verb, or between the substantive and its attribute. Thus Tuum in me odium (above). Exemplum Cæsaris ad te litterarum, *A copy of Cæsar's letter to you.* So Syracusas in Siciliâ ivit would mean *He journeying in Sicily went to Syracuse* (*in Siciliâ* belonging to *ivit*) ; not *He went to Syracuse in Sicily*, which would be in Latin, In Siciliam Syracusas ivit, *He went into Sicily to Syracuse*, or, Syracusas in Siciliâ sitas ivit, *He went to Syracuse (which is) situated in Sicily.*

USE OF INFLEXIONS OF PERSON AND GENDER.

§ 149.   As the finite verb has inflexions to denote differences of number and person, it must be put in the same person and number as its subject.

> Ex.   Equus currit, *The horse runs.*
> Equi currunt, *The horses run.*
> Nos amamus, *We love.*
> Tu regis, *Thou rulest.*

§ 150.   The subject, especially if a substantive pronoun, is, although exprest in English, frequently omitted in Latin wherever there is no risk of mistake.   Thus the pronouns of the first and second persons are usually omitted, the form of the verb being sufficient to indicate them ; and the third person of the verb naturally refers to the subject last mentioned, unless a new subject be exprest, or the person and number of the verb be different.   Thus *curro, curris, currimus, curritis* refer to the speaker and, person spoken to.

> Ex.   Rullus audit: currit ad urbem: jubet servos sequi, *Rullus hears: runs to the city: orders his slaves to follow.*   Here *Rullus* is subject to *currit* and *jubet.*

§ 151.   Certain verbs (*libet, piget, pudet, pœnitet, tædet*) expressive of the existence of personal feelings are used in Latin in the third person sing. only, and sometimes without any definite subject exprest.   They are called *impersonal* verbs.   (See § 90.)

> Ex.   Miseret me aliorum, *Pity seizes me for others.*

For a similar use of the passive voice see § 258, 3.   Other verbs, as *oportet, convenit, expedit,* &c., also called impersonals, have usually a sentence or infinitive mood for subject: all occasionally have a neuter pronoun (*quod* or *hoc*) apparently for subject.

§ 152.   When two or more subjects of different persons have the same predicate, the verb is put in the first person, if any one of the subjects be in the first person; if not, in the second, if any one of the subjects be in the second person.

Ex. Ego et Tullia valemus, *I and Tullia are well.*
Tu et Tullia valetis, *Thou and Tullia are well.*
Hæc neque ego neque tu fecimus, *Neither I nor thou have done this.*

§ 153. Nouns in the singular number, but denoting a multitude of persons, sometimes have the verb in the singular, sometimes in the plural.

Ex. Pars abiit, *A part has left.*
or Pars abierunt, *A part have left.*

§ 154. So we frequently have the plural in expressions like the following:

Alius alium vulnerant, *They wound (one one man), another another.*

Suam quisque domum incendunt, *They set on fire each his own home.*

§ 155. As the adjective has inflexions to denote differences of number, gender, and case, it must agree in all these respects with the substantive when used as epithet, and with its subject when used as secondary or oblique predicate.

(a) As epithet.
Ex. Terra dura, *Hard land.*
Terræ duræ, *Of hard land.*

(b) As secondary or oblique predicate.

Ex. Terra manet dura, *The land remains hard.*
Ego sum timidus (if the speaker be a man),
Ego sum timida (if the speaker be a woman), *I am timid.*
Scit mulierem esse timidam, *He knows the woman to be timid.*

Licet mulieri esse timidæ, *A woman may be timid* (lit. *It is allowed for a woman to be timid*).

Reddit Cæsarem felicem, *He makes Cæsar happy.*

§ 156. As the substantive has inflexions to denote differences of number and case, it must agree in these respects with the principal substantive when used as epithet (i.e. in apposition), and with its subject, when used as secondary or oblique predicate.

(*a*) As epithet:

Ex. Urbs Roma, *The city Rome,* or (as we say), *The city of Rome.*

Urbis Romæ, *Of the city Rome.*

(*b*) As secondary or oblique predicate:

Ex. Hæc urbs est Roma, *This city is Rome.*

Asia Scipioni provincia obtigit, *Asia fell to Scipio as his province.*

Cæsar factus est imperator, *Cæsar was made general.*

Scio Cæsarem esse factum imperatorem, *I know that Cæsar was made general.*

Puero datur nomen Egerio, *To the boy is given the name Egerius.*

Te judicem æquum puto, *I think you a fair judge.*

§ 157. This use of substantives, to add a further description, whether as epithet or secondary (or oblique) predicate, is not confined to the additions of a single expression only.

Ex. In tribunali Q. Pompeii, prætoris urbani, familiaris nostri, sedebamus. *We were sitting on the bench (in the court) of Q. Pompeius, the city prætor, our friend.*

Quattuor liberos habuit, tres filios, filiam unam. *He had four children, three sons and one daughter.*

§ 158. Relative adjectives (*qui, qualis, quantus,* &c.)

agree with the word to which they refer (called their *ante-cedent*) in number and gender, but are put in the case required by their own sentence.

> Ex. Terra in quâ vivimus fertilis est, *The land in which we live is fertile.*
>
> Divitiæ quantas habebat perditæ sunt, *All the wealth he possessed was lost* (lit. *The wealth, as much as he was possessing, was lost*).

§ 159. Adjectives are frequently used without the substantive which they qualify being exprest. In this case there is often some word in the passage to which they naturally refer; if not, if the adjective be of the masculine gender, *persons* are usually meant; if of the neuter gender, things are meant.

> Ex. Ipsorum linguâ Keltæ, nostrâ Galli appellantur, *In their own language they are called Kelts, in our (language) Gauls.*
>
> Docti censent, *The learned are of opinion* (i. e. learned *persons*).
>
> Suavia delectant, *Sweets delight* (i.e. sweet *things*).
>
> Imperatum facit, *He executes the command.*
>
> Qui hoc censent errant, *Persons who are of this opinion err.*
>
> Quæ imperata sunt facit, *He does the things which were ordered.*
>
> A primo, *from the first:* In perpetuum, *for ever.*

§ 160. Many adjectives being specially applicable to particular substantives are used without them and pass as substantives.

> Ex. Dextra, *The right,* i. e. Dextra manus, *The right hand.*
>
> Cāni (i. e. capilli), *White hairs.* Cumānum (i. e. prædium), *A villa* (or *estate*) *at Cumæ.*

§ 161. If an adjective qualifies two or more substantives of different genders, it is made to agree with the nearest to itself in the sentence : but if they are spoken of distinctly *as persons*, the masculine gender is used; if distinctly *as things*, the neuter gender is used.

Ex. Omnes agri et maria} *All the fields and seas.*
Agri et maria omnia}

Uxor mea et filius mortui sunt, *My wife and son are dead.*

Honores, imperia, victoriæ fortuita sunt, *Honours, commands, victories are chance things.*

§ 162. Both an adjective used as secondary or oblique predicate and a relative adjective may be considered as really agreeing with a substantive understood, which substantive is the real secondary or oblique predicate, and to which the adjective or relative is an epithet. The substantive understood is usually the subject of the predicative adjective, or the antecedent of the relative; but sometimes the sense admits of another substantive being understood; in that way we frequently find the adjective and relative in the neuter singular.

Ex. Triste lupus stabulis, *A wolf is a sad (thing) for the folds.*

Pars militum sunt cæsi, *A part of the soldiers are slain (men).*

Lupus quod est sævum animal (i.e. quod animal est sævum animal) appropinquat, *The wolf which is a savage animal approaches.*

§ 163. This substantive is sometimes *exprest* twice; sometimes only with the relative or as secondary (or oblique) predicate.

Ex. Erant omnino itinera duo quibus itineribus domo exire possent, *There were only two roads by which (roads) they could march from home.*

For the subjunctive *possent*, see § 235. 10.

Hæc est vera via, *This (way) is the true way.*

Interfecit quos milites invenit, *He killed what soldiers he found (He killed the soldiers which soldiers he found).*

§ 164. An infinitive mood, or a sentence when used in place of a substantive, is considered as of the neuter gender.

 Ex. Dulce est pro patriâ mori, *It is sweet to die for one's country.* (*Pro patriâ mori* is subject to *est.*)

   Via prima salutis, quod minime reris, Graiâ pandetur ab urbe, *The first way of safety will, what you least expect, be opened by* (or *from*) *a Graian city.* (The antecedent of *quod* is the whole of the principal sentence.)

USE OF INFLEXIONS OF CASE.

§ 165. The cases are chiefly used as follows: (originally they probably denote relations of space or place):

Nominative expresses name of person addressed or subject of sentence.

Accusative expresses (direct) object.

Dative expresses indirect object.

Ablative expresses adverbial additions of place, time, manner, circumstances, &c.

Genitive expresses adjectival addition or the object after adjectives and substantives.

§ 166. NOMINATIVE.

1. Name of the *person* (or *thing*) *spoken to.* (This is often called the *Vocative case.*)

 Ex. Musa veni, *Come, O Muse.*

N.B. In nouns of the second declension ending in *us* a shorter form is used, see § 21.

§ 167. 2. Name of *person* or *thing spoken about;* i. e. the subject of the sentence when the predicate is a finite verb.

> Ex. Cæsar loquitur, *Cæsar speaks.*
>
> Vos dicite, *Say ye.*

Hence frequently as secondary predicate when the predicate is a finite verb. See §§ 155, 156.

§ 168. ACCUSATIVE.

1. OBJECT OF VERB (or, rarely, of verbal substantives, cf. § 256).

(*a*) *Place towards* which.

N.B. In prose the preposition *ad* is generally prefixed, except before the names of *towns* and *islands* small enough to be considered as *one* place.

> Ex. Venit Romam, *He comes to Rome.*
>
> Domum reditio, *A return home.*

§ 169. (*b*) *Object of action* of a transitive verb.

> Ex. Percussit dextram, *He struck the right hand.*
>
> Cupit divitias, *He desires riches.*

§ 170. Under this head fall certain special usages :

(A) To this belongs the use of the accusative as subject to an infinitive mood as predicate; on which see below, § 246. 2.

> Ex. Dicit eum venire, *He speaks of him as coming (He says that he is coming).*

For the noun used as predicative accusative, see § 156.

§ 171. (B) If a verb (as verbs of *teaching, concealing, asking*) can have as a direct object, either a person or a thing, it may have both together.

> Ex. Docet Catonem Græcas litteras, *He teaches Cato Greek literature.*
>
> Cf. § 246. 1, *Docebo,* &c.

Non celavi te sermonem hominum, *I have not kept you in ignorance of people's talk.*

Cæsar frumentum Æduos flagitabat, *Cæsar constantly asked the Ædui for corn.*

The accus. of the *thing* remains even when the verb is in the passive voice, e.g. Primus Cato rogatus est sententiam, *Cato was first asked his opinion.*

§ 172. (C) In exclamations (really object after some verb understood).

Ex. O me miserum, *O (pity or help) me wretched.*
Testes egregios! *Fine witnesses!* (ironically).

§ 173. 2. Compass or measure of the action or quality (after verbs, adjectives, and nominal adverbs).

(a) *Space over which**; i.e. distance, length, &c.

Ex. Abest sex millia passuum, *He is six miles off.*
Nix minus quattuor pedes alta jacuit, *The snow lay less than four feet deep.*

§ 174. (b) *Time during which.*

Ex. Quáttuor dies vixit, *He lived for four days.*
Decessit Alexander, mensem unum annos tres et triginta natus, *Alexander died, aged thirty-three years and one month.*

§ 175. (c) *The extent of the action of the verb* exprest *either* by a neuter adjective of definition or quantity;

* In considering the meaning of the cases, and the translation into English, the meaning of the words themselves must be borne in mind: thus, where *totus* is added to the substantive, the *ablative* case is used to express the *space over which* (because the *whole over* which is conceived as one place *at* which); as, urbe totâ gemitus fit, *over the whole city* (i.e. in the city as a whole) *there is lamentation.* So on the other hand, *to fly in all directions* is in Latin 'in omnes partes fugere', *to fly into all parts.* Similarly with regard to the moods and tenses of verbs. See § 86. 259. 3.

R. G. 7

Ex. Hoc doleo, *This is the pain I feel.*

Quid prodest? *Of what use is it?*

Multum nocet, *He does much injury.*

Plurimum possunt, *They have most power.*

Quid me ista lædunt? *What hurt do those matters* (of yours) *do me?*

Nescio quid conturbatus esse videris, *You seem to be somewhat confused.*

Nescio quid (like a compound pronoun) qualifies *conturbatus.*

Similarly, Nostram vicem anxius, *Anxious on our account* (or *in our stead*). So *multum,* &c. used adverbially, § 62.

§ 176. *Or* by a substantive of the same meaning as the verb, accompanied by an oblique adjectival predicate.

Ex. Duram (*or* hanc) servit servitutem, *He has a hard* (or *this*) *service to perform.*

This is called the *cognate* accusative.

§ 177. (*d*) *Part concerned or affected* (only in poetry).

Ex. Similis vultum, *Like in looks.*

Tremit artus, *He trembles all over his limbs.*

§ 178. DATIVE is used to express the *indirect object*, both after transitive verbs, which have also a direct object, and after intransitive verbs, which have this indirect object only (with or without an accusative of the *extent*), and which in English are often translated by a transitive verb, and therefore without any preposition*.

* The following verbs in common use, although intransitive in Latin, at least in certain senses, and therefore requiring their object (generally a *person*) to be put in the dative, are usually translated by transitive verbs in English :

adversor, *oppose.*

æmŭlor, *rival* (in bad sense).

blandior, *soothe.*

crēdo, *trust, believe* (a person).

diffīdo, *distrust.*

displīceo, *displease.*

făveo, *favour.*

fido, *trust* (so confido).

grātĭfĭcor, *gratify, oblige.*

ignosco, *pardon, forgive.*

illūdo, *mock.*

179.   1. *Person* (or *thing*) *for* or *to whom* (i. e. the person or thing affected by an action or by the *existence* of a quality, although not directly acted on). (See App. D.)

Ex. Dat librum illi, *He gives him the book.*

Sedibus hunc refer ante suis, *First restore him to his fit abode.*

Nocet puero, *It is hurtful for the boy.*

Utilis reipublicæ est, *He is useful for the state.*

Vicinus urbi habitat, *He dwells near for* (or *to*) *the city.*

Nonnihil irascor tibi, *I am somewhat angry with you.*

Credit aliquid mulieri, *He entrusts something to the woman.*

Id Cassio persuadet, *He persuades Cassius of that* (lit. *He is a persuader to Cassius regarding that*).

Scuto uni militi detracto, *A shield having been snatched from one soldier.*

Hæc vobis illorum per biduum militia fuit, *Such was their two days' service that they have*

impĕro, *command* (persons, &c.).
indulgeo, *indulge.*
invĭdeo, *envy.*
mălĕdīco, *scold, abuse.*
mĕdeor, *heal.*
mĭnor, *threaten.*
mŏdĕror, *check.*
nŏceo, *hurt, damage.*
nūbo, *marry* (of a woman).
ŏbēdio, *obey.*
obsĕquor, *obey (comply with).*
obsisto, *thwart.*
obsum, *hinder.*
obtrecto, *disparage.*
occurro, *meet.*

offĭcio, *obstruct.*
ŏpĭtŭlor, *help.*
parco, *spare.*
pāreo, *obey.*
plăceo, *please.*
præcurro, *outstrip.*
præsto, *excel.*
præsum, *superintend.*
prŏpinquo, *approach.*
prōsum, *profit, benefit.*
sătisfăcio, *satisfy.*
servio, *serve.*
subvĕnio, *support.*
sŭpersum, *survive.*
supplĭco, *supplicate.*
tempĕro, *check.*

7—2

to shew you (or *Such, let me tell you, was their two days' service*).

Nequaquam visu ac specie æstimantibus pares, *By no means alike in the eyes of those who judged* (or *judge*) *of them by their appearance and display* (lit. *for those judging,* &c.).

Sese omnes Cæsari ad pedes projecere, *All threw themselves at Cæsar's feet* (for *Cæsar at his feet*).

§ 180.   Under this head fall certain special usages:

(A) *Person possessing* (after verb of *being*).

Ex.   Est mihi pater, *A father exists for me,* i.e. *I have a father.*

§ 181.   (B)   *Agent.* Rare in prose, except with gerundive and passive participle.

Ex.   Hæc mihi dicta sunt, *This is what I said* (lit. *These things are for me said things*).

Nihil restat illis faciendum, *Nothing remains for them to do.*

§ 182.   2. *Purpose for which.*

Ex.   Cui bono est, *Who gains by it?* (lit. *To whom is it for a good?*).

Duas legiones castris præsidio relinquit, *He leaves two legions to guard the camp* (lit. *For the benefit of the camp, for the purpose of a guard*).

Urbi condendæ eum præfecit, *He placed him over the building of the city.*

Decemviri legibus scribendis, *A commission of ten for drawing up laws.*

Suam virtutem irrisui fore indoluerunt, *They were vexed that their valour would be* (a matter) *for derision.*

§ 183.   ABLATIVE expresses adverbial qualifications, and usually requires a preposition (*from, at, in, by, with*) to translate it into English.

In consequence probably of an early confusion of the forms of the cases, the ablative is used to express both the place *from* which and the place *at* which, both the origin and the instrument or manner of an action or state; which notions properly belong to the genitive and dative* respectively.   This has restricted the uses of the genitive and dative, and occasioned some uncertainty in the meaning of the ablative, which is however practically removable by considering the meaning of the passage.

§ 184.   From the nature of the expressions put in the ablative a simple substantive is very frequently insufficient; and an adjective, or participle (agreeing with the substantive), is added as (oblique) predicate.   This construction is often called *ablative absolute.* Not unfrequently (see the last three examples in § 192) we have a subjective genitive similarly added.

§ 185.   1.   PLACE WHENCE.

(a)   *Place, &c. from which.*

N.B.   In prose a preposition (*ab* or *ex*) is generally prefixed except before the names of *towns* and *smaller islands.*

Ex.   Româ proficiscitur, *He sets out from Rome.*

Frumentum Rhodo advehit, *He brings the corn up from Rhodes.*

Pellit loco milites, *He drives the soldiers from their place.*

Data Id. Jun. Thessalonicâ, *Despatched on the Ides of June from Thessalonica* (*data* agrees with *epistola* understood).   (See App. G.)

* It should be remembered that the forms for the dative and ablative are the same in the plural of all declensions, and not unfrequently in the singular.

§ 186.   (b) *Thing from which* separation takes place (or exists).

   Ex.   Arcet tyrannum reditu, *He keeps the tyrant from returning.*

Solvit eum vinclis, *He releases him from chains.*

Mortui sensu carent, *The dead want feeling.*

Vacat culpâ, *He is free from fault.*

Coegimus decemviros abire magistratu, *We compelled the decemvirs to abdicate their office.*

Alienum existimatione meâ, *Foreign to my reputation.* (See App. D.)

Orbus rebus omnibus, *Deprived of everything.*

§ 187.   (c) *Origin.*

   Ex.   Mercurius Jove natus, *Mercury sprung from Jove.*

Animâ constamus et corpore, *We are composed of soul and body.*

L. Domitius Cn. F. Fab. Ahenobarbus, i.e. Lucius Domitius Cnæi filius Fabiâ (i.e. tribu) Ahenobarbus, *Lucius (son of Cnæus) Domitius Ahenobarbus of the Fabian tribe.*

§ 188.   To this head probably* belongs the ablative of the *standard of comparison.*

Usual only after comparative adjectives in nom. or acc. case.

   Ex.   Major Achille, *Greater than Achilles* (lit. greater if you take Achilles as your starting point).

* For in Greek the *genitive* is used. But the usage may also be explained as coming under 2. *d*, thus: a person is *magnus* of himself, but *major* only *in consequence* of some one else possessing size or excellence.

Vilius argentum est auro, virtutibus aurum,
*Silver is less valuable than gold, gold (less
valuable) than virtues.*

Opinione* celerius venit, *He is coming quicker
than was expected.*

§ 189.   **2.   PLACE WHERE.**

(*a*) *Place at which* (if the noun be of the 3d decl. *or
of* the plural number).

Ex.   Babylone habitat, *He lives at Babylon.*

Bellum terrâ marique comparat, *He is pre-
paring war by land and sea.*

Castris se tenet, *He keeps himself in his camp.*

Populi sensus et theatro et spectaculis per-
spectus est.   Nam gladiatoribus, &c., *The
feelings of the people were clearly seen at the
theatre and the shows.   For at the gladia-
torial exhibition,* &c.

§ 190.   With verbs of motion this ablative expresses the *road
by which.* (Cf. § 64. B.)

Ex.   Proximâ (sc. viâ) ibo, *I will go by the nearest
way.*

Portâ Collinâ urbem intrat, *He enters the city
at* (or *by*) *the Colline Gate.*

Pado frumentum subvehit, *He carries the corn
up the Po.*

§ 191.   (*b*)   *Time when* or *within which.*

Ex.   Sexto die venit, *He came on the sixth day.*

Vix decem annis urbem cepit, *He hardly took
the city in ten years.*

---

* So also, with (usually *before*) either adjectives or adverbs,
solito, justo, œquo, necessario, spe, exspectatione, exspectato.

Sex. Roscii mors quatriduo, quo is occisus est,
Chrysogono nuntiatur, *News of the death of
Sextus Roscius is brought to Chrysogonus in
four days from the time he was killed* (lit.
*in the same period of four days in which he
was killed*).

Initio æstatis, *When summer is* (or *was*) *com-
mencing.*

Imperante Tiberio, *When Tiberius was emperor.*

Regibus ejectis, *After* (or *on*) *the expulsion of
the kings.*

Cicerone et Antonio coss. (i. e. consulibus), *When
Cicero and Antonius were consuls.*

§ 192.   (c) *Amount at which,* or after comparative, *amount of
difference.* (See also p. 185, note.)

Ex. Vitam parvo* redemit, *He purchased his life
for* (i. e. *at* or *with*) *a small sum.*

Tritici modius fuerat denariis quinque, *A bushel
of wheat had been at five denaries* (or, *five
denaries had been the price of,* &c.).

Magno detrimento certamen stetit, *The contest
was waged with much loss* (lit. *stood at much
loss*).

Dignus pœnâ, *Worthy of punishment.*

(The substantive dependent on *dignus* is (in prose)
almost always put in the ablative.)

Multis partibus major, *Many times greater.*

Altero tanto longior, *Longer by as much again*
(lit. *by a second as great quantity*).

---

* When the *price* is indefinitely expressed by *nihilum, tantu-
lum,* or adjectives in the positive or superlative degree, the
ablative is used; when by *tantus, quantus,* or adjectives in the
comparative degree (e. g. *pluris*), the genitive is used. But after
verbs of *estimation* (except *æstimo*, which has both cases), the
genitive alone is used. Madvig.

§ 193. (*d*) *Attendant cause* or *circumstances, means* or *in-strument, manner, &c. from, under, with,* or *in which.* (The *manner* generally requires the addition of a nominal or pronominal adjective as oblique predicate, or the pre-position *cum* (§ 206. *c.* 3): the *instrument* does not.)

N.B. This use of the ablative might often be deduced from its other meaning under ɪ. (*c*).

Ex. More Carneadeo disputat, *He disputes in the manner of Carneades.*

Gladio regem ferit, *He strikes the king with a sword.*

Arcam lapidibus implet, *He fills the chest with stones.*

Dolo* hoc fecit, *He did it treacherously.*

Auctoritate tuâ opus mihi est, *I need your (personal) authority* (lit. *There is a work for me with your authority*).

Auctore Cassio lex lata est, *The law was passed under the advice of Cassius (Cassius being the adviser).*

Nullis impedimentis ibat, *He was marching without baggage.*

Cæsar equitatu præmisso subsequebatur omnibus copiis, *Cæsar having sent on his cavalry proceeded to follow with all his forces.*

Reipublicæ vel salute vel victoriâ gaudemus, *We rejoice at the commonwealth's—safety* (shall we call it?) *or victory.*

Quod benevolentiâ fit, id odio factum criminaris, *What is really done from kindness, you charge to have been done from hatred.*

Quid hoc populo obtineri potest? *What can be maintained* (or *what measure can be carried*) *with such a people as this?*

---

* In this adverbial way (without oblique predicate or *cum*) are used *ordine, ratione, more, jure, injuriâ, clamore, silentio, consensu, fraude, vi, vitio,* 'unduly,' *cursu, agmine,* &c.

Hannibal xv ferme millium spatio castra a Tarento posuit, *Hannibal pitched his camp at a distance of almost fifteen miles from Tarentum* (lit. *with an interval of*, &c.).

Injussu imperatoris de statione discedit, *He leaves his post without his general's order.*

Voluntate ejus reddere obsides Sequanis licebat, *The Sequani might have restored the hostages with his consent.*

N.B. The ablatives after fungor, *I busy myself* (*with*), fruor, *I enjoy myself* (*with*), utor, *I employ myself* (*with*), potior, *I make myself powerful* (*with*), vescor, *I feed myself* (*with*), nitor, *I support myself* (*with*), &c. are of this class*.

The *instrument* must be carefully distinguished from the *agent:* the former is a *thing* and is put in the ablative *without* a preposition; as, gladio interfectus est, *he was killed with a sword.* The agent is (generally) a *person*, and is put in the ablative with the preposition *ab;* as, ab Antonio interfectus est, *he was slain by Antony.*

§ 194. So (especially after substantives and adjectives and the verb *sum*) to express the *part concerned*, i. e. thing in respect of which a term is applied : or (with oblique predicate) the *characteristic quality.*

Ex. Æger pedibus, *Diseased in the feet.*

Mancipiis locuples, *Rich in slaves.*

Major natu, *Greater in respect of birth*, i.e. *older.*

Freti ingenio, *Relying on their ability.*

Natione Gallus, *A Gaul by nation.*

---

* The following verbs in common use are usually translated by transitive verbs in English, but have this (apparent) object in the ablative in Latin:

ăbūtor, *misuse, abuse.*
căreo, *want.*
ĕgeo, *need* (also with gen.).
fungor, *discharge.*
fruor, *enjoy.*
indĭgeo, *need* (frequently with gen.).
pluo, *rain* (generally impers.).
pŏtior, *enjoy, gain* (or with gen.).
ūtor, *use.*

So also (mihi) opus est, usus est, *I need* or *require*, have the *thing required* in the ablative.

Sunt quidam homines, non re sed nomine, *There are some persons, men not in reality, but in name.*

Eo felix, quod brevi mortuus est, *Happy in that (fact) that he died shortly.*

Agesilaus staturâ fuit humili, *Agesilaus was of low stature* (lit. *was of stature low*).

P. Valerius summâ virtute adolescens, *Publius Valerius, a youth of the greatest excellence.*

§ 195.   GENITIVE expresses adjectival additions of two kinds, viz. *subjective* and *objective*, according as the word put in the genitive case is the subject or object of the action, &c. indicated by the substantive upon which it depends. Ex. Helvetiorum injuriæ populi Romani, i.e. injuriæ quibus Helvetii populum Romanum affecerant. *Helvetiorum* is subjective genitive; *populi Romani* is objective.

§ 196.   1.   SUBJECTIVE.

  (*a*)   *Person* (or *thing*) *possessing* or *originating.*

  Ex.   Horti Cæsaris, *Cæsar's gardens.*

  Hectoris Andromache, *Hector's Andromache* (i.e. *Hector's wife Andr.*).

  Ubi ad Dianæ veneris, *When you have come to Diana's* (i.e. *temple,* as we say *to St John's*).

  Præsidium pudoris, *The defence which modesty affords.*

  Illius amicissimi, *His best friends.*

  Vitium proprium senectutis, *A vice peculiar to old age.*

  Est boni judicis scire, *A good judge would know* (lit. *it is the mark of,* or *belongs to, a good judge to know*).

  Carthaginienses tutelæ nostræ duximus, *We considered the Carthaginians to be under our protection.*

  Cæsar dicere solebat non tam suâ* quam rei-

_____

* A similar use of the possessive pronoun abl. fem. is found after *rēfert.* Quid tuâ id rēfert, *What concern is that of*

publicæ interesse ut salvus esset, *Cæsar was in the habit of saying, that it was not so much his interest as that of the state, that he should be preserved.*

§ 197.   (*b*)   *Containing whole* (called *partitive* genitive).

    Ex.   Pars militum, *A part of the soldiers.*

        Fortissimus Græcorum, *Bravest of the Greeks.*

        Extremum æstatis, *The end of summer.*

        Hoc præmi, *This piece of reward.*

        Nihil relicui fecerunt, *They left nothing undone* (*they left nothing of leavings*).

        Parum prudentiæ, *Too little prudence.*

        Ubinam gentium, *Where in the world?*

N.B. *All of us* is in Latin, *nos* omnes. So Trecenti con·juravimus, *Three hundred of us have conspired;* Tota Asia, *The whole of Asia;* Amici aderant quos multos habebat, *His friends, of whom he has many, were present.* The adjectives *summus, medius, ultimus, extremus, imus, supremus, relicuus, ceterus, adversus, aversus,* are used similarly; as, Summus mons, *The top of the mountain;* Relicua turba, *the rest of the crowd;* Adversa basis, *the front of the pedestal;* Aversa charta, *the back of the paper.*

§ 198.   (*c*)   *Size, kind,* or *description of which* a thing is.

    Ex.   Fossa centum pedum, *A ditch of a hundred feet* (i.e. *in length*).

        Acervus frumenti, *A heap of corn.*

        Tridui viam processit, *He advanced a journey of three days.*

        Vir consili magni, *A man of great policy.*

        Vidi ibi multitudinem hominum, *I saw there numbers of people.*

        Dies dictionis causæ, *The day for pleading his cause* (*causæ* is genitive of object).

yours? The genitive after *rēfert* is not so common. (Probably the real expression was *tuæ rei fert, tuæ* (*rei*) *interest;* cf. post*hac* for post*hæc.* DONALDSON.)

Tum illud cujus est audaciæ! *Then that other matter, what boldness it shews!*

Voluptatem virtus minimi facit, *Manly virtue counts pleasure of little worth.*

Tanti est tacere, *It is worth while to be silent* (lit. *Silence is of so much value*).

To this head we may refer the *genitive of definition.*

Vox voluptatis, *The word pleasure.*

Numerus trecentorum, *The number three hundred.*

Nomen carendi, *The term carere.*

§ 199.   2. Objective.

(*a*)   *Object of action* implied in *substantives* and *adjectives.*   (See App. D.)

Ex.   Timor hostium, *Fear of the enemy.*

Signum erumpendi, *A sign for breaking out.*

Præcepta vivendi, *Rules for life.*

Rogo ut rationem mei habeatis, *I beg you to have regard to my interests.*

Avidus gloriæ, *Greedy of glory.*

Tenax propositi, *Tenacious of his purpose.*

Reus furti, *Charged with theft.*

Prodigus æris, *Lavish of his money.*

Plenus odii, *Full of hatred.*

Similis tui, *Resembling you* (or *a copy of you*).

§ 200.   (*b*)   *Secondary object* of the thing after verbs of *accusing, condemning, acquitting, reminding,* the impersonal verbs *piget, pudet, miseret, pœnitet, tædet,* and sometimes after *impleo* and *compleo,* which all have also a direct object of the person.   (See also § 192, note.)

Ex.   Admonuit illum sceleris, *He reminded him of his wickedness.*

Accusat eum furti, *He accuses him of theft.*

Pœnitet me laboris, *I repent* (§ 90) *of my toil.*

Tædet me vitæ, *I am weary* (§ 90) *of life.*

Also sometimes after *memini, reminiscor, obliviscor, egeo, indigeo, potior,* and always after *misereor:* which have no direct object.

The first three often have an *accus.* instead of this *gen.*, the others (except *misereor*) often have an *ablative.*

Miserere meæ egestatis, *Have pity on my need.*

Memini illius diei, *I am mindful of that day.*

Potitur rerum, *He makes himself master of the government.*

Indigeo tui consili, *I am in need of your advice.*

§ 201.   3. *Place where:* if noun be of 1st or 2d declension, singular number.

Ex.   Romæ vivit, *He lives at Rome.*

Rhodi constitit, *He stopt at Rhodes.*

Patrem familias domi suæ occidere nolumus, *We are unwilling to slay the head of a household at his own house.*

N.B. In this last usage the case is really the *locative* (i.e. the original dative, cf. *ruri* and § 64. B), which happens to resemble the genitive in these declensions. So *humi*, and (in connection with *domi*), *belli*, *militiæ*, &c. Perhaps also *animi* in *pendemus*, &c. *animi.*

USE OF CASES WITH PREPOSITIONS.

§ 202. Prepositions are originally adverbs of place, and are prefixed to oblique cases of substantives to give greater precision to the general ideas *implied in the cases themselves.* They are much more frequent in prose than in poetry. Some are used with the *accusative*, some with the *ablative*, some with either, but with suitable differences of meaning.

(A) The following are used with the *accusative* only:

> *Ad, adversus, ante, apud, circum, cis, ob, penes, per, pone, post, prope, secundum, trans,* and all ending in *a* (except the preposition *a* itself) and in *ter.* (*Subter* rarely has the ablative.)

(B) With the *ablative* only:

> *Ab* (*abs, a*), *absque, clam, coram, cum, de, ex* (*e*), *palam, præ, pro, sine, tenus.* Also very rarely *procul, simul.*

(C) With *accusative* or *ablative:*

> *In, sub, subter, super.*

(D) The following are also used as *adverbs,* without any case:

> *Ante, circa, circiter, clam, contra, coram, extra, infra, intra, juxta, pone, post, præter, procul, prope, propter, simul, subter, supra, ultra,* and rarely (with numerals) *ad,* 'about.'

Use of the Accusative Case with Prepositions.

§ 203. The *accusative* case implies (1) *place whither,* (2) *place over* or *about which.* These meanings are made more definite by the prepositions as follows.

1. Place towards which.

(a) *To* (*but not into*).

> AD. Ad urbem venit, *He came to the city;* Devertit Clodius ad se, *Clodius turns aside to his own house;* Domum ad Ciceronem ivit, *He went to Cicero's house;* Litteras ad te dabo, *I will post a letter to you.* (Cf. App. G.)

This preposition is not generally required when the motion is towards a *town* mentioned simply by name. Thus, Romam venit, *He came to Rome.*

> (2) Of time *until:* Ad summam senectutem tragœdias fecit, *He made tragedies up to extreme old age.*

(3) *At* (presence *after motion*) of place : Ad fluvium eum expectabat, *He was expecting him at the river.* Senatus ad Apollinis fuit, *The Senate was assembled at Apollo's* (temple).

(4) Of time : Præsto fuit ad horam destinatam, *He was ready at the hour appointed.* Ad famam obsidionis delectus haberi cœptus est, *At the news of the blockade a levy was begun to be held.*

(5) Metaphorically : Omnes ad unum consentiunt, *All to a man agree.* Ad viginti millia erant, *There were present to the number of 20,000 men.* (Cf. § 202.)

(6) *In addition to :* Ad cetera vulnera hanc quoque plagam inflixit, *In addition to the other wounds he added this blow also.*

(7) *Looking at, in regard to :* Ad istorum normam sapientes, *Philosophers if you look to your friends' pattern.*

(8) *Intended for :* Canes ad venandum alit, *He keeps dogs for hunting.* (See App. D.)

AD compounded with VERSUS, *turned,* makes

ADVERSUS, *towards,* which is generally used metaphorically, *towards* and *against,* as, Mea adversus Cæsarem indignatio, *My indignation against Cæsar.* VERSUS is occasionally used as a preposition, and put after its case.

ERGA, *towards,* metaphorically, of *friendly* feelings; as, Mea erga te benivolentia, *My good will towards you.*

(b) *To this side of,*

CIS, CITRA : Citra urbem hostes elicit, *He entices the enemy to this* (i. e. *his*) *side of the city.*

(2) Metaphorically, *not amounting to :* Citra satietatem, *Not amounting to satiety.*

For other usages, see 2 (k).

(*c*) *Into, on to,*

> IN : In Italiam venit, *He came into Italy:* Deiotă-
> rum in equum sustulerunt, *They lifted Deiota-
> rus on to his horse.*
>
> (2) Of a limit of time, *for, against:* In pos-
> terum diem eam invitavit, *He invited her for
> the next day.*
>
> (3) In distributions : Quingenos denarios pre-
> tium in capita statuerant, *They had fixed* 500
> *denaries as the price per head.*
>
> (4) Metaphorically, *of a result:* Ex homine
> se convertit in beluam, *From a man he changes
> himself into a beast.*
>
> (5) *Towards:* Amore inflammati in ejus-
> modi patriam, *Fired with love towards such a
> country.* Cives servilem in modum cruciati, *Citi-
> zens tortured after the manner of slaves.*
> Hæc in rem sunt, *These things tend to one's
> interest.*
>
> (6) Metaphorically, *against:* In eum scripsit
> carmen, *He wrote a poem against him.* In nos
> viri, in nos armati estis? *Against us (do you show
> yourselves) men, against us are ye armed?*
>
> INTER, *in and amongst;* as, Inter falcarios venit,
> *He came amongst the scythe-makers.*
>
> > For other usages see 2 (*c*).
>
> INTRA, *within:* Intra mœnia compulsus, *Having
> been driven within the walls.*
>
> > For other usages, see 2 (*n*).

(*d*) *Outside of,*

> EXTRA; as, Extra terminos egredi non possum, *I
> cannot proceed beyond the bounds.*
>
> > For other usages see 2 (*n*).

(*e*) *To and beyond,*

> TRANS; as, Trans Rhenum ducit exercitum, *He leads
> his army across the Rhine.*

(*f*) *To and under,*

> SUB, SUBTER; as, Exercitum sub jugum mittit, *He
> sends the army under the yoke.* Res unum sub
> aspectum subjiciuntur, *The matters are brought
> under one glance.*
>
> (2) Of time, *close to,* i. e. generally *about* or
> *just after:* Sub noctem, *At nightfall.* Sub eas
> literas statim recitatæ sunt tuæ, *Immediately
> after those dispatches yours were read aloud.*

(*g*) *To and over,*

> SUPER; as, Super montem exercitum ducit, *He leads
> his army over the mountain.*
>
> (2) Metaphorically, *besides:* Punicum exerci-
> tum super morbum etiam fames affecit, *The
> Punic army besides sickness suffered also from
> famine.*

(*h*) *Following,*

> SECUNDUM; as, Secundum fluvium ibat, *He was
> going along the river.*
>
> (2) Metaphorically: Secundum naturam vivere,
> *To live in accordance with nature.*
>
> (3) Of time, *immediately after:* Secundum
> comitia, *Immediately after the comitia.*
>
> (4) Metaphorically: Secundum vocem vultus
> valet, *The look tells next to the voice.* Secundum
> ea multæ res hortabantur, *In favour of that
> course* (lit. *those things*) *many things were urg-
> ing him.*

§ 204.   2. PLACE OVER or ABOUT WHICH.

(*a*) *At,*

APUD; generally prefixed to *persons;* as, Apud me, *At my house.* Apud senatum verba fecit, *He made a speech before the senate.*

(2) Metaphorically: Apud Homerum, *In Homer's writings.*

PENES, *in the custody of;* as, Servi centum dies penes accusatorem fuere, *The slaves for a hundred days were in the custody of the accuser.*

(2) Metaphorically: Penes quos locutionis emendatæ laus fuit, *Who had a right to the praise of correct language.*

(*b*) *Through,*

PER; as, Per urbem venit, *He came through the city.*

(2) Of time: Per hiemem dormit, *It sleeps all through the winter.*

(3) Metaphorically, *by means of:* Per litteras rogat, *He asks through the medium of a letter.* Per Cæsarem facit, *He does it by the agency of Cæsar.* Per me vel stertas licet, *You may snore for all I care.* So in entreaties, swearing, &c.: Per te deos oro, *I implore you by the Gods.*

(4) *By way of:* Vastationem agrorum per contumeliam urbi ostentant, *They display to the city by way of insult the ravaging of the fields.* Per ludum et jocum, *In sport and joke.*

(*c*) *Between, among,*

INTER; as, Inter urbem ac Tiberim ager fuit, *The land lay between the city and the Tiber.*

(2) Of time: Inter hæc, *Whilst this was going on.*

8—2

(3) Metaphorically: Inter has sententias dijudicat, *He decides between these opinions.* Quod colloquimur inter nos, *Our talk amongst ourselves.* Inter suos honestissumus, *A man of excellent character amongst his friends.*

For other usages see 1 (*c*).

(*d*) *Beside and past,*

PRÆTER; as, Præter castra copias duxit, *He led his forces past the camp.*

(2) Metaphorically, *besides:* Præter auctoritatem vires habuit, *Besides his personal authority he had power also.*

(3) *Except:* Præter me nemini hoc videtur, *This seems so to none except me.*

(*e*) *Around,*

CIRCUM, *round:* Terra circum axem se convertit, *The earth revolves round its axis.*

(2) *About:* Circum hæc loca commorabor, *I shall stop about these parts.*

CIRCA, *about:* Plena templa circa forum, *Full were the temples about the Forum.*

(2) Of time, *about:* Circa lucem, *About daylight.*

CIRCITER, of time, *about:* Nos circiter Kalendas in Formiano erimus, *We shall be at our Formian villa about the Kalends.*

(*f*) *Near,*

PROPE; as, Prope urbem castra posuit, *He pitched his camp near the city.* (So propius, proxime.)

PROPTER: Propter Ciceronem sedet, *He sits near Cicero.*

(2) Metaphorically, *on account of:* Propter metum, *On account of fear.*

JUXTA, *close to;* as, Juxta murum castra posuit, *He pitched his camp close to the wall.*

(*g*) *Opposite to,*

OB; as, Mors ob oculos sæpe versata est, *Death was often present before his eyes.* So in the phrase, Ob viam alicui ire, &c., *To go, &c. to meet a person.*

(2) Metaphorically (so more frequently), *on account of:* as, Ob hanc causam, *For this cause.* Quam ob rem, *on which account.*

(*h*) *Before,*

ANTE; as, Ante ædes eum video, *I see him before the house.*

(2) Of time; as, Ante hunc diem, *Before this day.*

(3) Metaphorically: Quem ante me diligo, *Whom I love before myself* (i. e. *more than myself*).

(*i*) *Behind,*

PONE (rare): Pone ædem Castoris, *Behind the temple of Castor.*

POST: Post me erat Ægina, *Ægina was behind me.*

(2) Of time: Post hunc diem, *After this day.*

(3) Metaphorically; as, Erat Lydia post Chloen, *Lydia came* (in my affection) *after Chloe.*

(*k*) *On this side of,*

CITRA: Citra Rhenum Germani sunt, *The Germans are on this side the Rhine.*

For other usages see I (*b*).

(*l*) *On the other side of, beyond,*

ULTRA; as, Cottæ ultra Silianam villam est, *Cotta's is beyond Silius' villa.*

(2) Metaphorically: Ultra vires, *Beyond one's strength.*

(*m*) *Inside of, within,*

INTRA; as, Iliacos intra muros peccatur et extra, *Within the walls of Ilium and without are sins being committed.*

(2) Of time: Intra annos quattuordecim, *Within fourteen years.*

For other usages see I (*c*).

(*n*) *Outside of,*

EXTRA; as, Hi sunt extra provinciam trans Rhodanum primi, *These are the first people outside of the province across the Rhone.*

(2) Metaphorically: Extra jocum, *without joking.*

For other usages see I (*d*).

(*o*) *Below,*

INFRA; as, Infra oppidum eum expectabat, *He was waiting for him below the town.*

(2) Metaphorically: Omnia infra se esse judicat, *He holds all things to be beneath him.*

(*p*) *Above,*

SUPRA; as, Supra prætoris caput, *Above the head of the prætor.*

(2) Metaphorically: Supra hominis fortunam, *Above the fortune of man.*

WITH ABLATIVE CASE.

§ 205. The *ablative* case implies (1) *Place whence,* (2) *Place where.* These meanings are made more definite by prepositions, as follows:

1. PLACE WHENCE.

(*a*) *From,*

A, AB, ABS; as, A portu venio, *I come from the port.*
Domo a Cicerone ivi, *I went from Cicero's
house* (*from Cicero from his house,* cf. § 259. 7).

(2) Of the *starting point* in arranging, reckoning, &c., even with verbs of rest; as, A lævâ stat,
He stands on the left hand. A fronte, *In front.*
Unus a novissimis miles, *A soldier in the rear
rank.* A nobis stat, *He is on our side* (metaphorically). Græcus ille ab omni laude felicior,
*The Greek is happier in every point of excel-
lence.* In later writers we have such expressions
as, Antiochus Ti. Claudi Cæsaris a bibliothecâ,
Antiochus (*was*) *Tib. Claudius Cæsar's librarian.*

(3) Of time: Ab horâ tertiâ, *From the third
hour.* Cæsar ab decimæ legionis cohortatione
ad dextrum cornu profectus est, *Cæsar, after
his address to the tenth legion, proceeded to the
right wing.*

(4) Metaphorically: Ab injuriis defendere, *To
defend from wrongs.*

(5) Of the *source* of action, and so of *the
agent;* as, A patre cognovi, *I learnt it from
my father.* A patre culpari, *To be blamed by a
father.* (Very rare with the gerundive. Cf. § 181.)

PROCUL, *far from;* as, Procul mari, *Far from the
sea* (generally, procul *a* mari, &c.).

(*b*) *Down from, from off,*

DE: De muro se dejecit, *He threw himself from
the wall.* Nescio quis de circo maximo, *Some
one or other from the circus maximus.*

(2) Of time, esp. De nocte, *Whilst yet night.*
De nocte multâ, *In the deep of night.* De die

potare, *To carouse in the daytime.* 'Only used when the subject of the sentence is a *person.*' Freund, *s. v.* (rarely *just after*).

(3) Signifying *separation* of a part from a whole : Hominem certum misi de comitibus meis, *I sent one of my retinue that I could rely on.*

(4) *Resulting from, in consequence of :* De improviso, *Of a sudden.* De industriâ, *On purpose.*

(5) *Of, about, concerning :* De hac re dubito, *About this matter I doubt.*

(c) *Out of,*

E, Ex ; as, Ex urbe venit, *He came out of the city.*

(2) *From, whilst yet on :* Ex equo pugnare, *To fight on horseback.* Ex itinere oppugnat oppidum, *He attacks the town on the march,* i. e. without regularly sitting down before it. Ex omnibus partibus rupes habet, *It has rocks on all sides.*

(3) Of time, *just after :* Cotta ex consulatu profectus est, *Cotta set out immediately after his consulship.* Diem ex die ducit, *He puts it off from day to day* (lit. *Spends day after day*).

(4) *Out of, from :* Ex eo quærit, *He asks of him.* Unus ex tribus modis, *One of three ways.* So of the material : Statua ex ære facta, *A statue made of bronze.*

(5) *In consequence of :* Ex vulnere æger, *Ill of a wound.*

(6) *In accordance with :* Ex consuetudine, *In accordance with one's custom.* Ex animi sententiâ, *In accordance with one's real opinion.* Ex asse hæres factus, *Named heir to the whole property.* E re meâ est, *It is for my interest.*

(*d*) *Absence from,*

ABSQUE, *without* (only in the older writers).

SINE, *without;* as, Sine pecuniâ, *Without money.*

CLAM, *concealed from;* as, Clam uxore meâ et filio, *Without the knowledge of my wife and son.*

§ 206. 2. PLACE WHERE, i. e. at, or in, which.

(*a*) *In,*

IN; as, In corde, *In the heart.* In Italiâ, *In Italy.* In oppido Hispali, *In the town* (of) *Seville* (Hispalis).

N.B. *In* is used with names of *towns* when *urbs* or *oppidum* is prefixed.

(2) *In and amongst :* In eo numero fuit, *He was of that number.* Dolor in maximis malis ducitur, *Pain is reckoned among the greatest evils.*

(3) Of time: In vitâ, *In the course of one's life.*

(4) Metaphorically: In agris vastandis versatus, *Engaged in laying waste the fields.* Vitricum tuum fuisse in tanto scelere fatebare, *You were admitting that your stepfather had been (an actor) in so great a crime.*

(5) *In the case of :* Respondit se id quod in Nerviis fecisset facturum, *He answered that he should do the same as he had done in the case of the Nervii.* In eo potissimum populus abutitur libertate, per quem consecutus est, *The people abuse their liberty in the case of the very man by whose means they have gained it.*

(*b*) *On,*

IN : In equo sedit, *He sat on his horse.* In eo flumine pons erat, *On* (i.e. *over*) *that river there was a bridge.*

(*c*) *With,*

> Cum ; as, Cum Balbo vivit, *He lives with Balbus.*
> Cum populo Romano bellum gerunt, *They wage
> war with* (i. e. *against*) *the Roman people.*

> (2) Of things carried, worn, &c. ; as, Servus
> cum gladio comprehensus est, *A slave was seized
> wearing a sword* (but servus gladio, &c. would
> be, *a slave was seized by means of a sword*,
> abl. of instr.).

> (3) Metaphorically: Qui cum timore aut malâ
> spe vivunt, *Who live in fear or wicked hope.*
> Cum magno provinciæ periculo fieret, *It would
> be attended with great danger to the province.*
> Poetæ cum voluptate audiuntur, *Poets are lis-
> tened to with pleasure.* Cum curâ scribit, *He
> writes with care.*

N.B. *Cum* is always placed *after* the personal pronouns, and
generally after the simple relative ; as, *mecum, vobiscum, quâcum,
quibuscum.*

> Simul ; as, Simul nobis, *Together with us* (only in
> poets and late Latin).

(*d*) *In front of,*

> Præ ; as, Præ se armentum agens, *Driving the
> herd in front of him.*

> (2) Metaphorically, *compared with:* Præ no-
> bis beatus, *Happy in comparison with us.*

> (3) *In consequence of* (chiefly of a *hindrance*):
> Nec loqui præ mœrore potuit, *And he could not
> speak for grief.*

> Pro ; as, Pro rostris, *in front of* (i. e. on the fore
> part of) *the tribune.*

> (2) Metaphorically, *in behalf of:* Pro patriâ
> mori, *To die for one's country.*

(3) *Instead of:* Pro consule venit, *He came as the consul's deputy* (i. e. as Proconsul). Quum pro damnato esset, *When he was as good as condemned.*

(4) *In proportion to:* Plus quam pro meâ parte ago, *I do more than in proportion to my share.*

CORAM ; as, Coram genero meo, *In the presence of my son-in-law.*

PALAM (very rare); as, Me palam, *Openly before me.*

(*e*) *As far as,*

TENUS; as, Collo tenus, *As far as the neck.* Eâtenus (i. e. ea parte tenus), *So far.*

N.B. *Tenus* is always put after its case. With plural substantive it generally takes a genitive case; as, Labrorum tenus, *As far as the lips.* On this usage see § 207.

(*f*) *Under,*

SUB; as, Sub pellibus hiemare, *To winter under tents of skins.* Sub monte consedit, *He sat down at the foot of the mountain.*

(2) Of time, *just at :* Sub discessu tuo, *At the time of his departure.*

(3) Metaphorically: Sub dicione Romanorum esse, *To be under the power of the Romans.* Sub pacto, *Under an agreement.*

SUBTER (rarely found): Subter densâ testudine, *Under a close tortoise-shell* (i. e. shields locked together).

(*g*) *Over,*

SUPER: Ensis super cervice pendet, *A sword hangs over his neck.*

(2) Metaphorically, *upon, about :* Super hac re scribam, *Upon this matter I will write.*

§ 207. Ergo, *on account of;* causâ, gratiâ, *for the sake of;* instar, *like to;* and tenus, *reaching to,* are used with the *genitive* case, but are not strictly prepositions. The first three are ablatives (*ergo* is strictly a Greek dative, ἔργῳ) of the *manner;* the last two are indeclinable substantives (instar, *likeness;* tenus, *extent*); *instar* being in apposition, &c. to some part of the sentence; *tenus* being an accus. by § 173.

§ 208. Prepositions compounded with verbs, sometimes (1) retain their proper meaning, and even their ordinary use with particular cases, the preposition being either repeated with the noun (so esp. *ad, in, ex, sub, cum*) or not; (2) sometimes form with the verb a new meaning which may be suited to a different case. Many verbs have both constructions. If a *local* relation be clearly (even though figuratively) intended, a preposition is (in prose) usually prefixed to the noun.

E.g. (1) Trans Rhenum exercitum ducit; ⎫
Trans Rhenum exercitum traducit; ⎬ all in same
Rhenum exercitum traducit. ⎭ meaning.

(2) Vitium aliquod inest in moribus;
His artibus (*dat.*) major prudentia inest.

§ 209. In composition some prepositions have, besides their usual meanings, certain special meanings, which they but partially exhibit out of composition. The following deserve notice:

CUM (in comp. CON-, CO-), *thoroughly;* as, sĕquor, *follow;* consequor, *overtake:* cædo, *cut;* concido, *cut to pieces.*

PER has a similar meaning; as, suadeo, *recommend;* persuadeo, *persuade.* Especially with adjectives; as, perjucundus, *very pleasant.*

PRÆ, *at the end, along the edge;* as, rodo, *gnaw;* prærodo, e.g. lingua dentibus prærosa, *a tongue bitten at the end.*

SUB- (SUBS-, SU-), (1) *Up;* as, emo, *take;* sumo, *take up;* suspicio, *look up;* sursum, i.e. su-versum, *upwards.*

(2) *Secretly;* as, rapio, *snatch;* surripio, *snatch away secretly.*

(3) *Slightly;* as, accuso, *accuse;* subaccuso, *accuse in a manner.* Also with adjectives; as, subobscurus, *rather dark.*

§ 210. Other prepositions are only used in composition:

AMB- (AM-, AN-), *about;* as, amb-igo, *lead about;* am-plector, *fold oneself round;* an-ceps, *two-headed.*

DĬS- (DĬR-, DĪ-), implies *division;* as, dīlabor, *slip in different directions;* dissentio, *think differently;* dirimo, *destroy* (emo).

IN, a *negative* prefix; as, injustus, *unjust.* So also VĒ- (rare); as, vēcors, *senseless.*

RED- (RE-),

(1) *Back;* as, redeo, *go back;* rĕtraho, *draw back.*

(2) *Again;* as, rĕpeto, *reseek.*

(3) *Reversal;* as, rĕfigo, *unfix.*

SED- (SĒ-), *separation;* as, sēd-itĭo, *a secession;* sēcedo, *go apart, withdraw:* in old Latin used as a preposition, se fraude esto, *it shall be without risk.*

N.B. The '*d*' at the end of these last two words is found in many prepositions, and is probably the '*d*' which was the sign of the ablative in old Latin. Thus, prod (prod-eo) is *in front;* red, *in the back;* extrad, *on the outside;* antid (antidhac = antea), *in front.*

OF THE DIFFERENT KINDS OF SENTENCES.

§ 211. (A) A *simple* sentence contains only one assertion, and therefore only one primary predicate (i. e. finite verb).

§ 212. (B) A *compound* sentence contains two or more assertions *co-ordinate* to one another, and therefore contains two or more primary or verbal predicates connected by some conjunction, but independent of one another in construction; such as, et, *and;* aut, *or;* nec, *nor;* sed, *but;* igitur, *therefore;* enim, *for;* quanquam (when it means *and yet*), &c.; also by the relative *qui* when it has the same effect as *et is, nam is,* &c. Occasionally the sentences are put together without any connecting word, but so that such a conjunction might be added without affecting the sense. When the subject or object, &c. of the co-ordinate sentences are the same, such subject, &c. is usually exprest only once.

> Ex. Rem cognoscit et sententiam dicit, *He hears the case, and utters his opinion.*
>
> Cæsar venit: illi autem fugerunt, *Cæsar came: they however fled.*
>
> Cæsar adfuit: qui dixit, *Cæsar was present: and he said.*
>
> Nam, quod ad populum pertinet, semper dignitatis iniquus judex est; qui aut invidet aut favet, *For as regards the people, it is always an unfair judge of worth; for it is either envious or partial.*
>
> Pompeius fremit, queritur, Scauro studet, sed utrum fronte an mente, dubitatur, *Pompey chafes, complains, is zealous for Scaurus, but whether in appearance or in heart, people cannot tell.*

§ 213. (C) A *complex* sentence contains two or more sentences, of which one only is *principal*, and the others *subordinate* to it.

Subordinate sentences are either Substantival, Adjectival, or Adverbial sentences, according as they stand in the place of a Substantive, an Adjective, or an Adverb.

§ 214. I. *Substantival* sentences may occupy any place which a substantive in the nominative or accusative case may occupy, i.e. Subject, Object, Epithet (in apposition), and secondary or oblique predicate.

They are (in Latin) of four kinds:

1. Infinitive sentence*, the subject being in the accusative, and the predicate in the infinitive.

---

* Expressions with the infinitive mood are not strictly *sentences*, but fragments of sentences. They are here classed with substantival sentences, because they are used where in English we use substantival sentences, and because they represent in the *oratio obliqua* what would be proper sentences in the *oratio recta.*

Ex. Scio te hæc dixisse, *I know that you have said this. Te hæc dixisse* is object to *scio.*

2. Sentences introduced by the conjunction *quod.*

Ex. Gratum est quod venisti, *Your having come is pleasing. Quod venisti* is the subject to *est.*

3. Dependent questions.

Ex. Cognovi cur hæc scripserit, *I have ascertained why he wrote this.* Here *cur hæc scripserit* is object to *cognovi.*

4. Some sentences introduced by *ut* or *ne;* especially as objects after verbs of *entreating, commanding, effecting,* &c. (Originally adverbial sentences of *purpose, result,* &c.)

Ex. Peto non ut aliquid novi decernatur, sed ne quid novi decernatur, *I ask not that some new decree be made, but that no new decree may be made.* The clauses followed by *ut* and *ne* are objects.

Accidit ut ibi adessem, *It happened that I was there. Ut ibi adessem* is subject to *accidit.*

§ 215. II. *Adjectival sentences* are always introduced by a relative (adjective, or adverb), as, *qui, qualis, quantus,* &c. *ubi, quando,* and stand where an adjective may stand, i. e. either as epithet to a substantive, or secondary predicate to a subject.

Ex. Locus ubi constiti, *The place where I stood.*

Hic est quem quærimus, *This is the man we are seeking.*

§ 216. III. *Adverbial* sentences are used to qualify verbs or adjectives, and are introduced either by a conjunction, or relative adverb, as, *ut, si, quum, quo,* &c. The different significations of adverbial sentences with the conjunctions introducing them are as follows:

1. PLACE *where, whence, whither.* Ubi, qua, quo, unde, &c. (*Local* sentences.)

2. TIME *when, during which, until, after, before, as often as.* Quum, ut (*when*), ubi, dum, donec, postquam, priusquam, quoties, &c. (*Temporal* sentences.)

3. MANNER *in which;* as, ut (*as*), ceu, quasi, quam, tanquam, velut, &c. (*Comparative* sentences.)

4. PURPOSE; *that, in order that.* Ut, ut ne, ne. (*Final* sentences.)

5. RESULT; *so that.* Ut, ut non. (*Consecutive* or *illative* sentences.)

6. CONDITION; *if, provided that, supposing that.* Si, quasi, dum, modo, &c. (*Conditional* sentences.)

7. CAUSE; *because, since.* Quod, quum, quia, siquidem, &c. (*Causal* sentences.)

8. CONCESSION; *although.* Etsi, quanquam, ut. (*Concessive* sentences.)

Examples of these different kinds of adverbial sentences will be given below in treating of the moods. With them should be compared the use of oblique cases (except genitive) with and without prepositions, especially the ablative with an oblique predicate.

§ 217. A subordinate sentence may itself be a complex sentence, and thus what is subordinate to one sentence may be principal to another.

Ex. Ut iis bonis erigimur quæ exspectamus, ita lætamur iis, quæ recordamur, *As we are excited by the good things which we expect, so we rejoice in the good things which we remember.*

The principal sentence is *sic lætamur iis:* to this there are two subordinate sentences, viz.

(1) *quæ recordamur,* a simple adjectival sentence qualifying *iis.*

(2) *ut erigimur bonis iis, quæ exspectamus,* a complex adverbial sentence of manner.

Thus, *ut erigimur bonis* is subordinate to *sic lætamur,* but principal to *quæ exspectamus.*

OF THE FINITE VERB.

§ 218. If I speak of an event taking place or an action being performed, I may wish to assert positively that it is taking, or has taken, or will take place, that a thing is so or is not so. In such cases the Romans used the *indicative* mood. Or again, I may wish to speak of an action or event *not as a fact, but as an idea or supposition,* referring to it as possible, or as existing in some other person's thoughts, or as desirable, or as an idea to promote or retard the realisation of which other actions are done, or other things exist. In this case the *subjunctive* mood is used. Or again, instead of asserting that a thing is so or is not so, I may order a person to do it. In this case the *imperative* mood is used.

(A) INDICATIVE MOOD.

§ 219. I. The indicative mood is used in direct assertions or negations, or questions, and therefore it is the mood generally found in sentences *not subordinate* to others.

§ 220. II. In *subordinate* sentences only when they express *actual* facts or *simple* descriptions, &c. Thus in

1. *Substantival* with conjunction *quod.*

Ex. Adde quod ingenuas didicisse fideliter artes emollit mores, *Add the fact that to have learnt faithfully the liberal arts softens the manners.*

§ 221. 2. *Adjectival:* especially definitive of existing classes, or when substitutes for a simple term.

(a) Either with simple relative.

Ex. Apud Alexandriam, quæ in Egypto sita est, vixit, *He lived at the Egyptian Alexandria.*

Omnibus, unde petitur, hoc consili dederim, *To all defendants in a suit I would give this advice* (lit. *To all persons from whom (satisfaction) is sought, &c.*).

Jugurtha, quantas maximas potest, copias armat, *Jugurtha arms as large a number of troops as he possibly can* (arm).

(b) Or with doubled form of relatives and those with *cunque* attached; as, *quisquis, quantusquantus* and *quicunque.*

> Ex. Quicquid erit, scribes, *Whatever it be, you will write* (the news).
>
> Quoscunque de te queri audivi, quacunque ratione potui, placavi, *All that I have heard finding fault with you, I have appeased in whatever way I could.*

§ 222. III. In *adverbial* sentences of

1. *Place*, with conjunctions; *ubi, ubicunque, qua, quacunque, unde, quo,* &c.

> Ex. Nunc proficiscar quo ire constitui, *Now I will start for the place I settled to go to.*
>
> Ubicunque Patricius habitat, ibi carcer privatus est, *Wherever there is a Patrician's dwelling, there is a private prison.*

2. *Time;* with *postquam, priusquam, quum* (when the relation between the actions is regarded as entirely or predominantly one of time; and so when frequency of *actual* occurrences is implied), *ut, simul ac, dum, donec, quoad, quando, quoties,* &c.

> Ex. Dum latine loquentur litteræ, quercus huic loco non deerit, *So long as literature shall talk Latin, this spot will not be without its oak.*
>
> Quum cecinit receptui, impellit rursum, *After sounding for a retreat, he again rouses (to action).*
>
> Quum ver esse cœperat, dabat se labori, *At the beginning of every spring he used to give himself up to toil.* (See § 229. 4.)

3. *Manner;* with *ut*, 'as', *quomodo* (both interrogatively and relatively), *quí? utcunque,* &c.

Ex. Ut dixi, ita feci, *As I said, so I did.*

Dicam quam brevissime potero, *I will tell in the very fewest words I can.*

Orator utcunque animum audientium moveri volet, ita certum vocis admovebit sonum, *An orator, whatever be the emotion he shall wish to excite in the mind of his hearers, will adapt to it a special modulation of his voice.*

Ut quisque est vir optimus, ita difficillime esse alios improbos suspicatur, *The better a man is, the greater difficulty has he in suspecting others to be rogues.*

4. *Condition,* when the speaker is not so much supposing a *possible* case, as stating *positively* the circumstances under which a fact *is* or *was* occurring, or *will* occur or not: and this especially (but not exclusively) when the principal sentence has the indicative: with *si, nisi.*

Ex. Da certa piamina fulminis, si tua contigimus manibus donaria puris, *Grant sure atonements of the lightning, if we have* (as we have) *with pure hands touched thy shrines.*

Perficietur bellum, si urgemus obsessos, *The war will be finished, if we continue* (as we are doing) *to press the besieged.*

Nisi hoc ita est, frustra laboramus, *If this is not so, we are labouring in vain.*

5. *Cause* (stated as a fact, not a supposition), with *quod, quia, quoniam, siquidem, quando, quandoquidem* and (after laudo, gratias ago, &c.) *quum.*

Ex. Non pigritia feci, quod non meâ manu scribo, *It is not from laziness that I do not write with my own hand.*

Veni quia tu voluisti, *I came because you wished.*

Gratulor tibi, quum tantum vales apud Dolabellam, *I congratulate you on your great influence
with Dolabella.*

6. *Concession,* with *quanquam, etsi, utut.* (Cf. § 221. *b.*)

Ex. Utut illud erat, manere oportuit, *However that
was he (she, they) ought to have stayed* (lit. *It
was a duty to stay*).

TENSES OF INDICATIVE MOOD.

§ 223. The tenses of the indicative mood may be conveniently divided into primary and secondary.

The *primary* tenses denote time contemporaneous with,
antecedent, or subsequent to the time *at* which we are
speaking, or at some time at which we feign ourselves to
be present and watching events.

The *secondary* tenses denote time contemporaneous
with, antecedent, or subsequent to some other time *of*
which we are speaking, and which we affirm to be past.

§ 224.   ACTIVE VOICE.

	PRIMARY.	SECONDARY.
Antecedent.	*Perfect*; dixi, *I have said.*	*Pluperfect*; dixeram, *I had said.*
Contemporary.	*Present;* dico, *I am saying.*	*Imperfect;* dicebam, *I was saying.*
Subsequent.	*Future;* dicam, *I shall say.*	*Aorist;* dixi, *I said* (i. e. after something had happened*).

The *2nd* or *completed Future* is used to denote an
action completed at some future time, i. e. time antecedent
to some event in future time; as, dixero, *I shall have
said.*

* This arrangement is suggested by Burnouf (quoted by
Donaldson, *New Crat.* § 372; *Varron.* p. 411, 3rd ed.).

§ 225. In order to denote future time, especially if regarded from a point in the past or future, the participle in *urus* is used with the different tenses of the verb *sum:* thus,

PRIMARY.		SECONDARY.
Contemporary.	amaturus sum, *I am about to* (or *mean to*) *love.*	amaturus eram (or, in the poets, fueram), *I was at the time about to love,* &c.
Subsequent.	amaturus ero, *I shall be about to love,* &c.	amaturus fui, *I was* (*once*) *about to love,* &c.

And the same form is resorted to for the subjunctive future; as, *amaturus sim,* &c. (Cf. § 237.)

§ 226. PASSIVE VOICE.

		PRIMARY.		SECONDARY.
Antecedent.	*Perf.*	amatus sum, *I am* (or *have been*) *loved.*	*Plup.*	amatus eram (or fueram), *I had been loved,* sometimes, *I was loved.*
Contemporary.	*Pres.*	amor, *I am being loved.*	*Impf.*	amabar, *I was being loved.*
Subsequent.	*Fut.*	amabor, *I shall be loved.*	*Aor.*	amatus sum, *I was loved.* amatus fui, *I was* (*for some time*) *loved.*

Completed *Future;* amatus ero (or fuero), *I shall have been loved.*

The forms of some Latin tenses are used with different shades of meaning. Thus,

§ 227. (A) *Present* tense expresses

(1) Action at the time of speaking; as, scribo, *I am writing.*

(2) Action at a moment, rhetorically assumed to be present (frequent in vivid narrations).

> Ex.   Quum Caius moriebatur, accurrit Lucius, *When Caius was dying, Lucius runs to him.*

(3) Action extending over some time, including the time of speaking.

> Ex.   Jamdudum scribo, *I have been for a long time writing.*
>
> Tertium jam annum hic sumus, *We are here now for the third year.*

(4) Action about to be commenced.

> Ex.   Jam venio, *Lo ! now I come.*

(5) Action, without reference to any particular time (especially in stating abstract truths).

> Ex.   Virtus est verum bonum, *Virtue is the true good.*

§ 228.   (B) *Imperfect* tense expresses

(1) Continuous action contemporaneous with past action referred to.

> Ex.   Quum hæc dicebat abibam, *Whilst he was saying this I was going away.*

(2) Habitual action in past time.

> Ex.   Hæc dicebat, *He used to say this*, or *he kept saying this.*

(3) Action commenced, or attempted, or intended in past time.

> Ex.   Servabam eum, *I was on the point of saving him,* or *I tried to save him,* or *I proceeded to save him.*

§ 229.   (C) *Perfect* tense expresses an action done in past time. This, according to the point of view, may be regarded as

(1) (Greek *Aorist*). Action subsequent to another action in past time : so usually in a continued narrative.

Ex. Postquam hæc dixit *abiit, After that he had said this, he departed.*

(2) Action single or momentary in past time.

Ex. Quum hoc prœlium factum est Cæsar aberat, *Cæsar was absent at the time when this battle took place.*

(3) (Greek *Perfect*). Action completed before present time, or before time assumed to be present; as, Scripsi, *I have written.* Sometimes with emphasis ; as, Perii, *It is all over with me.* Fuit Ilium, *Ilium is a thing of the past.*

So of an action quickly completed; as, Terra tremit: fugere feræ, *The earth quakes: the beasts are fled and gone.*

(4) It is used also in subordinate sentences, in speaking of *repeated* actions, when the principal verb is in the present tense. (For this the pluperfect is used when the principal verb is in the imperfect, as in § 222. 2, and not often otherwise in (subordinate) temporal sentences unless, after *postquam*, some *lapse* of time between the actions is signified.)

§ 230. (D) The *Future* is in Latin (besides its other uses) used in subordinate sentences, qualifying a principal future sentence, and referring to the same time. (In English the present is generally found.)

Ex. Dicam quum potero, *I will say, when I can.*
Naturam si sequemur ducem, nunquam aberrabimus, *If we follow the guidance of nature we shall never go astray.*

But this future in the *oratio obliqua* becomes a *present* (or *imperfect*); as, Negat Cicero, si naturam *sequamur* ducem, unquam nos aberraturos. (Negabat, si *sequeremur*, § 248. 6.)

§ 231. (E) The *Completed Future* expresses

(1) Action already completed at a given future time.

Ex.   Quum tu hæc leges, ego illum fortasse convenero, *When you will be reading this, I shall perhaps have spoken with him.*

(2) Action completed simultaneously to another action in future time.

Ex.   Qui Antonium oppresserit, is bellum confecerit. *The man that shall have crushed Antony will* (therein) *have finished the war.*

(3) Future result of a past action.

Ex.   Si plane occidimus, ego omnibus meis exitio fuero, *If we are utterly fallen, I shall have been the destruction of all my friends.*

(4) Action postponed.

A frequent meaning in the comic poets, but confined in writers of the best period to the word *videro.*

Ex.   Recte secusne, alias viderimus, *Whether rightly or not, we shall see on some future occasion.*

(B) Subjunctive Mood.

§ 232. The subjunctive mood expresses the *supposition* or *conception* of a fact as opposed to the assertion of it. All its uses may be ultimately referred to this, but for convenience they may be classed in subordinate divisions as follows.   Either the fact or truth supposed may be considered as the cause or condition of another fact or truth : or itself dependent on conditions or on other statements being true : or it may be imagined as an idea to be realized, a purpose to be carried out, a command, a wish, a result.   In conditional sentences we have the first two classes, the former as the protasis, the latter as the apodosis : the former stating the circumstances, not which *do* exist, but which we suppose *will have* (or *would have had*) *to* exist in order that a thing may take place, and which consequently limit and determine the mode of its existence : the latter stating the thing which takes place not as a certainty but as contingent on the fact and truth of the other.   The third class is exemplified by those sentences which contain the conjunction *ut.*

I. Action, event, truth, &c. of which the existence is *supposed,*

(1)   as a bare supposition. (Hypothesis or Concession.)

(2)   as a condition. (Condition.)

(3)   to be the attendant cause or circumstance of another action. (Cause).

II.   Action &c. of which the existence is *assumed,*

(4)   if certain other things exist. (Conditional existence.)

(5)   according to the report or opinion of others. (Oratio obliqua.)

(6)   because it is a qualification of some other supposed or assumed action. (Dependent on infinitive or subjunctive moods.)

III.   Action, &c. of which the existence is *intended* or *desired :*

(7)   Wish.

(8)   Command or duty.

(9)   Purpose.

(10)   Result or consequence.

§ 233.   It must be always remembered that a writer may *sometimes* (especially in relative sentences, putting a definition, § 221, for a natural result, § 235, 9), if he chooses, express a supposition positively, as if it were a fact, and therefore use the indicative mood ; or, on the other hand, express a fact as if it were only a *supposition,* and therefore use the subjunctive mood.   If, however, he wish to *imply by the form* of expression that it is a *supposition,* or *conception* (though it may be also a fact), he uses the subjunctive ; otherwise he uses the indicative.

§ 234.   The student must further bear in mind, especially if he connect the use of the indicative and subjunctive moods with particular conjunctions, that a sentence which ordinarily would have had the indicative mood may have the subjunctive for some collateral reason.   Thus a subjunctive of the classes numbered 4 or 7, &c. will be often found (especially where the 2nd pers. sing. stands for the indefinite *one*) where otherwise we should have expected the indicative.

Ex.   Si stare non possunt, corruant, *If they cannot stand, why let them fall.*

Camillus, quamquam exercitum assuetum imperio, qui in Volscis erat, mallet, nihil recusavit, *Camillus,*

> *although he would have preferred* (i.e. if he had had
> the choice) *the army which was amongst the Volsci,
> accustomed as it was to his rule, still made no objection.*
> Regularly we should have had *malebat.*

So usually in sentences under 5 and 6.

§ 235. The subjunctive mood is generally found in
subordinate sentences, qualifying a principal sentence and
introduced by relatives and conjunctions, especially *qui*
(*quæ, quod*), *si, quum*, and *ut*. The conjunctions, besides
connecting the sentences, serve also to render the general
meaning (§ 218. 232) more precise. The different shades of
meaning may be enumerated as follows, but it will be seen
that they are closely related, and that several of the examples might be referred to other heads than the one under
which they are here placed.

1. An ACTION MERELY SUPPOSED ; but with conse-
quent assertion exprest or implied; e.g. *concessive* sentences.

> Ex. (*a*) Dicat aliquis, *A man may say,* (cf. §. 259. 2).
>
> > Hæc sint falsa sane: invidiosa certe non sunt,
> > *Suppose these-assertions to be false: invidious
> > they are not.*
> >
> > Vendat ædes vir bonus, &c., *Suppose an honest
> > man to sell his house,* &c. (See the passage
> > in Cic. *Off.* III. 13.)
>
> (*b*) With conjunctions, e. g. *ut, quamvis, forsitan.*
>
> (*Licet* is not a conjunction but a verb. Its use comes under 9.)
>
> > Ut desint vires, tamen est laudanda voluntas,
> > *Grant that strength be wanting, yet the will
> > is praiseworthy.*
> >
> > Quamvis desint, &c., *Suppose strength to be
> > wanting to any extent you please.*

2. An ACTION SUPPOSED AS THE CONDITION OF ANOTHER
ACTION (i. e. in the protasis * of a conditional sentence).

---

* The *protasis* is the relative or conditional clause; the *apodosis* is the corresponding demonstrative or conditioned clause.

(*a*)   Without conjunction (the verb being generally put first in the clause):

Ex.   Partem opere in tanto, *sineret* dolor, Icare haberes, *Some place in this great work, had grief permitted, Icarus, thou wouldst have had.*

Dares hanc vim Crasso, in foro saltaret, *Had you (been giving,* i.e.*) offered this power' to Crassus, he would have been dancing in the forum.*

(*b*)   With relative, esp. *qui quidem, qui modo.*

Ex.   Omnium oratorum, quos quidem ego cognoverim, acutissimum judico Q. Sestorium, *Of all orators, at least whom I have known, I judge the acutest to be Q. Sestorius.*

Quod sciam, *As far as I know* (i.e. *if I know*).

(*c*)   With conj. e.g. *si, dum* ('provided that'), *modo, dummodo.*

Si hic *sis,* aliter sentias, *If you should be in my position, you would feel differently.*   (For *sentias,* see 4. *a.*)

Manent ingenia senibus, modo permaneat studium et industria, *Old men retain their abilities, do but their interest and industry remain unimpaired.*

(*d*)   With apodosis not exprest, especially with conj. *quasi, tanquam si, ceu.*

Ex.   Sed quid ego his testibus utor, quasi res dubia aut obscura sit? *But why do I resort to these witnesses as* (I should do) *if the matter were doubtful or obscure?* (*quasi* is *qua* faciam *si*).

O si angulus ille proximus accedat, *O if that corner close to should but be added!*

3.   AN ACTION THOUGHT AS THE ATTENDANT CAUSE OR CIRCUMSTANCE *under* or *notwithstanding which other actions or events take place.*

(*a*) With relative; *qui, præsertim qui.*

Ex. Jamdudum ego erro, qui tam multa verba faciam,
I have long been making a mistake in speaking at such length.

Egomet, qui leviter Græcas litteras attigissem, tamen Athenis commoratus sum, *I, although I had but slightly touched Greek literature, yet tarried at Athens.*

(*b*) With conj. esp. *quum*, which thus gets to mean '*since*,' '*whereas*,' '*notwithstanding*' (so quum præsertim), '*if ever*'; also after *ubi, quicunque*, in the last meaning.

Quæ quum ita sint, hoc dico, *And since this is the case, I say as follows.*

Quum in jus duci debitorem vidissent, convolabant, *If ever they caught sight of a debtor being led into court, they used to fly together to his assistance.*

Eo quum pervenisset, ad reliquas legiones mittit, *When he had come thither, he sends to the rest of the legions.*

Dion, quum crudeliter a Dionysio violatus esset, tamen eodem rediit, *Dion, notwithstanding that he had been cruelly outraged by Dionysius, still returned to the same place.*

With the imperfect and pluperfect in historical narration, after *quum* (as in the last two examples), the use of the subjunctive is very frequent, and *implies* (without positively asserting) that the action, event, &c. was not merely coincident or antecedent in time, but that it exercised, or might have exercised an *influence* over the other action or event. In English we often mark *time* only.

4. AN ACTION SUPPOSED AS EXISTING IF SOMETHING ELSE EXIST (i.e. in the apodosis of a conditional sentence).

(*a*) With Condition exprest:

Ex. Si hic sis, aliter *sentias, You would feel differently if you should be in my position.* (For
sis, see above, 2. *c.*)

Quidnam homines putarent, si tum occisus esset
quum, &c., *What, pray, would men have been
thinking, if he had been slain when, &c.*

(*b*) With Condition not exprest:

Tu *velim* ad me venias, *I should like you to
come to me* (i. e. if you can do so. For *venias,*
cf. 9).

Themistocles quidem nihil dixerit, in quo ipse
Areopagum adjuverit, *Themistocles will* (if
he *have* tried to do so) *have named nothing
in which he helped the Areopagus* (for *adjuverit,* see 6).

Canes venaticos diceres, *You* (or *one*) *would
have said they were hounds* (i. e. if you [or
one] had not known to the contrary).

Mihi pœnarum illi plus quam optarem dederunt,
*To me they have given more satisfaction than
I should (now) have wished.*

5. An Action reported as stated, or known, or
thought by some one else; in a subordinate sentence.

(*a*) Ex. Laudat Panætius Africanum, quod fuerit ab-
stinens, *Panætius praises Africanus for being*
(as Panætius asserts) *abstinent.* (If the writer's
own opinion were given we should have had
fuit.)

Romani, quia consules prospere rem gererent,
minus his cladibus commovebantur, *The Romans were not so much disturbed by these
disasters, because they considered the consuls
to be managing the matter successfully.* (*Because* [as a matter of fact] *the consuls were
managing matters successfully,* would have
required *gerebant.*)

So especially after *non quod, non quia, non quo*, introducing a reason alleged, but false.

> Pugiles in jactandis cæstibus ingemiscunt, non quod doleant animove succumbant, sed quia profundendâ voce omne corpus intenditur, venitque plaga vehementior, *Boxers groan when wielding their gauntlets, not that* (as people may think) *they are in pain, or their heart fails them, but because by exerting the voice all the body is put on the stretch, and the blow comes with greater force.*

(*b*) Dependent interrogative:

> Quæsivi quid faceret, *I inquired what he was doing.*
>
> Videte ut hoc iste correxerit, *See how the defendant corrected this.*
>
> Haud scio an crudele sit spectaculum, *I know not whether it be* (i.e. *I almost think that it is*) *a cruel spectacle.*
>
> Rem frumentariam, ut satis commode supportari posset, timere se dicebant, *They kept saying that they were afraid, that the corn could not be conveniently brought up* (*afraid about the corn, how it could be,* &c. See 259. 4. *e*).

> > Relative clauses must be distinguished from interrogative, e.g. Senes omnia quæ curant meminerunt; qui sibi, cui ipsi debeant, *Old men remember all things which they care about; who owe them money, and whom they owe money to.*

6. An action qualifying another supposed action, i.e. in sentences subordinate to subjunctive moods or infinitives, and not expressing independent declaration of *facts.*

> Non enim is sum qui, quidquid videtur, tale dicam esse quale videatur, *For I am not the man to say that whatever we see* (i.e. *all visible things,* cf. § 221) *is of the kind it appears to be.*

Si luce quoque canes latrent, quum deos salutatum aliqui venerint, opinor, iis crura suffringantur, quod acres sint, quum suspicio nulla sit, *If in daylight also dogs should bark, when persons have come to address the gods, they would, I imagine, have their legs broken for being so watchful, when there is no ground for suspicion.* (If *si* were removed all the verbs would be in the indicative.)

N.B. To this and the preceding class belongs the use of the subjunctive in the *oratio olliqua,* for which see § 248.

7. AN ACTION SUPPOSED AND WISHED.

(*a*) Ex. Valeant cives mei : sint incolumes, sint beati, *Farewell to my fellow-citizens : safe and happy may they be.*

Interceam si valeo stare, *May I die if I have strength to stand.*

(*b*) With conj. *utinam :*

Utinam eum inveniam, *That I may but find him!*

8. AN ACTION SUPPOSED AND COMMANDED. (cf. § 248. 4.)

(*a*) Ex. Aut bibat aut abeat, *He must either drink or leave.*

Puer telum ne habeat, *Don't let the boy have the dart.*

Sed de hoc tu ipse videris, *You yourself must look to this.* (Madvig considers *videris* an indicative, cf. § 231. 4.)

Ne dixeris, *Do not say.*

Adservasses hominem, &c., *You should have kept the man, &c.* (See Cic. *Verr.* v. 65.)

Frumentum ne emisses, *You ought not to have bought the corn* (in past time).

Imitemur majores nostros, *We should imitate our ancestors.*

In prohibitions, if exprest in the third person, the present and perfect are frequent; if in the second person, the perfect both active and passive is preferred, and the present is very rare.

(*b*) In interrogative sentences (if negative, with *non*).

Ex. Quid hoc homine faciatis? *What are you to do with such a fellow as this?*

Cur plura commemorem? *Why should I mention more?*

Hæc quum viderem, quid agerem? *Seeing this, what was I to do?* (Cic. *Sest.* 19. See the answer, *ib.* 20.)

So also in a dependent sentence:

Non satis constabat quid agerent, *They did not rightly know what they were to do.*

9. AN ACTION STATED AS AN IDEA TO BE REALIZED, a purpose to be carried out.

N.B. In English the (so-called) infinitive is regularly used to express a purpose, in Latin very rarely, and only in poetry.

(*a*) Ex. Fac cogites, *Mind that you think.*

Cave putes, &c., *Beware of thinking, &c.*

Intereat necesse est, *Die he must.*

Sine te exorem, *Let me prevail upon you.*

Licet scribat, *He is allowed to write* (lit. *It is allowed that he write*).

Exercitum locis habeam opportunis, provinciam tuear, omniaque integra servem, dabo operam. *I will exert myself to have the army in good positions, protect the province, and keep everything unharmed.*

(*b*) With a relative.

Misi ad Antonium qui hoc ei diceret, *I sent one to Antonius to tell him this.*

Non habet unde solvat, *He has not wherewith to pay.*

(c) With conj. *ut*, 'in order that,' *dum*, *quoad*, or in negative sentences, *ut ne, dum ne, ne, quominus,* &c.

Ex. Legum omnes servi sumus, ut liberi esse possimus, *We are all bond to laws that it may be possible for us to be free.*

Cura ut valeas, *Take care of your health.*

Vereor ne hoc sit, *I fear lest this be* (i.e. *that it is*) *the case.* Cf. § 259. 4. *e.*

Caius orat Dolabellam ut ad Julium proficiscatur, *Caius implores Dolabella to set out on his journey to Julius.*

Oppidum oppugnare instituit, ne quem post se hostem relinqueret, *He commenced besieging the town, that he might not leave any enemy in his rear.*

Dum reliquæ naves eo convenirent, ad horam nonam in ancoris expectavit, *He waited at anchor to the ninth hour to allow of the other ships assembling there.*

Non recusabo quominus omnes mea scripta legant, *I will not object to all men reading my writings.*

Elephantos in primam aciem induci jussit, si quem injicere ea res tumultum posset, *He ordered the elephants to be led into the first line, in hopes that this manœuvre might cause some confusion.*

10. AN ACTION STATED AS THE NATURAL RESULT OF OTHERS.

(a) With relative.

Ex. Digna res est, quam diu multumque consideremus, *The matter is worthy of our long and full consideration.*

Plus tamen ferociæ Britanni præferunt, ut quos nondum longa pax emollierit, *The Britons, however, exhibit more mettle* (than the Gauls), *inasmuch as a long peace has not yet enervated them.*

Non is es, qui gloriere, *You are not the person to boast.*

Quid habes quod mihi opponas ? *What have you to bring against me ?*

Innocentia est affectio talis animi, quæ noceat nemini, *Innocence is that kind of affection of the mind, which is hurtful to no one.*

 (*b*) With conj. *ut* (*ut non* in negative sentences), *quin.*

Ex. Reliquos ita perterritos egerunt, ut non prius fugâ desisterent, quam in conspectum agminis nostri venissent, *The rest they drove before them in such a panic of fear, that they did not stop flying, before they had come into sight of our line of march.*

Accidit ut illo tempore in urbe essem, *It so happened that I was in the city at that time.*

Proximum est ut doceam, &c., *The next thing is that I should show, &c.*

Mos est hominum ut nolint eundem pluribus rebus excellere, *It is the habit of the world not to allow that the same person excels in more points than one.*

Sunt qui putent, *There are persons such as to think* (or, *There are persons who may be supposed to think.* So *sunt* &c. *qui* generally in prose).

Nemo est quin dubitet, *There is no one but hesitates.*

Tenses of the Subjunctive.

§ 236. As the time in subordinate propositions is determined by the time of the principal sentence, the present and perfect subjunctive are used in sentences dependent on primary tenses, the imperfect and pluperfect subjunctive in sentences dependent on secondary tenses. The historical present is considered as primary or secondary at the will of the writer. The tenses are generally distinguished *from one another* in the same way as the tenses in the indicative mood.

§ 237. If future time require to be distinctly marked, the periphrasis of the future in *rus* with *sim* or *essem* is resorted to (§ 225). Otherwise the present and imperfect supply the place of a simple future, and the perfect and pluperfect of a completed future.

(In Virg. *Æn.* VI. 871, 879, we have an illustration of the way in which *past* tenses come to be used in reference to *future* time; because the speaker throws himself in imagination into the future, and speaks from that point of view.)

The following examples show the use in the sentences most frequently occurring. It will be seen that some sentences admit of a greater variety of tenses than others :

§ 238. I. In *dependent interrogative* and *consecutive* sentences.

1. *Dependent interrogative* (5. *b*).

(*a*) Vidi(*perf.*)
    Video   quid facias, *I see*   *what you are*
    Videbo   *I shall see*   *doing.*
                     I have seen

(*b*) .... quid feceris, ... *what you did* or *have done,* or *will have done.*

(*c*) .... quid facturus sis, ... *what you will do.*

(*aa*) Videram   *I had seen*   *what you were*
     Videbam quid faceres, *I was seeing* *doing.*
     Vidi(*aor.*)   *I saw*

(*bb*) .... quid fecisses, ... *what you had done* or *would have done.*

(*cc*) .... quid facturus esses, ... *what you were about to do.*

10—2

2. *Consecutive Sentences* (10. *a, b*).

(*a*)

Eo factum est (*perf.*) Eo fit Eo fiet	ut milites animos demittant,	*Só it has resulted So it results So it will result*	*that the soldiers lose heart.*

(*b*) .... demiserint, ... *have* (or *will have*) lost heart.

(*c*) .... demissuri sint ...... *will eventually lose heart.*

(*aa*)

Eo factum erat Eo fiebat Eo factum est (*aor.*)	ut milites animos demitterent,	*So it had resulted So it was resulting So it resulted*	*that the soldiers lost heart.*

Sometimes *demiserint* of a distinct historical fact.

(*bb*) .... demisissent .... *had lost heart.*

(*cc*) .... demissuri essent ...... *were eventually to lose heart.*

§ 239. II. *In imperative and final sentences.*

Present is used in sentences subordinate to primary tenses: imperfect in sentences subordinate to secondary tenses.

1. *Imperative.*

Ex. (*a*)

Mandavit (*perf.*) Mandat Mandabit	occludat portas,	*He has enjoined He enjoins He will enjoin*	*him to shut to the gates.*

(*aa*)

Mandaverat Mandabat Mandavit (*aor.*)	occluderet,	*He had enjoined He was enjoining He enjoined*	*him to shut to the gates.*

2. *Final.*

Ex. (*a*)

Occlusit (*pf.*) Occludit Occludet	portas ut hostes excludat,	*He has shut, shuts, &c. the gates to shut out the enemy (that he may shut out the enemy .*

(*aa*) Occluserat ⎫ portas ut hostes excluderet, *He had*
  Occludebat ⎬ *shut, was shutting, &c. the gates to shut*
  Occlusit(*aor.*)⎭ *out the enemy (that he might shut out).*

§ 240. III. *Optative and conditional sentences.*

Present and perfect are used to imply that the wish
may be realized, or the condition occur.

Imperfect and pluperfect to imply that the wish cannot
now be realized, or the condition cannot now occur.

 1. *Optative.*

  (*a*) O veniat mihi ille iterum, *May he come again
to please me.*

  (*b*) Venerit mihi ille iterum, *May he but have come, &c.*

  (*aa*) Veniret mihi ille iterum, *Were he but coming
again to please me.*

  (*bb*) Venisset mihi ille iterum, *Had he but come again
to please me.*

 2. *Conditional.*

  (*a*) Si pereat, doleam, *If he were* (or *should be*) *perishing, I should be grieving.*

  (*b*) Si perierit, doluerim, *If he have perished, I* (*shall*)
have grieved.

  (*aa*) Si periret, dolerem*, *If he had been perishing, I
should have been grieving.*

  (*bb*) Si perisset, doluissem, *If he had perished, I
should have grieved.*

---

* This may often be translated like the pluperfect, but it implies a state or continuous action, not a completed act.

§ 241. If this last conditional expression be in a dependent sentence, so that the subjunctive mood would be required on that account also, a periphrasis is resorted to; as,

> Ostendis quomodo, si perisset, doliturus fueris, *You show how you would have grieved, if he had perished.*

> Ostendisti, &c. ....fuisses, *You show-ed, &c.* (*fuisses* only in dependent *interrogative*).

The subjunctive is in translating into English often not distinguished from the indicative, especially in sentences under § 235. 3, 5, 6, 10 (*b*). The examples given above will suggest other modes of translating.

(C) IMPERATIVE MOOD.

§ 242. The *imperative* mood is used in commands and entreaties, generally (from the nature of its meaning) in the second person with the subject (pronoun of the second person) suppressed, but with the *name* of the person addressed in the nominative (or *vocative* in nouns of the second declension*).

Ex. Patres conscripti, subvenite misero mihi, *Conscript fathers, succour me in my wretchedness* (literally, *succour me wretched*).

§ 243. The future imperative is used with express reference to the time following, or some particular case that may occur, and thus frequently in legal forms.

Ex. Quum valetudini tuæ diligentissime consulueris, tum consulito navigationi, *Do not think of sailing until you have most carefully taken thought for your health.*

Servus meus Stichus liber esto (in a will), *My slave Stichus is to be free.*

---

* The imperative mood stands in the same relation to the indicative that a vocative case does to a nominative case. So *ama* is to *amas*, *amate* to *amatis*, as *domine* to *dominus*. A final '*s*' was easily lost in Latin, if we may judge from the early poetry; see Appendix F.

Dic quibus in terris, &c., et Phyllida solus habeto, *Tell
me in what lands, &c., and then you may keep Phyl-
lis to yourself.*

N.B. Commands are also, and prohibitions are in
prose always (except in legal forms where we find the fut.
imp.), exprest by the subjunctive mood, see § 235. 8.

OF THE INFINITE VERB.

§ 244. Besides the indicative, imperative, and subjunctive moods, verbs have other special forms and usages,
one as a substantive, and another as an adjective. The
former is called the *infinitive mood,* the latter the *participle.*

INFINITIVE MOOD.

§ 245. The *infinitive* is used as a substantive to express the action of the verb *as an abstract notion* but
(generally) referred to a subject *. It has inflexions for differences of voice and tense, but not for person, and exercises
all the functions of a verb in requiring objects and qualificatory expressions, but is never (except possibly in one
peculiar idiom, infr. 5) a *direct* predicate, though frequently
a predicate of an accusative case.

§ 246. 1. As *object* after another verb and sometimes
(chiefly in poetry) after adjectives.

The verbs so followed by an infinitive are generally such as
involve a reference to another action (of the same subject) to complete their meaning: e. g. verbs expressing *will, power, duty,
resolution, custom, commencement,* &c. Examples of such will be
found throughout this Syntax.

Ex. Pompeius quoque statuit prælio decertare, *Pompey
also determined to fight it out in a pitched battle.*

---

* See the abstract character well exemplified in Cic. *Tusc. D.*
I. 36.

Vincere scis, Hannibal, victoriâ uti nescis, *You understand conquering, Hannibal, but do not understand using your victory.*

Docebo eum posthac tacere, *I will teach him silence
for the future* (see § 171).

Cupit scire, *He desires knowledge.*

Cupidus scire, *Desirous of knowledge* (in prose generally cupidus *sciendi*).

2. As oblique predicate, with its subject in the accusative case, the whole expression forming the object after
verbs.

The verbs so followed are such as *naturally* have a *thing* or
fact, not a person, for their object: e. g. verbs expressing *knowledge, opinion, declaration, wish, permission, satisfaction, surprise,*
&c. Sometimes expressions equivalent to a verb, e. g. *testis sum,*
&c., have a similar object.

Ex. Promittebat se venturum esse, *He was promising to
come* (or, *that he would come*).

Scimus te venisse, *We know of your having come*
(or, *We know that you have come*).

Miror te ad me nihil scribere, *I wonder at your not
writing to me.*

Sapientem civem me et esse et numerari volo, *I wish
(myself) both to be and to be accounted a wise citizen.*

Varus promissa non servari querebatur, *Varus kept
complaining of the promises not being kept.*

Herus me jussit Pamphilum observare, *Master bade
me watch Pamphilus* (or, *ordered my watching
Pamphilus*).

Quid me impedit hæc probare? *What prevents my
proving this* (or, *approving of this*)?

Cæsar castra vallo muniri vetuit, *Cæsar forbade the
camp's being fortified with a rampart.*

This infinitive is retained even when the finite verb is put in the passive voice, and the subject of the infinitive becomes the subject of this passive verb.

Ex. Ille dicitur mortuus esse, *He is said to be dead.*

Consules jussi sunt exercitum scribere, *The Consuls were ordered to enrol an army.*

Regnante Tarquinio Superbo in Italiam venisse Pythagoras reperitur, *Pythagoras is found to have come into Italy in the reign of Tarquinius Superbus.*

3. As *subject* of a sentence, either (*a*) absolutely or (*b*) with its own subject in the accusative case.

The predicate of such a sentence is usually *either est* with a substantive, adjective or participle (e. g. *dictum, dicendum est*), or an impersonal verb (§ 151).

Ex. (*a*) Dulce et decorum est pro patriâ mori, *Sweet and comely is death in our country's cause.*

Oportet me hoc dicere, *It behoves me to say this.*

Certum est mihi omnia audacter dicere, *I am determined to tell the whole matter boldly* (lit. *To tell, &c. is for me a settled thing*).

(*b*) Te venire pergratum est, *Your coming is very pleasant to me.*

Senatui placuit Crassum Syriam obtinere, *The Senate approved of Crassus' holding Syria* (lit. *Crassus' holding Syria pleased the Senate*).

4. Infinitive sentence used in exclamations (object or subject to a verb understood).

Ex. Ergo me potius in Hispaniâ tum fuisse quam Formiis, *There now! that I should have been in Spain, rather than at Formiæ just then.*

At te Romæ non fore! *Oh! but to think of your not going to be at Rome.*

Mene incepto desistere victam? *(Can it be supposed) that I should be conquered and give up my design?*

5. As predicate to a subject in the nominative case
(possibly with some such idea as *incipiebant* understood),
to express actions just commenced and rapidly following
one another.

(This is sometimes called the *historic infinitive.*)

Ex. Postquam ædes irruperunt, diversi regem quærere,
*When they broke into the palace, they went in dif-
ferent directions to seek the king.*

Jamque dies consumptus erat, quum tamen barbari
nihil remittere, atque, uti reges præceperant, acrius
instare, *And now the day was spent, when the
foreigners still relaxed no efforts, and, as their
chiefs had instructed them, began to press more
vigorously.*

Tenses of the Infinitive.

§ 247. The tenses of the infinitive are regulated by the
time of the infinitive verb being *contemporaneous* with,
antecedent, or *subsequent* to that of the verb on which it
depends.

(*a*) Antecedent: (See also App. p. 196.)

Spero te scripsisse, *I hope that you have written
already.*

Speravi te scripsisse, *I hoped that you had written
already.*

Magna laus est tantas res solum gessisse, *It is a great
praise to have performed such important exploits
alone.*

In the passive script*us fuisse* corresponds to script*us fui* or
eram: script*us esse* to script*us sum* or scrib*ebar.*

(*b*) Contemporaneous: (Other examples in § 259. 2.)

Ex. Dico te scribere, *I say that you are writing.*

Dixi illud scribi, *I said that that was being written.*

Voluit scribere, *He wished to write.*

Delendam esse Carthaginem censeo, *My opinion (and vote) is that Carthage must be annihilated.* (See § 254.) (*esse* is often omitted.)

(*c*) Subsequent:

Credo te scripturum esse, *I believe that you are about to write.* (*esse* is often omitted.)

Credebam te deceptum iri, *I was in the belief that you would be deceived.* (See p. 54.)

For the future infinitive, both active and passive, a periphrasis with *fore* or *futurum esse* is often made use of.

Ex. Credo fore ut amem, amer, *I believe that I shall love, be loved.*

Credidi fore ut amarem, amarer, *I believed that I should love, be loved.*

The completed future passive (or deponent) is expressed by *fore* with the past participle, as

Hoc dico me satis adeptum fore, si ex tanto in omnes mortales beneficio nullum in me periculum redundârit, *This I say, that I shall have gained enough, if from so great a benefit towards all mankind, no danger shall have flowed back upon me.*

OF REPORTED SPEECH.

§ 248. When a statement is directly made, a question directly put, or a supposition exprest as the speaker's own, the language is said to be direct (*oratio recta*). So also in the report of a speech when the first person is retained; as, *Cæsar said: I am about to march,* &c.

When a statement, question, or supposition is reported as made, put, or exprest by another than the narrator, but without retaining the first person, the language is said to be oblique or indirect (*oratio obliqua*); thus, *Cæsar said that he was about to march.*

(1) The moods used in the *oratio obliqua* are the infinitive and subjunctive, never the indicative.

(2) All statements in *principal* sentences (in the indicative mood) in the *oratio recta* become infinitives in the *oratio obliqua.*

Those relative sentences in which *qui = et is* or *nam is, quum = et tum,* &c. are put in the infinitive.

(3) Questions *in the indicative mood* in *oratio recta,* are put in the infinitive if of the first or third person : in the subjunctive if of the second person.

(4) All *subordinate* sentences, as also all sentences in the subjunctive and imperative moods in *oratio recta,* are put in the subjunctive.

(5) The tenses of the infinitive are present, or perfect, or future according as the time would have been present, perfect, or future in the *oratio recta.*

(6) The tenses of the subjunctive are usually (because dependent on a past tense, "he said,") secondary, viz. imperfect and pluperfect, especially in commands or questions ; but if the verb on which the whole *oratio obliqua* depends be in the present, then the present and perfect *may* be used, as they would be in the *oratio recta,* and sometimes even when the governing verb is in the past.

§ 249. N.B. When an indicative mood is found in the midst of *oratio obliqua,* it expresses an assertion of the narrator, not of the person whose speech is being reported; as,

> Cæsar per exploratores certior factus est, ex eâ parte vici, quam Gallis concesserat, omnes noctu discessisse, *Cæsar was informed by scouts, that from that part of the village, which he had granted to the Gauls, all had departed in the night.* The *quam Gallis concesserat* is Cæsar's explanation for the benefit of his readers: the scouts would describe it to him by the local relations.

§ 250. The above rules will be best illustrated by the following extracts :

See also Cæsar, *Bell. Gall.* I. 17, 18, 20, 31, 35, 36, 44, 45. Livy, I. 50, 53 ; IV. 2 ; V. 20. Tacit. *Ann.* XIII. 43 ; XIV. 1. Cicero, *Orat. pro Milone,* 35.

ORATIO RECTA.	ORATIO OBLIQUA.
Divico ita loquitur. Si pacem populus Romanus cum Helvetiis *faciet,* in eam partem *ibunt* atque ibi *erunt* Helvetii	Is ita cum Cæsare egit : Si pacem populus Romanus cum Helvetiis *faceret* in eam partem *ituros* atque ibi *futuros* Helve-

ubi *tu* eos constitue*ris* atque esse volue*ris:* sin bello persequi persever*as*, reminisc*itor* et veteris incommodi populi Romani et pristinæ virtutis Helvetioru*m*. Quod improviso unum pagum adortus *es*, cum ii qui flumen transier*ant* suis auxili*um* ferre non pot*erant,* ne ob eam rem aut *tuæ* magnopere virtuti tribue*ris* aut *nos* despexe*ris*. *Nos* ita a patribus majoribusque *nostris* didic*imus* ut magis virtute, quam dolo contend*amus* aut insidiis nitamur. Quare ne com*miseris* ut *hic* locus ubi constit*imus* ex calamitate populi Romani et internecione exercitus nomen capi*at* aut memoriam prod*at*.

tios ubi eos *Cæsar* constitu*isset* atque esse volu*isset :* sin bello persequi persever*aret* reminisc*eretur* et veteris incommodi populi Romani et pristinæ virtutis Helvetiorum. Quod improviso unum pagum adortus *esset*, cum ii qui flumen transis*sent* suis auxilium ferre non pos*sent,* ne ob eam rem aut *suæ* magnopere virtuti tribue*ret* aut *ipsos* despiceret *: se* ita a patribus majoribusque *suis* didic*isse*, ut magis virtute, quam dolo contend*erent* aut insidiis niterentur. Quare ne commit*teret* ut *is* locus ubi constit*issent* ex calamitate populi Romani et internecione exercitus nomen cap*eret* aut memoriam prod*eret*.

Respondet Cæsar: Eo *mihi* minus dubitationis da*tur* quod eas res quas vos (legati Helvetii) commemora*vistis* memoria teneo *:* atque eo gravius fero quo minus merito populi Rom. accid*erunt;* qui si alicujus injuriæ sibi conscius fuisset, non fu*it* difficile cavere: sed eo decept*us est* quod neque commissum a se intelli*gebat* quare timeret neque sine causa timendum put*abat*. Quod si veteris contumeliæ oblivisci *volo*, num etiam recentium injuriarum, quod *me* invito iter per provinciam per vim tempta*stis*, quod Hæduos, quod Ambarros, quod Allobroges vexa*stis* memoriam deponere possum *?* Quod *vestra* victoria tam insolenter gloria*mini*

His Cæsar ita respondit: Eo *sibi* minus dubitationis da*ri* quod eas res, quas legati Helvetii commemoras*sent* memoria tene*ret* atque eo gravius ferre quo minus merito populi Rom. accid*issent :* qui si alicujus injuriæ sibi conscius fuisset, non fu*isse* difficile cavere ; sed eo decept*um* quod neque commissum a se intelli*geret* quare timeret neque sine causa timendum put*aret*. Quod si veteris contumeliæ oblivisci ve*llet*, num etiam recentium injuriarum, quod *eo* invito iter per provinciam per vim tempta*ssent*, quod Hæduos, quod Ambarros, quod Allobroges vexas*sent* memoriam deponere po*sse ?* Quod *sua* victoria tam insolenter gloria*rentur*, quodque tam diu quodque tam diu *me* impune injurias tulisse admir*amini* eodem pertin*et*. Consuer*unt* enim d*ii* immortales, quo gravius homines ex commutatione rerum doleant, quos pro scelere eorum ulcisci velint, his secundiores interdum res et diuturniorem impunitatem concedere. Cum *hæc* ita sint, tamen si obsides a *vobis mihi* d*abuntur*, uti ea quæ pollic*emini* facturos intelliga*m*, et si Hæduis de injuriis quas ipsis sociisque eorum intul*istis*, item si Allobrogibus satisfaci*etis*, *equidem* cum *vobis* pacem faci*am*.

se impune injurias tulisse admir*arentur*, eodem pertin*ere*. Consues*se* enim deo*s* immortales, quo gravius homines ex commutatione rerum doleant, quos pro scelere eorum ulcisci velint, his secundiores interdum res et diuturniorem impunitatem concedere. Cum *ea* ita sint, tamen si obsides ab *iis sibi* dent*ur*, uti ea quæ pollic*eantur* facturos intelliga*t*, et si Hæduis de injuriis quas ipsis sociisque eorum intul*erint*, item si Allobrogibus satisfaci*ant*, *sese* cum *iis* pacem *esse* fact*urum*.

CÆSAR, *B. G.* I. 13, 14.

In hunc modum loquuntur: Quid *est* levius aut turpius quam auctore hoste de summis rebus capere consilium?

Tribuni militum nihil temere agendum existimabant: Quid *esse* levius aut turpius quam auctore hoste de summis rebus capere consilium?

CÆSAR, *B. G.* V. 28.

Quid de prædâ faciendum cense*tis*?

Quid de prædâ faciendum cense*rent*?   LIV. V. 20.

Quod vero ad amicitiam populi Romani adtul*erint*, id iis eripi quis pati poss*it*?

Docebat...Quod vero ad amicitiam populi Rom. adtul*issent*, id iis eripi quis pati poss*et*?

CÆSAR, *B. G.* I. 43.

Ar*a est* in vestibulo templi Laciniæ Junonis cujus cinis nullo unquam move*tur* vento.

Fama est ar*am esse* in vestibulo templi Laciniæ Junonis cujus (=et ejus) cinerem nullo unquam move*ri* vento.

LIV. XXIV. 3.

Of the use of the Participles.

§ 251. The *Particiles* exercise the functions of a verb in requiring objects and qualificatory expressions, but have adjective inflexions. Like other adjectives, they frequently (esp. in the neuter gender) assume the character of a substantive.

I. 1. Used *predicatively* (very frequent).

Ex. Currit intuens hostes, *He runs keeping his eye on the enemy* (or *He keeps*, &c. *as he runs*).

Abiit mane profectus, *He started early and left.*

Jacet interfectus, *He lies slain.*

Venit nos visurus, *He comes to see us.*

Post natos homines, *Since the creation of men.*

Barbarus eum ob iram interfecti domini obtruncavit. *A barbarian cut him down out of revenge for the murder of his master.*

In suspitionem incidit regni appetiti, *He became suspected of having aimed at a despotism* (regni appetendi, *of aiming at,* &c.).

See also § 191, 192, 259. 5.

2. Used *as an epithet.*

Ex. Carbo ardens cecidit, *A glowing coal fell.*

Tempus venturum docebit, *Future time will show.*

Res bene gestæ, *Successful exploits.*

3. Used *as substantive;* as, Docti, *learned men;* factum, *a deed;* amans, *a lover;* futurum, *the future.*

If such a participle be used completely as a substantive, an epithet to it may be an adjective; otherwise an adverb. Thus we have, præclarum factum, *a glorious deed;* also, recte factum, *a good deed* (lit. *a thing rightly done*). Facete dictum, *a witty saying.*

160 *Participles.*

§ 252. II. The participle in *dus* has two usages:

(*a*) *Substantival**. The neuter is used as a verbal substantive, and inflected accordingly for the different cases.

Ex. Est nobis obtemperandum legibus, *It is for us to obey the laws*, or, *We must obey the laws* (lit. *There is for us an obeying the laws*).

Leges ad obtemperandum faciles, *Laws easy to obey.*

Non est solvendo, *He is insolvent* (lit. *He is not for paying*).

Summa voluptas ex discendo capitur, *The highest pleasure is received from learning.*

Est nobis studium agendi aliquid, *We have a fondness for doing something.*

§ 253. The gen., dat., and abl. are used where the infinitive, if declinable, would have been used in those cases respectively: but the genitive is never dependent on a verb; and the accusative is only used after prepositions, especially *ad* and *inter*. The accusative is never, the dative and (if accompanied by a preposition) the ablative, are rarely used with a *direct* object dependent on them. The adjectival form (see next §) is used instead. Thus, *ad placandos deos*, not *ad placandum deos*. The nominative is used to express an *obligation*, and is confined to intrans. verbs.

In the acc., gen., dat., and abl., this form is called a *gerund*.

§ 254. (*b*) *Adjectival.* If the verb be transitive, instead of the object being put in the accusative case, it is *generally* attracted into the same case as the participle, which is then made to agree with it in gender †.

* It was even considered so completely a substantive that the genitive was used (not after Cicero) with a genitive case dependent on it; as, Facultas agrorum latronibus condonandi, *A power of granting (of) lands to brigands.* Cic. *Philipp.* v. 3. Perhaps however, both genitives are immediately dependent on *facultas*, *A power over lands, of granting them*, &c.

† This adjectival use seems to differ from the substantival as *by laws-obeying* differs from *by obeying laws*.

That the participle in '*dus*' (probably originally a present

Ex. Sunt nobis leges legendæ, *We must read the laws*
(lit. *The laws are for us to read*).

Venit ad leges legendas, *He came to read the laws.*

Damus operam legibus legendis, *We devote our ex-
ertions to reading the laws.*

Legibus legendis bene meruit, *He deserved well by
his reading the laws.*

Studium legum legendarum, *The desire of reading
the laws.*

In this use (and the subst. nom.) the participle is called the
gerundive.

active participle; comp. volvendus, e. g. volvenda dies, *rolling
time*, oriundus, secundus) is not really passive is shown satis-
factorily by Donaldson and Key.

1. The gerunds which are of the same form, are *active.*

2. Deponents have no passive, and yet the participle in *dus*
is used just as from an active verb.

3. Similar intransitive uses of present participles are common
in other languages ; as, *Before the city was built or building* (or,
a-building, i. e. *on* or in building), which corresponds to the
Latin, Ante conditam condendamve urbem.

4. Infinitives (to which the gerundive approximates in
character only with adjectival inflexion) often exhibit a certain
oscillation as to the subject and object of the action exprest
by them, e.g. *He is the man to do it :* here *man* is the doer. *He
is the man to hit,* here *man* might be either subject or object of
the action. So in Greek, καλὸς ἰδεῖν, *fair to view*, compared with
δεινὸς λέγειν, *good at talking.* With the Latin gerund and
gerundive may be compared the German, Die Schuld ist zu
bezahlen, *The debt is to be paid (for us to pay).* Die zu bezahlende
Schuld, *The debt to be paid.*

The expression of *obligation* usually attributed to the nominative case both of the substantive and adjective (i.e. gerund and
gerundive) is not due to the form itself. How easily such a
notion may be attached by custom to words which of themselves
do not contain it may be seen by comparing the English phrases,
We are about to do it, where mere futurity is implied, *We are to
do it,* where obligation is implied. So *It is to be done,* may mean
either Potest fieri or faciendum est, i.e. fiat necesse est.

R. G. 11

(The *nominative* construction is often conveniently translated by the passive in English, *These laws must be read by us.*)

Similarly,

> Conon muros Athenarum reficiendos curavit, *Conon had the walls of Athens restored* (lit. *Conon took charge of the restoring of the walls of Athens*).

> Demus nos philosophiæ excolendos, *Let us give ourselves to philosophy to refine.*

§ 255. Sometimes as a mere epithet (rare):

> Vir minime contemnendus, *By no means a man (for us) to despise.*

> Malum vix ferendum, *An evil scarcely to be borne.*

SUPINES.

§ 256. The verbal substantive of the fourth declension is used in the accusative and ablative cases in certain expressions, where in English we use respectively the active and passive infinitive. The accusative may have an object in the same construction as the verb from which it is derived would.

N.B. These forms are called the active and passive *supines.*

1. Accusative after verbs expressing motion:

Ex. Ivit petitum pacem, *He went to seek peace (to a seeking peace).*

> Quamprimum hæc risum veni, *Come as soon as possible to (enjoy a) laugh at these things.*

> Lacedæmonii senem sessum receperunt, *The Lacedæmonians received the old man to sit (among them).*

2. Ablative, especially after adjectives of quality:

Ex. Turpe dictu, *A thing disgraceful to be said (disgraceful in the saying).*

§ 257. We have the dative of the same form in such expressions as habere contemptui, *to hold for* (an object of) *scorn.* So Quoniam eo natus sum, ut Jugurthæ scelerum ostentui essem, *Since I was born to serve for an exhibition of* (i. e. *to exhibit) the crimes of Jugurtha.*

Of the Passive Construction.

§ 258. Any sentence may be exprest passively as well as actively. See also § 245. 2.

1. If the verb be *transitive*, the object of the active verb becomes the subject of the passive verb, and the subject of the active verb is put in the ablative with the preposition *ab.*

Ex. Lucius interficit Marcum, *Lucius slays Marcus.*

Marcus interficitur a Lucio, *Marcus is being slain by Lucius.*

An oblique predicate of the object becomes a secondary predicate of the subject. Thus, *Lucius creat Marcum consulem,* becomes *Marcus creatur consul a Lucio.*

2. If the verb be *intransitive* and have an indirect object in the dative, the passive (3rd person sing.) is used impersonally, the object remains in the dative, and the subject is put as before in the ablative with *ab.*

Ex. Lucius nocet Marco, *Lucius (is injurious to,* i.e.*) hurts Marcus.*

Marco nocetur a Lucio, *Injury accrues to Marcus from Lucius* (or, *Marcus is hurt by Lucius).*

11—2

3. The passive impersonal construction is often used to express actions done generally without any particular agent being specified.

Ex. Ejus testimonio creditur, *Credit is given to his evidence.*

Cui parci potuit? *Who could have been spared?*

Itur in silvam, *People go into the wood.*

His persuaderi ut diutius morarentur non poterat, *They could not be induced to tarry longer.*

MISCELLANEOUS OBSERVATIONS.

§ 259. 1. (*a*) The reflexive pronouns *se, suus*, almost always refer to the subject either of their own sentence or, if that be subordinate (not unfrequently), to the subject of the principal sentence, *eum* or *illum* to some one not the subject; as,

Ex. Dicit eum non se consulem creatum esse, *He says that he (the other man), not himself, is created consul.*

Sibi autem mirum videri, quid in suâ Galliâ Cæsari negoti esset, *It was (he said) amazing to him what business Cæsar had in his (the speaker's) Gaul.*

Dixit neminem secum sine suâ pernicie contendisse, *He said that no one had fought with him* (i. e. the speaker) *without destruction to himself* (i. e. the opponent).

(*b*) But *suus* sometimes refers to another word *in the sentence.*

Ex. Hannibalem sui cives e civitate ejecerunt, *Hannibal was banished from the state by his own fellow-citizens* (lit. *his own fellow-citizens banished*, &c.)

> Catilina admonebat alium egestatis, alium cupiditatis suæ, *Catiline reminded one of his poverty, another of his lusts* (or, *used to remind*).

2. An assertion of *power, duty,* &c. is exprest by auxiliary verbs (not by the subjunctive), thus,

> Possum facere, *I can do.*

> Poteram facere, *I could have done at the time,* or, *I could have been doing.*

> Non potui facere, *I could not have done.*

> Licet facere, *I may do.*

> Licebat facere, *I might have done at the time,* or, *I might have been doing.*

> Licuit facere, *I might have done.*

> Debeo facere, *I ought to do.*

> Debebam facere, *I ought to have been doing,* or, *to have done at the time.*

> Debui facere, *I ought to have done.*

The auxiliary is usually in the indicative, except in a dependent sentence. (Cf. § 234.)

3. (*a*) The use of auxiliary verbs in the apodosis of conditional sentences should be noted. The auxiliary is put in the *indicative* in order to indicate that it is not the power, duty, lawfulness, &c. which is conditional, but only the *performance* of the act. Thus,

> Antoni gladios potuit contemnere, si sic omnia dixisset. The *si dixisset* really qualifies *contemnere,* not *potuit.*

> Si victoria, præda, laus, dubia essent, tamen omnes bonos reipublicæ subvenire decebat. Sall. *Jug.* 85.

(*b*) So also the future in *rus* is used with *eram* (where a specified point of past time is spoken of), or *fui* (of past time merely), or (if the construction require it) *fuisse* (not the subjunctive, unless in a dependent sentence) in the apodosis of conditional sentences; as,

> Illi ipsi aratores qui remanserant relicturi omnes agros erant, nisi ad eos Metellus Roma litteras misisset, *Would have left their lands* (lit. *were purposing at the time to leave*).

(*c*) Similarly the Latins said, Æquum, longum, &c. est, erat, fuit, fuerat; where we should say, *It would be, would have (now) been, would have (then) been, would have (previously) been, right,* &c.

4. Sentences that are or may be introduced in English by the conjunction *that* are variously exprest in Latin.

Such sentences are frequently in apposition to a substantive (*ea res, hic sermo,* &c.), or neuter pronoun, generally in nom., acc. or abl. cases. (Such a pronoun corresponds strictly to the English word *that**.)

(*a*) *That=in order that, so that,* expressing a consequence intended or actual, i.e. a purpose or result, requires *ut* or *qui* (*quæ, quod*) with subjunctive. (Examples in § 235. 9, 10.)

Such sentences follow verbs (and phrases) of *effecting, praying, providing, advising, commanding, striving,* &c.: also *talis, adeo, ita,* &c.

Verbs of *wishing* and *commanding* have also an acc. with inf. So almost always *jubeo, patior, veto* (see § 246. 2).

(*b*) *That* after verbs (and phrases) of *perceiving, knowing, thinking, saying,* (mental) *feeling,* &c. requires accusative with infinitive. (Examples in § 246. 2.)

Verbs of (mental) *feeling* have also *quod* with indicative of actual facts (§ 222. 5).

---

* A sentence like the following gives exactly the English idiom (*ne* being originally a simple negative, not a conjunction). Non minus id contendunt et laborant ne ea quæ dixerint enuntientur, *They contend and labour not less that the things which they have said be not divulged.*

(*c*) *That = the fact that, because* (except after such verbs as have been mentioned supr. *b*), expressing actual facts, requires *quod* with indicative (in *oratio recta;* see § 220).

Ex. Eumeni inter Macedones viventi multum detraxit, quod alienæ erat civitatis, *It was very prejudicial to Eumenes while living among the Macedonians, that he belonged to a foreign state.*

Hoc uno præstamus vel maxime feris, quod exprimere dicendo sensa possumus, *In this one point we have the greatest superiority over beasts, that we have the power of expressing our feelings by speech.*

Quod me vetas quicquam suspicari, geram tibi morem, *In that you forbid my harbouring any suspicion, I will do as you wish.*

(*d*) *That* when preceded by *it*, the clause being really subject to an impersonal verb, or to *est* with a secondary predicate, has several constructions, viz.:

I. After *accidit, fit, sequitur, proximum est, accedit,* &c. expressing a consequence, we find *ut* with subjunctive. (See § 235. 10. After *accedit* we find also *quod* with indic. of *facts*.)

II. After *oportet, convenit* ('it is proper'), *expedit, pudet,* &c. we find the acc. with inf. *Oportet* (signifying *necessity,* not *duty*) and *necesse est* have also subj. (without *ut*).

III. After such expressions as *mos est, verisimile est, gloriosum est,* &c.

  1. *That...should, is to,* may be translated by *ut* with subj.

  2. *That...is, are, was,* &c. by *quod* with indic.

  3. Abstract notions (with either English translation) by acc. with inf. after some expressions of the kind.

Ex. Hoc vero optimum est, ut quis nesciat, &c., *Now this is excellent* (ironical), *that a man should not know,* &c.

Ad multas res magnæ utilitatis erit, quod Gaius adest, *It will be found to be of great service for many purposes that Gaius is here* (or, *Gaius' being here will,* &c.).

Accusatores multos esse in civitate utile est, *A number of accusers in the state is a useful thing* (or, *That there should be*, &c.; or, *That there are*, &c.).

(*e*) *That* after verbs of fearing requires a negative in Latin where it does not in English, and *vice versâ;* thus,

Vereor ne pater veniat, *I fear that my father will come* (lest my father should come, § 235. 9. *c*).

Vereor $\begin{cases} \text{ut pater veniat,} \\ \text{ne pater non veniat,} \end{cases}$ *I fear that my father will not come* (I am afraid as to how my father is coming, § 235. 5. *b*).

5. The past participle active in English is generally exprest in Latin by

(1) Past participle of *deponent* verb. Ex. Locutus, *Having spoken.*

(2) *Quum* c. plup. subj. Ex. Quum Cæsarem interfecisset, $\left.\begin{array}{l} \textit{Having} \\ \textit{killed} \\ \textit{Cæsar.} \end{array}\right.$

(3) Abl. with obl. pred. Ex. Cæsare interfecto,

An expression of this kind referring to the subject or object, &c. of the sentence must be put in the nominative or accusative, &c. respectively.

Ex. Cohortes pulsæ a Cæsare diffugerunt, *The cohorts, being routed by Cæsar, fled in different directions* (not. Cohortibus a Cæsare · pulsis diffugerunt, if *Cohortes* be the subject to *diffugerunt*).

Manlius cæsum Gallum torque spoliavit, *The Gaul being slain, Manlius despoiled him of the chain* (not Manlius cæso Gallo torque eum spoliavit).

Such expressions may often be better translated by two finite verbs; e. g. *Manlius slew the Gaul and despoiled him of the chain.*

6. Several uses of prepositions in English are liable to lead to error in translating into Latin.

(*a*) 'To' before a substantive in Latin must generally be translated by the dative, except when it comes after verbs of motion, when *ad* with the accusative is required.

(*b*) 'With' requires *cum* with the ablative; (1) when it denotes *accompanied by*, especially if it precede a person's name, i. e. *He went with John;* (2) when it denotes *manner* (not *means* or *instrument*), and the substantive stands singly without attribute of any kind. See § 206. *c*. 3.

(*c*) 'By' when used with names of persons, by whose agency or instrumentality anything was done, should be translated by *per* with accusative after an active voice, by *a, ab*, with an ablative after the passive voice; when it denotes *past*, e. g. after a verb of motion, by *præter* c. acc.

(*d*) 'In' dependent upon a noun requires that a participle be added in Latin, or that *in* with the accusative should be used, i. e. *He went to his house in town*, I vit in urbem domum, or, Ad domum in urbe sitam (not domum in urbe). See note to § 147.

(*e*) 'For'=*instead of, on behalf of*, requires *pro* with the ablative.

(*f*) 'Without' prefixed to a participle in English is exprest in Latin by a negative (never by *sine* with a gerund); thus,

> Miserum est nihil proficientem angi, *It is miserable to be tortured without making any advance by it.*

> Consul non expectato auxilio collegæ pugnam committit, *The Consul joins battle without waiting for the reinforcements of his colleague.*

> Hæc dijudicari non possunt nisi ante causam cognoverimus, *These things cannot be decided without our having first learnt the cause.*

7. The Latin idiom prefers to make all the parts of a sentence dependent on the primary predicate.

(*a*) Thus a notion which might be made dependent on a substantive, and be exprest by the genitive, is often put in the dative, as dependent on the predicate; e. g. thus, *Cæsari* ad pedes se projecerunt (§ 179), rather than *Cæsaris* ad pedes se projecerunt.

(*b*)   So in expressions of *place*, e. g. Domo a *Cicerone* ivi (§ 205. *a*); not a *Ciceronis* domo.

Ivit in urbem domum (supr. 6. *d*).

See also the examples at end of Appendix G.

OF THE USE OF CERTAIN CONJUNCTIONS IN CO-ORDINATE SENTENCES (chiefly from Madvig).

§ 260.   Co-ordinate sentences, regularly exprest, either have a conjunction with every member, or with all but the first.   In the former case the writer shows that he has foreseen the distribution of his sentence into two or more co-ordinate clauses or parts; in the latter case the first clause expresses the original idea, the others are in the nature of after-thoughts.   The following are the most important usages (in prose chiefly) requiring notice:

1.   *Copulative* conjunctions, i.e. those which connect both sentences and meaning: *et, quĕ* (appended to the first word of a clause), *atquĕ* (or before consonants *ac*).

(*a*)   *et...et* simply connect, whether words or sentences.

(*b*)   *quĕ...et* connect only words; as, Seque et ducem, *Both himself and his leader.*

(*c*)   *quĕ...quĕ*, rare in prose; but used with a double relative; as, Quique Romæ, quique in exercitu erant, *Both those at Rome and those in the army.*

When used only with second member, *quĕ* marks the second member as a supplement to the first: *ac* (*atque*) puts the second member forward more forcibly.   The distinction is, however, not always preserved.

Ex. Omnia honesta inhonestaque, *All things becoming, and the unbecoming too.*

Omnia honesta atque inhonesta, *All things, the unbecoming no less than the becoming.*

In joining three or more perfectly co-ordinate words, we may either omit the conjunction entirely, as, Summâ fide, constantiâ, justitiâ, or connect each of them with the preceding (prefixing a conjunction to the first also, or not, as we like), as, Summâ fide et constantiâ et justitiâ: or we may omit it between the first members and annex *que* to the last; as, Summâ fide constantiâ justitiâque.

2. *Disjunctive* conjunctions, i. e. those which connect the sentences, but disconnect their meaning: *aut, vel, ve* (appended to first word of clause), *sivĕ* (or *seu* before consonants only).

(*a*) *aut...aut* connect things mutually exclusive, especially where an alternative is offered; as, Aut Cæsar aut nullus, *Either Cæsar or nobody.* Aut hoc aut illud, *Either this or that* (but not both).

(*b*) *vel...vel* give a choice of *expression*, or connect things not mutually exclusive, or with either of which the assertion is equally true; as, Vel metu, vel spe, vel pœnâ potest Galliam vincere, *He can conquer Gaul, either with fear, or hope, or reward* (i. e. with any or all).

(*c*) *vĕ...vĕ.* Only in poets; similar to *vel...vel.*

(*d*) *seu (sive)...seu (sive)* connect (as mere conjunctions) only nouns and adverbs, and are used of unessential distinctions; as, Seu casu seu consilio deorum, *Whether by chance or by the plans of the gods* (no matter which). (If used with verbs they are equal to *vel si...vel si*).

When used only with second member, *aut* implies an essential distinction of ideas; *vel* (often *vel potius, vel etiam*), *vĕ, seu (sivĕ)* (often *seu potius*, where a correction of something previously said is meant) are used to introduce expressions regarded as supplementary to, or possible corrections or substitutions for, a former expression.

3. *Adversative* conjunctions, i. e. those which contrast the meaning, while they connect the sentences: *sed, autem, verum, at* (autem does not begin a sentence, but is placed after the first word).

(*a*) Sed, *but,* introduces a sentence which alters or sets aside the former; as, Ingeniosus homo sed in omni vita inconstans, *A clever man, but unstable throughout life.*

(*b*) Autem, *however,* introduces a different statement in continuation of a former, but in no way limiting it; as, Gyges a nullo videbatur, ipse autem omnia videbat, *Gyges used to be invisible to everyone, and yet he himself see everything.*

Nunc quod agitur agamus, agitur autem, &c., *Now let us attend to the real matter on hand, and that is, &c.*

(*c*) *At* introduces an emphatic observation different from the preceding. It is especially used in lively discourses introducing objections, or interrogative exclamations; as,

At memoria minuitur, *But* (you say) *the memory grows weak.* So especially *at enim.*

Una mater Cluentium oppugnat. At quæ mater! *Only his mother assails Cluentius. But what a mother!*

(*d*) *Verum* (also *verum etiam*) is similarly used, but expresses the correction of the preceding more strongly.

4. *Negative* conjunctions, něque (*nec* before consonants), něvě (*neu* before consonants).

[Non is *not:* haud has similar meaning, but is not usual with verbs (except in *haud scio*); nē is used in sentences denoting a will, wish, command, or design.]

(*a*) něque...něque, *neither...nor.*

(*b*) něque...et, *both not...and.*

(*c*) et...něque, *both...and not.*

(*d*) nēve...nēve = et nē...et nē.

Nē...quidem (the emphatic word being put between the particles) is *not even,* or *neither* (when we use this word in the *second* member, without *nor* following); as, Ne matri quidem dixi, *Not even to your mother did I mention it.*

Si non sunt, nihil possunt esse; ita ne miseri quidem sunt, *If they do not exist, they cannot be anything; neither then are they miserable.*

Neque in the second member is often joined with *tamen, vero, enim: nĕvĕ=et nĕ* or *aut nĕ* is used in the second member to express a negative *purpose*, &c. when *ne* or *ut* has been used in the first.

Of the use of Particles in Interrogative Sentences.

§ 261. Questions are either simple or alternative. The Latins generally distinguish interrogative sentences by particular particles.

(1) *Simple questions.*

(*a*) *Nĕ* (appended to the important word), when the answer may be either *yes* or *no;* as, Sentisne? *Do you feel?*

(*b*) *Nonnĕ,* when the answer *yes* is expected; as, Nonne sentis? *Do you not feel?*

(*c*) *Num,* when the answer *no* is expected; as, Num sentis? *You do not feel, do you?*

(Affirmative answers are *etiam, ita, vero, sane, ita vero, ita est, sane quidem;* or with the proper pronoun, as, *Ego vero.* Or the verb is repeated, as, *Sentio.*

Negative answers are *non, minime, minime vero;* or with the pronoun, as, *Minime nos quidem;* or with the verb, as, *Non sentio.* When the contrary, &c. is asserted by way of reply, we have *Imo, imo vero,* 'No, on the other hand;' 'Nay, rather.')

(2) *Alternative questions.*

(*a*) *Utrum...an;* as, Utrum nescis, quam alte ascenderis, an id pro nihilo habes, *Are you ignorant what a height you have reached, or do you count it for nothing?*

(*b*) *Nĕ* (appended)...*an.* Pacemne huc fertis an arma? *Is it peace or arms that ye bring?*

(*c*) *An* (with second member of question). Sortietur an non? *Will he draw the lot or not?*

(*d*) *Nĕ* (only in dependent questions and with second member). In incerto erat vicissent victine essent, *It was uncertain at the time whether they were conquerors or conquered.*

N.B. *An* is frequently used in a question apparently simple, but in reality the first member is supprest, and this is in fact indicated by the use of *an,* which always belongs to the second member of an alternative question.

Ex. Quando autem ista vis evanuit ? An postquam homines minus creduli esse cœperunt ? *But when did that efficacy you talk of pass away? (Need I ask) or was it (not) from the time when men began to be less credulous ?*

APPENDICES.

APPENDIX A.

LATIN DECLENSIONS OF GREEK NOUNS.

(Chiefly from Madvig, Kennedy, and Donaldson.)

MANY words, chiefly proper names, were adopted from the Greek, and retained, some more, some less, their Greek mode of declension. They belong to the 1st, 2nd, or 3rd declensions of Latin nouns. Many have also a purely Latin form.

1st DECLENSION in *ās, ēs, ē*. Greek nouns differ from Latin only in the singular. Some in *ās* have also a form in *ă* for nominative; as, *Mĭdă*, or *Mĭdās* (Μίδας):

Sing.

Nom.	Ænēās (Αἰνείας)	Anchīsēs ('Αγχίσης)	ĕpĭtŏmē (ἐπιτομή)
Voc.	Ænēā	Anchīsē, *or* -ā	ĕpĭtŏmē
Acc.	Ænēam, *or* -ān	Anchīsēn	ĕpĭtŏmēn
Gen.	Ænēæ	Anchīsæ	ĕpĭtŏmēs
Dat.	Ænēæ	Anchīsæ	ĕpĭtŏmæ
Abl.	Ænēā	Anchīsē, *or* -ā	ĕpĭtŏmē

2nd DECLENSION in *ŏs, ōs, ūs, on* neut.:

Sing.

Nom.	Dēlŏs (Δῆλος)	Andrŏgĕōs ('Ανδρόγεως)	Panthūs (Πάνθους)	Nom. ⎫ cōlŏn
Voc.	Dēlĕ	Andrŏgĕōs	Panthū	Voc. ⎬ (κῶλον)
Acc.	Dēlŏn, *or* -um	Andrŏgĕōn, *or* ō, *or* -ōnă	Panthum	Acc. ⎭
Gen.	Dēlī	Andrŏgĕō, *or* -ī	Panthī	Gen. cōlī
Dat. ⎫ Abl. ⎬ Dēlō		Andrŏgĕō	Panthō	Dat. ⎫ cōlō Abl. ⎬

In the plural we find a few forms: nom. cănēphŏræ, (*female*) *basket-bearers;* and gen. plur. Georgicōn, *of farming matters.*

Such as the following have inflexions belonging to the 3rd decl., as well as those belonging to the 2nd or 1st decl.

Sing.

Nom. Orpheūs ('Ορφεύς)	Perseūs (Περσεύς) *also*	Persēs (1st decl.)
Voc. Orpheū	Perseū	Persē, *or* -ă
Acc. Orphĕum, *or* -ĕă	Persĕă	Persēn
Gen. Orphĕī, *or* -eī, *or* -ĕŏs Persĕī		Persæ
Dat. Orphĕō, *or* -ĕī, *or* -eī Persĕō, *or* Persī		Persæ
Abl. Orphĕō, *or* eō	Persĕō, *or* -eō	Persē, *or* -ā

So also *Achilles* and *Ulixes,* which are otherwise of the 3rd decl., have genitives *Achillĕī* and *Ulixĕī* as well.

3rd DECLENSION:

Sing.

Nom. Thălēs	Pĕriclēs	Păris
Voc. Thălĕ, *or* -ēs	Pĕriclēs, *or* -e	Părĭ
Acc. Thălem, *or* -ēn, *or* -ētăPericlem, *or* -ĕa		Parĭn, *or* -im, *or* -Ĭdă, *or* -ĭdem
Gen. Thălĭs, *or* -ētĭs	Periclĭs, *or* -ī	Parĭdĭs
Dat. Thălī, *or* -ēti	Periclī ˙	Părĭdī
Abl. Thălē, *or* -ētĕ	Periclĕ, *or* -ī	Părĭdĕ (*or* -ī?)

Sing. Nom. Erinnўs   Plur. Nom.⎰Erinnўĕs, *or* -ўs
      Voc. Erinnў   Voc.⎱
      Acc. Erinnnўn, *or* -ym,   Acc. Erinnўăs, *or* -ўs
         or -ўă
      Gen. Erinnўĭs, *or* -ўs, *or* ўŏs   Gen. Erinnўum
      Dat. Erinnўĭ, *or* -ў   Dat.⎰(Erinnўsĭn, *or* -ўbus?)
      Abl. Erinnўĕ, *or* -ў   Abl.⎱

Sing. Nom. Nērĕĭs   Plur. Nom.⎰Nērĕĭdĕs
      Voc. Nērĕĭ   Voc.⎱
      Acc. Nērĕĭdă, *or* -dem   Acc. Nērĕĭdăs, *or* -dēs
      Gen. Nērĕĭdŏs, *or* -dĭs   Gen. Nērĕĭdum
      Dat. Nērĕĭdi   Dat.⎰Nērĕĭdĭbŭs(*or*-ĕĭsĭn!)
      Abl. Nērĕĭdĕ   Abl.⎱

Sing.		Plur.	
Nom.	crāter	Nom.	
Voc.	crāter	Voc.	} crātērĕs
Acc.	crātēră, *or* -em	Acc.	crātērăs
Gen.	crātērĭs	Gen.	crātērum
Dat.	crātērī	Dat.	
Abl.	crātērĕ	Abl.	} crātērĭbŭs

Sing.		Sing.	
Nom.		Nom.	} Dīdo
Voc.	} Ēchō	Voc.	
Acc.		Acc.	Dīdō, *or* -ōnem
Gen.	Ēchūs	Gen.	Dīdūs, *or* -ōnĭs
Dat.	} Ēchō	Dat.	Dīdō, *or* -ōnī
Abl.		Abl.	Dīdō, *or* ōnĕ

Gen. Plur. in *ōn* is sometimes found; as, *metamorphōseōn.*
The acc. sing. in *ă*, and plur. in *ăs*, from imparisyllabic nouns are
very common.

APPENDIX B.

TERMINATIONS OF DERIVATIVES.

(Mainly an abridgment from Madvig.)

THE following are the most frequent terminations of derivative substantives, adjectives, and verbs, with their most usual
meanings. They are generally affixed to the root, which is sometimes slightly modified. (The short connecting vowel is here
generally mentioned as part of the termination.)

I. 1. SUBSTANTIVES, derived from *substantives,*

(a) and denoting *persons.* end in
-*ārius, e.g.* argentarius, *a banker,* (argentum).

(b) denoting *office,* or *employment,* or *condition,* have
these endings, (all affixed to personal names),
-*ium, e.g.* sacerdotium, *priesthood ;* (sacerdos).
-*ātus, e.g.* consulatus, *consulship ;* (consul).
-*ūra, e.g.* prætura, *prœtorship ;* (prætor).
-*īna, e.g.* doctrina, *teaching ;* (doctor).

R. G. 12

(c) denoting *place*, end in

-*ārium*, *e.g.* seminarium, *seed-plot;* (semen).
-*ium*, affixed to personal names in *or; e.g.* audito-
rium, *lecture-room;* (auditor).
-*īnum*, affixed to personal names in *or; e.g.* pistri-
num, *bakehouse;* (pistor).
-*īle*, affixed to names of animals; *e.g.* ovile, *sheep-
fold;* (ovis).
-*ētum*, affixed to names of plants; *e.g.* quercetum,
oak-grove; (quercus).

(d) denoting *material objects*, end in

-*al*, *e.g.* animal, *a breathing thing;* (anima).
-*ar*, *e.g.* calcar, *a spur;* (calx).

Some rarer terminations are seen in the following words:
prædo, *a robber*, (præda); lectīca, (lectus); fabrīca, (faber);
militia, (miles); ærugo, (æs).

(e) *Diminutives*, end in

-*ŭlus*, -*a*, -*um*, affixed to nouns of 1st and 2nd
decl., and to some few of the 3rd; *e.g.* servulus,
a little slave; arcula, *a small box;* rēgulus, *a petty
king*, or *chieftain;* (servus, arca, rex).
-*ŏlus*, -*a*, -*um*, (if vowel precede), *e.g.* filiolus, *a little
son;* (filius).
-*lus*, -*a*, -*um*, with assimilation of preceding consonant; *e.g.* tabella, *tablet;* agellus, *small plot of
land;* (tabula, ager).
-*culus*, -*a*, -*um*, affixed to nouns of 3rd, 4th, or 5th
decl.; *e.g.* flosculus, *flowret;* virguncula, *little girl;*
versiculus, *versicle;* diecula, *short time;* (flos, virgo,
versus, dies).
-*illus*, -*a*, -*um*, *e.g.* sigillum, *seal;* lapillus, *little
pebble;* (signum, lapis).

I. 2. SUBSTANTIVES, derived from *adjectives*,

and denoting *quality*, end in

-*tas*, or -*ĭtas; e.g.* bonitas, *goodness;* pietas, *duti-
fulness;* libertas, *liberty;* (bonus, pius, liber, *free*).
-*ia*, affixed mostly to adjectives of one termination
(§ 13. 2. *c*), *e.g.* audacia, *boldness;* (audax).

-tia, or *-ĭtia; e.g.* justitia, *justice;* (justus).
-tūdo, e.g. altitudo, *height;* (altus).

Rarer terminations are seen in gravēdo, (gravis), sanctimōnia (sanctus).

I. 3. SUBSTANTIVES, derived from *verbs,*

(*a*) and denoting *agents,* end in
-tor, or *-sor,* (*i.e.* or affixed to supine form), *e.g.* adjutor, *helper;* tonsor, *barber;* (adjuvo, tondeo).
-trix, or *-strix,* fem. of above, *e.g.* adjutrix, tonstrix.

(*b*) denoting *action,* have endings

affixed to root of verb,
-or, e.g. amor, *love;* favor, *favour;* (amo, faveo).
-ium, e.g. imperium, *a command;* gaudium, *delight;* (impero, gaudeo).
-io, e.g. oblivio, *forgetfulness;* (obliviscor).

affixed to supine form,
-io, e.g. tractatio, *treatment;* divisio, *division;* (tracto, divido).
-us, e.g. auditus, *hearing;* visus, *seeing;* (audio, video).
-ūra, e g. conjectura, *conjecture;* (conjicio).

(*c*) denoting thing, *i.e. means,* and sometimes *place,* end in
-men, (sometimes denotes *action*), *e.g.* velamen, *veil;* lumen, (*i.e.* lucmen), *light;* tegmen, *covering;* molimen, *effort;* (velo, luceo, tego, molior).
-mentum, e.g. ornamentum, *an ornament;* tormentum, (for torcmentum), *hurling-machine;* (orno, torqueo).
-cŭlum, -clum, e.g. operculum, *lid;* (operio).
-crum, if the word have an *l* near the affix, *e.g.* sepulcrum, *tomb;* (sepelio).
-ulum, -clum, if the root end in *c* or *g, e.g.* vinculum, *a bond;* (vincio).
-bŭlum, -blum, e.g. pābulum, *fodder;* (pasco).

12—2

-*brum*, -*bra*, if the word have an *l* near the affix,
e.g. flabrum, *blast;* dolabra, *mattock;* (flo, dolo).
-*trum*, (before which affix *d* becomes *s*), *e.g.* aratrum,
plough; rostrum, *beak;* (aro, rodo).

Rarer terminations are seen in the following words: prurĭgo,
(prurio); cupīdo, (cupio); erro, *a wanderer;* (erro); tūtēla,
(tutor); quĕrella, (queror); (i. e. *l*, when the preceding syllable
is long: *ll*, when it is short. LACHMANN).

II. 1. ADJECTIVES, derived from *substantives.*

A. From *common* nouns,

(a) and denoting the *material*, or *resemblance*, end in

-*eŭs*, *e.g.* ligneus, *wooden;* virgineus, *maidenly;*
(lignum, virgo).
-*neus*, -*nus*, or -*ĭnus*, (esp. of woods), pōpulneus, *of
poplar-wood;* ilignus, *of holm-oak;* fraternus,
brotherly; cedrĭnus, *of cedar-wood;* (pōpulus, ilex,
frater, cedrus).
-*ĭcius*, latericius, *of brick;* gentilicius, *relating to the
clansmen;* (later, gentilis).
-*āceus*, *e.g.* chartaceus, *of paper;* (charta).

(b) denoting *to what a thing belongs*, end in

-*ius*, (usually from personal nouns in *or*), *e.g.* impera-
torius, *belonging to a general;* regius, *kingly;* (imperator, rex).
-*ĭcus*, (chiefly in poetry), *e.g.* bellicus, *relating to
war;* (bellum).
-*ĭvus*, *e.g.* festivus, *festive;* captivus, *captive;* (festus,
captus).
-*ĭlis*, *e.g.* civilis, *of a citizen;* sextilis, *of the sixth
(month);* (civis, sextus).
-*ālis*, *e.g.* fatalis, *fated;* naturalis, *natural;* (fatum,
natura).
-*āris*, if the word have *l* near to the affix, *e.g.* pŏpu-
laris, *popular;* (pŏpulus).
-*īnus*, *e.g.* libertinus, *belonging to a freedman;* equi-
nus, *of horses;* (libertus, equus).

-*ānus, e.g.* urbanus, *of the city;* primanus, *of the fourth* (legion); (urbs, primus).
-*ārius, e.g.* agrarius, *connected with land;* septuagenārius, *of seventy (years)*; (ager, septuaginta).

(c) denoting *fulness,* end in

-*ōsus, e.g.* damnosus, *ruinous;* lapidosus, *full of stones;* (damnum, lapis).
-*ŭlentus,* or *-ŏlentus, e.g.* fraudulentus, *fraudulent;* violentus, *violent;* (fraus, vis).

(d) denoting what a thing is *furnished with* (participial forms), end in

-*ātus, e.g.* barbatus, *bearded;* (barba).
-*ītus, e.g.* turritus, *turreted;* (turris).
-*ūtus, e.g.* cornutus, *horned;* (cornu).
-*tus, e.g.* onustus, *laden;* (onus).

The following words exhibit rarer terminations: rustĭcus, (rus); aquātĭlis, (aqua); diutĭnus, (dies, or diu); legitĭmus, (lex); æternus, (ætas, i.e. ævitas); campester, (campus); subitāneus, (subitus); honōrus, (honor).

B.   from *Proper Names of Persons.*

The names of Roman clans in *-ius* are properly adjectives, and are used as such of a man's public works, *e.g.* Gens Fabia, the Fabian *clan;* M. Fabius, *Marcus of the Fabian clan;* hence lex Fabia, *a law (or statute) procured by a Fabian,* (as we say *Lord Campbell's Act,* meaning an Act of Parliament proposed by Lord Campbell); via Appia, *a road constructed by one of the Appian clan.*

(a) From these words are derived adjectives, ending in

-*ānus,* relating to an individual of a family; *e.g.* bellum Marianum, *the war against Marius.*

So Romans adopted by another took the name of their adopted father, and appended to it an adjective of this kind derived from their own clan; *e.g.* C. Julius Cæsar Octavianus, was the name of Augustus, originally of the Octavian clan.

(*b*) From Roman surnames are derived adjectives, ending in

-*iānus, e.g.* Ciceronianus; (Cicero).
-*ānus,* (more rarely), *e. g.* Sullānus, Gracchānus; (Sulla, Gracchus).
-*īnus,* (rare), *e.g.* Verrīnus, Plautīnus; (Verres, Plautus).
-*ĕus,* (in poets and later writers), ˉ*e.g.* Cæsareus, Romuleus; (Cæsar, Romulus).

(*c*) From Greek names are derived adjectives, ending in

-*ēus, e.g.* Aristoteleus; (Aristoteles).
-*ĭcus, e.g.* Platonicus; (Plato).

C. from *Proper Names of Places;*

(*a*) from Latin names, end in

-*ānus,* from names ending in *a, æ, um, i, e.g.* Romanus, Fundānus; (Roma, Fundi).
-*īnus,* from names in *ia* and *ium, e.g.* Amerīnus, Lanuvinus; (Ameria, Lanuvium).
-*ās,* (gen. *ātis*), from names in *a, æ, um,* (esp. *na, næ, num*), *e.g.* Arpinas, Fidenas; (Arpinum, Fidenæ).
-*ensis,* from names in *o,* and some in *a, æ, um, e.g.* Sulmonensis, Cannensis; (Sulmo, Cannæ).

(*b*) from Greek names, end in

-*ius, e.g.* Rhodius; (Rhodus).
-*ātes, e.g.* Spartiates; (Sparta).
-*ītes, e.g.* Abderites; (Abdera).
-*ōtes, e.g.* Heracleotes; (Heraclea).
and others.

D. Names of nations are themselves adjectives, with the terminations previously noticed, *e.g.* Latinus. Others in *scus,* or *cus, e.g.* Volscus, Græcus. Others are for the most part substantives, *e.g.* Italus, Thrax; from these are formed adjectives ending in

-*ĭcus, e. g.* Italicus, Arabicus.
-*ius,* from Greek words, *e.g.* Thracius.

II. 2. ADJECTIVES derived from *verbs*.

   (*a*) denoting *action*, end in

      -*ax*, affixed to root, *e.g.* minax, *threatening;* pugnax, *pugnacious;* (minor, pugno).

   (*b*) denoting *state*, end in

      -*ĭdus*, affixed chiefly to root of intransitive verbs of 2nd conj.; *e.g.* calidus, *hot;* timidus, *afraid;* (caleo, timeo); rapidus, *hurrying;* (rapio).

   (*c*) having passive signification, end in

      -*ĭlis*, affixed to root and supine form, *e.g.* fragilis, *brittle;* docilis, *teachable;* fissilis, *cleavable;* (frango, doceo, findo).
      -*bĭlis*, affixed to root and supine form, *e.g.* amabilis, *loveable;* flexibilis, *pliable;* (amo, flecto).
      -*īcius*, (affixed to supine form), commenticius, *feigned;* insiticius, *grafted;* (comminiscor, insero).

Other rarer terminations are seen in the following: fa cundus, *eloquent*, (for, *I speak*); querŭlus, *querulous*, (queror); conspi cuus, *visible*, (conspicio).

The participles also are often used as mere adjectives; see § 81. 7; 251. 2.

III. Derivative VERBS are derived from *substantives, adjectives*, and other *verbs*.

   1. Verbs of the 1st conjugation are mostly transitive.

They are derived

   (*a*) from substantives, *e.g.* fraudo, *I cheat;* vulnero, *I wound;* (fraus, vulnus).

   (*b*) from adjectives, denoting originally (but not always) to *make* a thing what the adjective denotes, *e.g.* maturo, *I ripen;* memoro, *I make mention of;* (maturus, memor).

   (*c*) from verbs, denoting frequent repetition.

      -*ĭto*, affixed to root of verbs of 1st conj. or supine form of 3rd conj., *e.g.* dictito, *say frequently;* visito, *visit frequently;* (dicto, viso).

-*to*, or -*so*, *i.e.* inflexion of 1st conj. affixed to supine form of 3rd conj., denoting a new idea in which is involved frequent repetition of the original action, *e.g.* pulso, *beat;* tracto, *handle;* (pello, *thrust;* traho, *draw*).

(*d*) *illo*, diminutives; *e.g.* cantillo, *quaver;* (cano, hence probably cantus, cantillus, whence cantillo).

(*e*) mostly intransitive. Deponents formed from substantives and adjectives, and denoting *to be something*, or *occupy oneself with something; e.g.* ancillor, *be a maid-servant;* græcor, *act like a Greek;* aquor, *fetch water;* (ancilla, Græcus, aqua).

2. Verbs of 2nd conj. are frequently intransitive.

They are derived

From substantives and adjectives, *e.g.* luceo, *be light;* floreo, *flourish;* (lux, flos); albeo, *be white;* (albus).

3. Verbs of 3rd conj. are derived

From other verbs, and end in

-*sco*, denoting commencement of action, chiefly from verbs of 2nd conj., *e.g.* horresco, *shudder;* (horreo). See § 109. Sometimes the simpler form in *eo* is not found, *e.g.* maturesco, formed (as if from matureo) from maturus.

4. Verbs of 4th conj. chiefly transitive (similar to verbs of 1st conj.), are derived

(*a*) from substantives, *e.g.* finio, *finish;* punio, *punish;* (finis, pœna).

(*b*) from adjectives, *e.g.* mollio, *soften;* superbio, *be proud;* (mollis, superbus).

(*c*) *ūrio*, affixed to supine form, denoting inclination; *e.g.* esurio, *hunger;* parturio, *be in labour;* (edo, pario).

APPENDIX C.

OF THE CONSTRUCTION OF CERTAIN VERBS.

MANY Latin verbs have a different construction or use from what would be expected from their ordinary English equivalents. The following are some of the most usual instances, which have not been otherwise noticed in the preceding pages.

(Partly from Madvig and Donaldson.)

Abdico me magistratu, } Abeo magistratu, {	*I resign the magistracy.*
Absum propius a Brundisio,	*I am nearer to Brundisium.*
Adigo aliquem {jusjurandum, ad jusjurandum, jurejurando,	*I put a man to his oath.*
Animadverto aliquem,	*I notice a man.*
Animadverto in aliquem,	*I take notice of,* i.e. *I punish* (often *with death*) *a man.*
Attendo {aliquid, animum ad aliquid,	*I attend to something.*
Aversor scelus,	*I turn away in horror from the crime.*
Cœptus sum laudari (not *cœpi*, with pass. inf.),	*I began to be praised.*
Caveo {aliquem, ab aliquo,	*I am on my guard against some one.*
Caveo hanc summam tibi,	*I give you security for this amount.*
Cedo tibi possessione hortorum,	*I give you up possession of the gardens.*
Circumdo {muros urbi, urbem muris,	*I throw a wall round the city.*
Colloco filiam {viro, in matrimonio,	*I give my daughter* {*a husband. in marriage.*
Commuto mortem cum vitâ,	*I get* (more usually, *give*) *death for life.*
Condemno aliquem {capitis* (not mortis), capite,	*I condemn a man to death.*

* A definite penalty of money or land is always put in the ablative, e. g. damnari *decem millibus, tertia parte agri.*

Condono filium patri,	*I pardon the son out of regard to the father.*
Confero culpam in aliquem,	*I throw the blame on a man.*
Consolor alicujus dolorem,	*I console a man in his distress.*
Convenio aliquem,	{*I have an interview with a man.* {In law, *I sue a man.*
Conveniunt hæc vitia in aliquem,	*These faults are appropriate to a man's character.*
Convēnit tempus {inter nos, {mihi tecum, (not *convenimus de tempore*),	*We have agreed upon the time.*
Defendo { injurias, { aliquem ab injuriis,	*I ward off injuries.* *I defend a man from injury.*
Desitus sum laudari (not *desii*, with pass. inf.),	*I ceased to be praised.*
Dicto audiens sum Cæsari,	*I am obedient to Cæsar.*

(Dicto audiens, i. e. *a hearing person for an order*, has become a compound adjective.)

Doceo aliquem {aliquid, {de aliquâ re,	*I acquaint a man with a thing.*
Dubito, dubius sum {quid hoc sit, {an hoc sit,	*I am doubtful* {*what this is.* {*whether it be so.*
Non dubito quin * hoc sit,	*I do not doubt this being so.*
Cave dubites Quid est quod dubites } {quin hoc facias { or hoc facere,	*Mind you don't hesitate* {*to do* *Why should you hesitate* {*this.*
Excuso {tarditatem litterarum, {me de tarditate litt.,	*I apologize for my tardiness in writing.*
Facio damnum,	*I suffer loss.*
Habeo pecuniæ magnam copiam,	*I have money in great abundance.*
Habeo aliquid conscientiæ,	*I make a thing a point of conscience.*
Impero provinciæ milites,	*I command a province to furnish troops.*
Intercedo rogationi,	*I put a veto on the proposed law.*
Intercedo pro aliquo magnam pecuniam,	*I stand security for a large sum for a person* (*I intercede* is supplicor, deprecor).
Interdico {aliquem sacrificiis {(Cæsar), {alicui aqua et igni {(Cicero),	*I forbid a man to attend* (or *to make*) *sacrifices.* *I forbid a man the use of fire and water.*

* *Quin* follows *negative* and *quasi-negative* expressions only. *Dubito* without a negative has only dependent interrogatives.

Intercludo $\begin{cases} \text{alicui fugam,} \\ \text{aliquem fugâ,} \end{cases}$	*I shut a man out from flight.*
Invehor multa in aliquem,	*I inveigh at length against a man.*
Minor tibi $\begin{cases} \text{mortem,} \\ \text{baculo,} \end{cases}$	*I threaten you* $\begin{cases} \text{with death.} \\ \text{with a stick.} \end{cases}$
Muto oves pretio,	*I get (more usually, give) sheep at a price.*
Nego hoc esse,	*I say this is not so.*
Paro bellum,	*I prepare for war.*
Pendeo ex te,	*I depend on you.*
Peto aliquid ab aliquo,	*I ask a man for something.*
Præsto tibi $\begin{cases} \text{damnum,} \\ \text{impetus populi,} \end{cases}$	*I am answerable to you* $\begin{cases} \text{for the loss} \\ \text{for the outbreaks} \\ \text{of the people.} \end{cases}$
Præsto tibi fidem,	*I keep my word to you.*
Probo librum alicui,	*I gain a man's approval of a book.*
Prohibeo regionem populationibus,	*I prevent the districts being plundered.*
Quæro ex (*or* ab *or* de) aliquo causam,	*I ask a man the cause.*
Recipio in me,	*I pledge myself.*
Recipio alicui,	*I pledge myself to some one.*
Vaco huic negotio,	*I am at liberty to attend to this matter.*
Vacat mihi,	*I have time.*
Valeo apud aliquem,	*I have influence with a person.*
Veto $\begin{cases} \text{te ire,} \\ \text{ne eas (rare),} \end{cases}$ (not *Jubeo non* or *ne*).	$\begin{cases} \textit{I forbid your going.} \\ \textit{I command you not to go.} \end{cases}$

The desire to give early notice of a negative's being in the sentence, as seen in the uses of *nego, veto,* and *cave* (s. v. *dubito*), led the Romans to say, non poterat (or nequibat) facere, *he could not do it;* nec fecit, *and he did not do it;* nec quisquam alius, *and no other* (not *et nemo*); neu quisquam, not *ut nemo,* &c.

Some verbs and phrases which are generally followed by *ut* with subj. take an acc. with inf. when they denote an *opinion:* e. g.

	With subj.	With inf.
adducor,	*I am induced,*	*I am induced to believe.*
auctor sum,	*I advise,*	*I assure.*
cogo,	*I compel,*	*I prove.*

concedo,	*I permit,*	*I grant.*
contendo,	*I strive,*	*I maintain.*
conficio,	*I accomplish,*	*I prove.*
decerno,	*I decree,*	*I judge.*
efficio, see conficio.		
moneo,	*I advise,*	*I remind (that so and so is).*
persuadeo,	*I persuade (to act),*	*I make a person believe.*
statuo,	*I determine (that a person shall),*	*I assume.*

APPENDIX D.

Of the Cases dependent on Adjectives.

The lists, &c. chiefly from Madvig.

It will have been seen from a comparison of § 179, 186, 194, and 199 that the 'Dative, Ablative, and Genitive after Adjectives' have very different origins and usually very different meanings, -preserving in fact their regular characteristics: the Dative being the indirect object, that is, the person (or personified thing) indirectly affected by the existence of the person or thing which possesses the quality denoted by the adjective; the Ablative being either an adverbial adjunct, expressing the attendant circumstances, part concerned, &c., or the thing from which separation takes place; and the Genitive being either the possessor, or the object after a transitive adjective, fulfilling the same functions that a nominative or accusative does with the verb.

But with certain words these meanings may become coincident, so that we find some adjectives used with more than one case, without much practical distinction. Thus we have, Alienum illi causæ, *A thing which is for that case a foreign one.* Alienum existimatione mea, *Foreign from my reputation;* Alienum meæ dignitatis, *Not belonging to my dignity.* But so ex-

tended a range of cases, with similar meaning, is very unusual.
An oscillation between dative and genitive, or ablative and genitive is not so uncommon.

1. The following adjectives have the *dative* of the indirect
object or *genitive* either of the possessor, the adjective being used
substantively, or of the object. (Instead of the *genitive* of the
possessor a possessive pronoun is found, § 56.)

æmulus,	dispar,
æquus,	dissimilis (see similis. So
æqualis,	also other compounds),
affinis,	familiaris,
alienus (also with abl.),	inimicus,
cognatus,	iniquus,
communis,	invidus,
contrarius,	necessarius, *intimate,*
par,	sacer,
propinquus,	superstes,
propior (also with accus.,	supplex,
§ 204. *f*),	similis (of living beings al-
proprius (rarely *dat.*),	most always with *genitive*),
proximus (see *propior*),	superstes.

E. g. Siculi Verri inimici, *Sicilians hostile to Verres.* Ini-
micissimus Ciceronis, *Cicero's bitterest enemy.*

Mihi familiare, *Familiar to me.* Familiarissimus meus, *My
most confidential friend.*

Locus propinquus urbi, *A place near for the city.* In propin-
quis urbis locis, *In the city's neighbourhood.*

Nec diu superstes filio pater, *Nor was there for the son a
father long surviving him.* Superstes omnium suorum, *Outliving
all his friends.*

Par similisque ceteris, *A man of similar character for the
others to consort with.* Versus similes meorum, *Verses, copies of
my own.*

Affinis ei turpitudini, *Akin to* (i. e. *involved in*) *that disgrace.*
Affinis rei capitalis, *An accomplice in a criminal matter.*

Civitas Ubiorum socia nobis, *The state of the Ubii allied to
us;* but, socia generis, *sharing the race.*

2. Many other adjectives, e. g. commodus, obnoxius, &c. are used with a similar *dative.*

Aptus, habilis, idoneus, accommodatus, paratus, are used either with a dative or with *ad* and the accusative.

E. g. Oratores aptissimi concionibus, *Speakers well suited for popular meetings* (or *addresses*). Orator ad nullam causam ido-neus, *A speaker not fit to plead any case whatever.*

N. B. In many examples, commonly given, the dative be-longs to the predicate generally, not to the adjective specially.

3. The following are used with the *ablative* or *genitive;* the former as an ablative of the *means,* or the *part* of a man's pos-sessions, &c., *in respect of* which the particular quality is predicated, the latter as the case usually dependent on adjectives. With the ablative, *full* may be considered to mean *filled with:* with the genitive (of the object) *pouring forth, possessing in abundance.*

dives,	uberrimus (*gen.* rare),
fertilis (in good prose *gen.*),	refertus (*gen.* of persons only),
plenus (usually *gen.*)	completus, do.
opulentus.	

E. g. Referta Gallia negotiatorum est, plena civium Roma-norum, *Gaul is stuffed full of traders, contains Roman citizens in crowds.* Vita undique referta bonis, *Life on all sides crammed with blessings.*

Ager fertilis frugum, *Land fruitful of corn.* Gens Italiæ opulentissima armis, viris, pecunia, *A race in all Italy with the amplest resources in arms, men, and money.*

Locuples, præditus, onustus, &c. have *ablative* only. (The last two are obviously participial forms.) Refertus, completus are true participles, and therefore might be expected to take the *ablative* only. But *completus* follows *compleo :* and *refertus* fol-lows the analogy.

[Madvig (apparently) considers the ablative after *dignus* and *indignus* to be of this class. Key considers it to be the ablative of comparison, and this is at least plausible.]

4. The following have, as might be expected from their meaning, besides a *genitive* of the object, an *ablative* of the thing

lacked (§ 186). But the genitive is not much used in prose after
the last five:

alienus (see above),	liber (with names of persons
egenus,	always ablat. with *ab*),
immunis,	nudus,
inanis,	orbus (rarely with *gen.*),
indigus,	purus,
	vacuus.

E. g. Inanissima prudentiæ, *Most void of* (legal) *skill.* Nulla
epistola inanis aliquâ re utili, *Not a letter without something
useful in it.* Omnia plena consiliorum, inania verborum.

Frugum vacuus, *Devoid of corn.* Mœnia defensoribus vacua,
Walls without defenders.

Extorris with *ablative* only.

Inops, pauper, with *genitive* only.

APPENDIX E.

LIST OF SOME WORDS EASILY CONFUSED.

(Partly from Kennedy and Donaldson.)

ăcer, *maple;*	ācer (adj.), *vigorous.*
arma (pl.), *arms, weapons;*	armus, *shoulder* (of animals).
ăpis, *bee;*	Āpis, *an Egyptian god.*
ăsīlus, *gadfly;*	ăsỹlum, *place of refuge.*
cælo (1st), *I engrave.*	cēlo (1st), *I conceal;*
cælum, *graving tool;*	cælum, *heaven.*
cănis, *dog;*	cānus (adj.), *hoary.*
căno (3rd), *I sing;*	cāneo, *I am hoary.*
cassis (-ĭdis, fem.), *helmet;*	cassis (-is, masc.), *hunter's net.*
cĕdo (§ 89), *give;*	cēdo, *I yield.*

cēdo, cessi, *yield;* cædo, cĕcīdi, *strike;* cădo, cĕcĭdi, *fall.*

clāva, *club;* clāvus, *nail;* clāvis, *key.*

cŏlus, *distaff;*   cōlum, *strainer.*

cŏlo (3rd), *cultivate;*   cōlo (1st), *I strain.*

cŏmĕs (-ĭtis), *companion;*   cōmis (adj.), *affable;*

cŏma, *hair;*   cōmo (3rd), *I arrange.*

cŏmĕdo (-ōnis), *messmate;*   cōmœdus, *comedian.*

cŭpĭdus (adj.), *desirous;*   cŭpīdo, *desire.*

dĕcus (-ŏris), *distinction;*   dĕcor (-ōris), *grace;*

dĕcŏro (1st), *I decorate;*   dĕcōrus (adj.), *graceful.*

dĕdĕre, *they have given;*   dĕdĕre, *to give up.*

dĭco (1st), *I dedicate;*   dīco (3rd), *I tell.*

diffĭdit, *he has cloven;*   diffīdit, *he distrusts.*

dŏlo (1st), *I chip, hew;*   dŏleo, *I have pain.*

ĕdo, *I eat;*   ēdo, *I give forth.*

ĕs, *thou art;* ēs, *thou eatest;* æs, *bronze.*

ēdŭco (1st), *I train;*   ēdūco (3rd), *I lead forth.*

făbŭla, *a little bean;*   fābŭla, *story.*

fĭdē, *by good faith;*   fidĕ, *trust thou.*

forfex, *scissors;* forpex, *curling irons;* forceps, *pincers.*

frĕtum, *sea;*   frētus, *relying.*

fŭgo (1st), *I put to flight;*   fŭgĭo (3rd), *I flee.*

hĭrundo, *a swallow;* hĭrūdo, *leech;* ărundo, *reed.*

ĭdem, *same thing;*   īdem, *same man.*

lăbor, *labour;*   lābor, *I slip.*

lĕvis (adj.), *light;* lēvis (adj.), *smooth;* lævus, *left-handed.*

lĕgo (3rd), *pick, read;*   lēgo, *depute, appoint.*

lĕpus (lepŏris), *hare;*   lĕpor (lĕpōris), *elegance.*

lĭcet, *it is lawful;* lĭceo, *I am valued;* lĭceor, *I bid for.*

lўra, *lyre;*   līra, *furrow.*

mălus (adj.), *bad;* mālum, *apple;* mālo, *I prefer;*

māla, *jaw, cheek;* mālŭs, *mast* of a ship; also *apple-tree.*

mănĕ, *wait thou;*   mānĕ, *morning.*

merx (mercis), *merchandise;*   merces (mercēdis), *hire.*

mulceo, *I soothe;*   mulgeo, *I milk.*

mĭsĕrĭs, *for the wretched;*   mīsĕrīs, *thou shalt have sent.*

nĭteo, *I shine;*   nītor (3rd), *I strive.*

nŏta, *a mark;* nŏtus, *south wind;* nōtus, *known.*

oblĭtus, *smeared;*   oblītus, *forgetful.*

occĭdens, *setting* (sun);   occīdens, *slaying.*

ŏpĕrior (4th), *I am being covered;* oppĕrior (4th), *I am waiting for.*

ŏs (ossis), *bone;*   ōs, ōris *mouth, face.*

părio (3rd), *I bring forth;* păro (1st), *I prepare;* pāreo (2nd), *I obey.*

pendo (3rd), *I hang up, weigh;* pendeo (2nd), *I am hung up.*
pĭla, *a (racquet) ball;*   pīla, *a pillar;*
pĭlus, *a hair;* pīlum, *pike;* pīleus, *cap.*
plăga, *a region;*   plāga, *a blow.*
pŏpŭlus, *a people;*   pōpŭlus, *poplar.*
pŏtĕs, *thou art able;*   pōtēs, *shouldst thou drink.*
prŏcĕres, *nobles;*   prōcērus, *tall.*
prōdĭte, *betray ye;*   prōdīte, *come ye forth.*
prŏfectus, *having started;*   prōfectus, *having been accomplished.*
prūnus, *a plum;* prūna, *a live coal;* prŭīna, *hoar frost.*
rĕfert, *he brings back;*   rēfert, *it is of consequence.* (§ 196, note.)
sĕdeo, *I sit;* sēdes, *a sat;* sīdo, *I settle.*
sĭnus, *fold* (of dress);   sīnum, *bowl.*
tĕrgus (ŏris), *hide* (of beasts); tĕrgum, *back* (of man).
trĭbūlis, *fellow tribesman;* trĭbŭlus, *caltrop;* trībŭlum, *threshing machine.*

ŭtī (adv.), *as, that;*   ūtī, *to use.*
văs, vădis, *bail;*   vas, vāsis, *vessel.*
vĕlīs, *shouldst thou wish;*   vēlīs, *with sails.*
vĕnio, *I come;* vēni, *I came;* vēneo (4th), *I am sold.*
vĭres, *Thou art green;*   vīres (plur.), *strength.*

APPENDIX F.

SPECIMENS OF OLD LATIN.

THE following extracts from old Latin laws and inscriptions which have been preserved to us will show the student some old forms of words and some old spelling. Both will be found very suggestive in etymological inquiries. A transcription in more recent Latin is given in italics. The punctuation throughout is modern.

(Chiefly from Donaldson's *Varronianus;* see also his *Lat. Gram.* Appendix I.)

1. From a Tribunitian law, 493 B.C.

Set, qui aliuta faxsit, ipsos Jovei sacer estod ; et sei qui im, quei eo plebei scito sacer siet, ocisit, pariceidas ne estod.

Si quis aliter fecerit ipse Jovi sacer esto ; et siquis eum, qui eo plebis scito sacer sit, occiderit parricida ne esto.

2. From the XII. Tables, 450 B.C.

Sei volet, suo vivito : ni suo vivit, qui em vinctum habebit, libras farris endo dies dato ; si volet plus dato. (Of a debtor imprisoned.) Em is *eum;* endo is *in.*

Tertiis nundinis partis secanto : si plus minusve secuerunt, se fraude esto. (Of the creditor's rights over the person of an insolvent debtor.) Partis is acc. pl. Se (i. e. *sine*) fraude esto : *It shall be without risk (to the creditors).*

Si pater filium ter venum duit, filius a patre liber esto. Duit is for *det.*

Si morbus ævitasque vitium escit, qui in jus vocabit, jumentum dato : *If disease or age shall prevent (a defendant's appearing to a summons), the plaintiff shall furnish a beast* (to draw or carry him). Escit (apparently an inchoative form) is for *erit.*

3. Epitaph on L. Cornelius Scipio, cir. 260 B.C.

L. Cornelio' L. F. Scipio
Aidiles . Cosol . Cesor.

Honc oino' ploirume cosentiont Romani
Duonoro' optimo' fuise viro'
Luciom Scipione'. Filios Barbati
Cosol Cesor Aidiles hic fuet apud vos.
Hec cepit Corsica' Aleria'que urbe'
Dedet tempestatebus aide' mereto.

L. Cornelius L. F. Scipio Ædiles, Consul, Censor.

Hunc unum plurimi consentiunt Romani
Bonorum optimum fuisse virum
L. Scipionem. Filius Barbati
Consul, Censor, Ædiles, hic fuit apud vos.
Hic cepit Corsicam, Aleriamque urbem.
Dedit tempestatibus ædem merito.

4. From an inscription on the Columna Rostrata, referring to the exploits of C. Duilius, who was Consul B.C. 260.

En eodem macistratod bene rem navebos marid Consol primos ceset, socios clasesque navales primos ornavet paravetque, cumque eis navebos claseis Pœnicas omneis et maxsumas copias Cartaciniensis, præsented sumod dictatored olorum, in altod marid pucnad vicet.

In eodem magistratu bene rem navibus mari consul primus gessit, socios classesque navales primus ornavit paravitque, cumque iis navibus classes Punicas omnes et maximas copias Carthaginienses, præsente summo Dictatore illorum, in alto mari pugnâ vicit.

5. From Q. ENNIUS (who died 169 B.C.).

Pellitur e medio sapientia, vei geritur res
Spernitur orator bonus, horridu' miles amatur;
Haut docteis dicteis certanteis, sed male dicteis,
Miscent inter sese inimicitias agitanteis
Non ex joure manu' consertum sed magi' ferro
Rem repetunt regnumque petunt, vadunt solida vei.

vei = *vi;* horridu', manu', magi' = *horridus, manus, magis;* docteis, dicteis = *doctis, dictis;* certanteis, agitanteis = *certantes, agitantes.*

6. From the Senatus consultum de Bacchanalibus, B.C. 186 referred to by Livy XXXIX. 14 (given in full by Donaldson, *Varron.* p. 270).

Neiquis eorum Sacanal habuise velet; sei ques esent, quei sibei deicerent necesus ese Bacanal habere, eeis utei ad pr. urbanum Romam venirent...... Bacas vir ne quis adiese velet ceivis Romanus, neve nominus Latini neve socium quisquam,... neve post hac inter sed coniourase neve comvovise neve conspondise neve conpromesise velet,... sacra in oquoltod ne quisquam fecise velet, neve in poplicod neve in preivatod, neve exstrad urbem sacra quisquam fecise velet, nisei pr. urbanum adieset isque de senatuos sententiad, dum ne minus senatoribus c. adesent quom ea res cosoleretur iousisent, censuere... sei ques esent quei arvorsum ead fecisent, quam suprad scriptum est, eeis rem caputalem faciendam censuere; atque utei hoce in tabolam ahenam inceideretis. Ita senatus aiquom censuit. Uteique eam figier ioubeatis ubei facilumed gnoscier potisit.

Nequis eorum Bacchanal habuisse vellet; si qui essent, qui sibi dicerent necesse esse Bacchanal habere, ei uti ad prætorem urbanum Romam venirent......Bacchas vir ne quis adiisse vellet civis Romanus neve nominis Latini neve sociorum quisquam,...neve post hac inter se conjurâsse neve convovisse neve conspondisse, neve compromisisse vellet,...sacra in occulto ne quisquam fecisse vellet neve in publico neve in privato, neve extra urbem sacra quisquam fecisse vellet, nisi prætorem urbanum adiisset isque de senatûs sententia, dum ne minus senatoribus centum adessent quum ea res consuleretur, jussissent, censuere...si qui essent qui adversum ea fecissent, quam supra scriptum est, eis rem capitalem faciendam censuere; atque uti hoc in tabulam ahenam incideretis. Ita senatus æquum censuit. Utique eam figi jubeatis ubi facillime nosci possit.

Compromisisse vellet]. This use of the perf. inf. with verbs expressing *will* and *power* (§ 246, 1. not 2 or 3), was imitated by the poets, e. g. Fratres tendentes opaco Pelion imposuisse Olympo. Hor. *Od.* III. 4. 52).

7. From the old Roman law on the Bantine table (probably not older than the middle of the 7th century A.U.C.).

Seiquis mag. multam inrogare volet, ei multam inrogare liceto, dum minoris partus familias taxsat, liceto.

If any magistrate shall wish to impose a fine, it shall be allowed him to impose a fine provided that he fix it at a less part of his property (than the fine named before). Partus = *partis.* This shows the origin of dumtaxat, *estimating,* i. e. *precisely, only.*

APPENDIX G.

OF THE TENSES, &c. IN THE EPISTOLARY STYLE.

(Partly from Key, *Lat. Gr.* § 1160, 1161. See also
Madvig, § 345.)

THE use of the tenses in epistolary writing is occasionally
very peculiar. The letters of the Romans being sent nearly
always by private hand, and the roads with the facilities for
travelling being very defective, a long time often elapsed between
the writing and the receiving a letter. Hence it was not uncommon for the writer to make allowance for this interval, and
to use those tenses which were suited to the time when the letter
should be read, viz. the imperfect and pluperfect for the present
and perfect, and the participle in -*rus* with *eram* to express an
immediate purpose. The perfect also frequently refers to the
time of the letter in which it occurs. This use of the secondary
tenses seems much more Cicero's habit (partly due to the familiar
nature of much of his correspondence) than that of others, if we
may judge from such letters as are included in the collection
entitled *Ciceronis Epistolæ ad Familiares.* Nor is it at all common in Pliny's letters.

Nihil habebam quod scriberem; neque enim novi quidquam
audieram, et ad tuas omnes epistolas rescripseram pridie; sed
quum me ægritudo non solum somno privaret, &c. (Cic. ad Att.
ix. 10. § 1.) The receiver of the letter would repeat this as
follows: *Tum quum Cicero hanc epistolam scripsit, nihil habebat
quod scriberet; neque enim novi quidquam audicrat et ad omnes
meas epistolas rescripserat pridie, sed quum eum ægritudo,* &c.

Etsi nil sane habebam novi, quod post accidisset quam dedis-
sem ad te Philogĕni* litteras, tamen quum Philotimum Romam

---

* Notice that the letter-carrier is in *dative* case; the person
addressed is *accusative* with *ad*. So, Ad te ideo antea rarius
scripsi, quod non habebam idoneum *cui* darem, nec satis sciebam

remitterem, scribendum aliquid ad te fuit, &c. (Cic. ad Att. vi.
3. § 1.) *Although I have indeed nothing new to report that has
occurred since I gave my last to Philogenes to take to you, yet as I
am sending Philotimus back to Rome, I am bound to write something to you.* (The tenses would naturally have been *habeo,
acciderit, dederim, remittam, est.*)

Triginta dies erant ipsi, quum has dabam litteras, per quos
nullas .a vobis acceperam. (Cic. ad Att. iii. 21.) *It is now
exactly thirty days since I heard from you.*

For additional examples see e.g. Cic. ad Att. iv. 3. § 5. v. 10.
§ 1. 15. § 3. 16. § 1, 4. &c. ad Q. Fr. ii. 7. &c. Plin. *Epist.* vii.
19, § 11.

The secondary tenses occur where the writer has specially
in mind the particular time of his writing, and is describing the
feelings and occurrences of the moment; and so most frequently
at the beginning and end of letters. But they are not always
adopted where they might be; and we often find the primary
tenses in close connection with the others. Thus:

Ego tuas opiniones de his rebus exspecto. Formias me con-
tinuo recipere cogitabam. (Cic. ad Att. vii. 15, at end of letter.)
*I expect to hear your thoughts on these matters. I am at this
moment thinking of taking myself off at once to Formiæ.*

Ipse, ut spero, diebus octo quibus has litteras dabam cum
Lepidi copiis me conjungam. (Plancus apud Cic. ad Fam. x. 18.
sub fin.) *I hope myself to join Lepidus' forces within eight days
from the time of despatching this letter.*

Vos quid ageretis in republica, quum has litteras dabam, non
sciebam. Audiebam quædam turbulenta, quæ scilicet cupio esse
falsa, ut aliquando ociosa libertate fruamur, quod vel minime
mihi adhuc contigit. (Trebonius apud Cic. ad Fam. xii. 16.)
*What is the state of politics at present with you, I am at the time
of writing this ignorant: I hear however that there are some dis-
turbances, which you may be sure I wish may prove not to be the
case, so that we may at length enjoy our liberty in ease: a thing
which as yet has fallen very little indeed to my lot.*

quo darem, *The reason why I did not write to you so frequently
before, (as I should otherwise have done,) was because I had not
any safe person to carry a letter, nor was I sure of your address*
(quo, *whither*). Both dative, and *ad* with accusative, are used for
the person addressed after *scribo, mitto,* &c.

This mode of writing a letter, as if it were a subsequent narrative, led sometimes to an oblique mode of giving the date of the letter.

Puteolis magnus est rumor Ptolemæum esse in regno...Pompeius in Cumanum Parilibus vēnit; misit ad me statim qui salutem nuntiaret. Ad eum postridie mane vadebam, quum hæc scripsi. (Cic. ad Att. iv. 10.) *We have a strong report down here that Ptolemy has been restored to his throne...Pompey arrived at his villa yesterday. He forthwith sent one of his people with his compliments to me. I am going to pay him a visit this morning.*

Puteoli, April 22nd. (The festival of Pales being on the 21st.)

A Roman letter always begins with a greeting, and the date is either interwoven with the letter or appears at the end. The greeting contains the names of the sender and receiver of the letter, sometimes with full titles, (especially if the letter be at all formal,) sometimes without, and the words *salutem dicit* (i.e. *says 'salve'*) (S. D.), or, *salutem plurimam dicit* (S. P. D.), or, simply *salutem* (S.), exprest by initials, either between the names of the sender and receiver, or after both. Thus:

Cæsar Imp. Ciceroni Imp. S. D. *Cæsar General sends greeting to Cicero General.*

Cn. Magnus Procos, S. D. M. Ciceroni Imp. *Cnæus (Pompeius) Magnus Proconsul, sends greeting to Marcus Cicero General.*

Cicero Dolabellæ Cos. suo S. *Cicero to his dear Dolabella Consul greeting.*

M. Tullius M. F. M. N. Cicero Imp. S. D. C. Cælio L. F. C. N. Caldo Quæst. *Marcus Tullius, son of Marcus, grandson of Marcus, Cicero General sends greeting to C. Cœlius, son of Lucius, grandson of Caius, Caldus Quæstor.*

Cicero App. Pulchro ut spero Censori S. D. *Cicero to Appius Pulcher, Censor as I hope, sends greeting.*

Plancus Imp. Cos. Des. S. D. Coss. Prætt. Tribb. Pl. S. P. Pl. Q. R. *Plancus General Consul elect sends greeting to the Consuls, Prætors, Tribunes of the Commons, Senate, Burghers, and Commons of Rome.*

Tullius Terentiæ suæ et pater suavissimæ filiæ, Cicero matri et sorori S. D. P. *Tullius sends hearty greeting to his dear Terentia, and the father* (i. e. *Cicero himself*) *to his darling daughter, Cicero* (i.e. *the son*) *to his mother and sister.*

The date is given thus:

Dat. v. Id. Decembr. a Pontio ex Trebulano. *Despatched on Dec. 9 from Pontius' house at Trebula* (lit. from his Trebulan villa, cf. § 160. 185).

Ab Appii foro horâ quartâ. *From Appii Forum at the 4th hour.*

Kal. Jan. M. Messala, M. Pisone Coss. *Jan. 1st, in the Consulship of Marcus Messala and Marcus Piso.*

D. Liberalibus. *Despatched on the festival of Liber* (i. e. March 17).

Dat. xiiii. Kal. Quinct. Thessalonicâ. *Thessalonica, June 17.* (Written before B.C. 45.)

viii. Idus Jan. Cularone ex finibus Allobrogum. *Jan. 6, Cularo,* (now *Grenoble,*) *in the territories of the Allobroges.*

Pliny's letters (excepting those to Trajan) end with *Vale.* Cicero's sometimes do so; but as a general rule have no formal conclusion.

APPENDIX H.

Of the Roman Way of expressing the Date.

(Partly from Madvig, *Suppl. to Gram.*)

The division of time into weeks of seven days with distinct names was not used by the ancient Romans (before the introduction of Christianity). The months were distinguished by the names adopted by us from the Romans, excepting that, before the time of the Emperor Augustus, *Julius* and *Augustus* had the names of *Quinctīlis* and *Sextīlis* (i. e. fifth and sixth month, March being the first). The days of the month were computed from three leading days in each, which were called respectively *Calendæ (Kal.)*, *Nonæ (Non.)*, and *Idus (Id.)*; to these the name of the month was appended as an adjective. The *Calendæ* was the first day of every month; the *Nonæ* and *Idus* the fifth and thirteenth, except in the months of March, May, July, and October, in which they were the seventh and fifteenth respectively. From these days they counted backwards, the days between the 1st and the Nones being reckoned as so many days before the Nones; the days between the Nones and Ides as so many days before the Ides; and the remaining days of the month as so many days before the Kalends of the *next* month. The day immediately preceding any of these reckoning points was called *pridie Nonas*, &c.; the day next but one before was the *third* day before (since the Nones, &c. were themselves included in the reckoning), and so on.

There are two abbreviated modes of denoting the date, e. g. the 27th of March might be marked as VI *Kal. Apr.*, or *a. d.* VI *Kal. Apr.* The first is for *sexto (die ante) Kalendas Apriles;* the second for *ante diem sextum Kalendas Apriles.* The later expression appears to have originally signified *before (on the sixth day) the Kalends of April;* the exact day being thrown in parenthetically, and attracted from the ablative into the accusative case in consequence of following *ante.* · Similarly we find the date some-times denoted by the number of days preceding a festival; as, *a. d.* v *Terminalia,* i.e. 19th Feb. (the festival of the god of boundaries being on the 23rd Feb.). This expression was con-sidered as one word, before which *in* or *ex* may stand; as, Ex ante diem III Nonas Junias usque ad pridie Kalendas Septem-bres, *from the 3rd to the 31st August;* differre aliquid in ante diem xv Kalendas Novembres, *to put off something to the 18th October.*

The readiest way of reckoning the day is, (1) if the date lie between the Kalends and Nones, or between the Nones and Ides, to subtract the number of the day mentioned from the number of the day on which the Nones or Ides fall, and add *one* (for the inclusive reckoning): (2) if the date lie between the Ides and the Kalends, to subtract the number of the day mentioned from the number of the days in the month, and add *two* (i. e. one for the inclusive reckoning, and *one* because the Kalends are not the last of the month in which the date lies, but the first of the following month).

In leap year the intercalated day was counted between *a. d.* VI *Kal. Mart.* and *a. d.* VII *Kal. Mart.* and denominated *a. d. bissextum Kal. Mart.,* so that *a. d.* VII *Kal. Mart.* answers as in the ordinary February to Feb. 23, and *a. d.* VIII. *Kal. Mart.* to Feb. 22nd, &c. (Hence the name of leap year, *annus bissextilis.*)

Before the reformation of the Calendar by Julius Cæsar, B. C. 45, the number of days in the months were in March, May, July, and October, 31 ; in February 28 ; in all the rest 29. (Hence, as these four months were two days longer, the Nones and Ides were two days later.) This should be remembered in reading Cicero's letters, many of which were written before 45 B.C. After that year the number of days in each month was the same as it is with us to this day.

The following examples suppose the date to be *subsequent to* B. C. 45. The usual abbreviated form is given. [It must be remembered that Kalendæ, Nonæ, and Idus are feminine, and the months *adjectives;* that the date (' *on the first,*' &c.) is in the ablative (*Kalendis, Nonis, Idibus*); and that *a. d.* VI *Non. Mart.* &c. is for *ante diem sextum Nonas Martias.*]

Day of English month.	January (So also Aug., Dec.).	April (So also Jun., Sept., Nov.).	March (So also May, Jul., Oct.).
1	Kal. Jan.	Kal. Apr.	Kal. Mart.
2	a. d. IV Non. Jan.	a. d. IV Non. Apr.	a. d. VI Non. Mart.
4	Prid. Non. Jan.	Prid. Non. Apr.	a. d. IV Non. Mart.
5	Non. Jan.	Non. Apr.	a. d. III Non. Mart.
6	a. d. VIII Id. Jan.	a. d. VIII Id. Apr.	Prid. Non. Mart.
7	a. d. VII Id. Jan.	a. d. VII Id. Apr.	Non. Mart.
8	a. d. VI Id. Jan.	a. d. VI Id. Apr.	a. d. VIII Id. Mart.
12	Prid. Id. Jan.	Prid. Id. Apr.	a. d. IV Id. Mart.
13	Id. Jan.	Id. Apr.	a. d. III Id. Mart.
14	a. d. XIX Kal. Feb.	a. d. XVIII Kal. Mai.	Prid. Id. Mart.
15	a. d. XVIII Kal. Feb.	a. d. XVII Kal. Mai.	Id. Mart.
16	a. d. XVII Kal. Feb.	a. d. XVI Kal. Mai.	a. d. XVII Kal. Jun.
30	a. d. III Kal. Feb.	Prid. Kal. Mai.	a. d. III Kal. Jun.
31	Prid. Kal. Feb.		Prid. Kal. Jun.

APPENDIX I.

OF THE ROMAN COMPUTATION OF MONEY.

(Partly from Madvig. *Suppl. to Gram.*)

SUMS of money were generally computed among the Romans by the *sestertius* (*nummus sestertius*, or *nummus* simply), a silver coin, first coined B.C. 269, when it was equal to $2\frac{1}{2}$ asses (§ 72), and subsequently, B.C. 217, reduced to four asses, about 2d. These are counted regularly, e. g. *trecenti sestertii, duo millia sestertiorum*, or *sestertiûm, decies centum millia sestertiûm*, i. e. 1,000,000 sesterces, or (omitting *centum millia*) *decies sestertiûm*.

The word *sestertium* appears to have been misunderstood and eventually treated as a neuter substantive (but never as a nom. or acc. sing.). Thus, when used with numeral adverbs, it is

declined in the singular number; as, sestertio decies fundum
emi, *I bought the farm for a million sesterces.*   When used with
cardinal numbers it is used in the plural; as, septem sestertia
seven (thousand) sesterces.   It will be seen that in the former case
sestertium denotes 100,000 sesterces; in the latter 1000 sesterces.
It is best in English always to use *sesterce* as the translation of
sestertius, and multiply for *sestertium.*

> duo sestertii, 2 *sesterces.*
> decem sestertii, 10 *sesterces.*
> centum sestertii, 100 *sesterces.*
> mille sestertium, 1000 (*of*) *sesterces.*
> duo millia sestertium, } 2000 *sesterces.*
> duo sestertia,
> centum, } millia sestertium, } 100,000 *sesterces.*
> centena,
> centum sestertia,
> bis centena millia sestertium, } 200,000 *sesterces.*
> bis sestertium,
> decies, &c., 1,000,000 *sesterces.*

HS is used as a symbol for sestert*ius* (§ 72), sestert*ium*, sestert*ia;* and the context frequently can alone decide which is
meant.   Sometimes a line is drawn over the numeral figure to
denote thousands.

HS. X. may mean decem sestertii   = 10 *sesterces.*
decem sestertia   = 10,000 *sesterces* (or HS.X.)
decies sestertiûm = 1,000,000 *sesterces.*

The distributive adjectives (as well as the cardinals), e.g.
centena, are used in these expressions of multiplication, without
meaning 100,000 *each* person &c.   (They here mean 100 taken
each of ten &c. times).

APPENDIX K.

(Partly from Kennedy, Donaldson, Madvig).

(1) *First Names* (Prænomina).

A.	Aulus.	M'.	Manius.
App.	Appius.	Mam.	Mamercus.
C. or G.	Caius or (more correctly) Gaius.	N. or Num.	Numerius.
		P.	Publius.
Cn. or Gn.	Cnæus or (more correctly) Gnæus.	Q.	Quintus.
		S. or Sex.	Sextus.
D.	Decimus.	Ser.	Servius.
K.	Kæso.	Sp.	Spurius.
L.	Lucius.	T.	Titus.
M.	Marcus.	Ti.	Tiberius.

Women's names are exprest by inverted characters; as, ꓳ for Caia.

(2) *Titles of Persons, &c.*

ÆD. CUR.	Ædilis Curulis.	O. M.	Optimus Maximus (title of Jupiter).
COS.	Consul.		
COSS.	Consules.	P. C.	Patres Conscripti.
D.	Divus.	P. M.	Pontifex Maximus.
DES.	Designatus.	PRÆT. PRÆTT.	Prætor, Prætores.
F.	Filius.		
III VIRI A.A.A. F.F.	Tres viri auro argento ære flando feriundo.	PROC.	Proconsul.
		PROQ.	Proquæstor.
		P. R.	Populus Romanus.
III VIR. R.C.	Triumvir reipublicæ constituendæ.	QUIR.	Quirites.
		RESP.	Respublica.
IMP.	Imperator.	R. P. P. R. Q.	Respublica Populi Romani Quiritium.
N.	Nepos.		

S. P. Q. R.   Senatus Populusque
　　　　　　　Romanus.
S. P. P. Q. R. Senatus   Populus
　　　　　　　Plebesque Romana.
Tʀ. Pʟ.   Tribunus Plebis.
Tʀ. Pᴏᴛ.   Tribunicia Potestate.

X. V.   Decemvir.
X. Vɪʀ. Sᴛʟ. Jᴜᴅɪᴋ. Decemvir
　　　　stlitibus (i. e. litibus)
　　　　judicandis.
XV. V. S. F. Quindecimviri sa-
　　　　cris faciundis.

The name of the tribe to which a person belonged is sometimes added to the name in an abbreviated form ; thus, *Pup.* for
Pupiniā. See § 185, and Cælius' letter in Cic. *Epist. ad Fam.*
vɪɪɪ. 8, § 5.

(3) *Sepulchral.*

F. C.   Faciundum curavit.
H. C. E.   Hic conditus est.
H. S. E.   Hic situs est.

OB.   Obiit.
P. C.   Ponendum curavit.
V.   Vixit.

(4) *In voting on trials.*　　*In voting on laws.*

A.   Absolvo.
C.   Condemno.
N. L.   Non liquet.

A. P.   Antiquam (legem) probo.
V. R.   Uti rogas.

(5) *Epistolary.*

D.   Data (est epistola).
S. D.   Salutem dicit.
S. P. D.   Salutem plurimam dicit.
S.   Salutem (dicit).
S. V. B. E. E. V.   Si vales, bene est: ego valeo.
S. T. E. Q. V. B. E. E. Q. V.   Si tu exercitusque valetis bene
　　est: ego quoque valeo.
S. V. G. V.   Si vales gaudeo. Valeo.

See also Appendix G.

(6) *In decrees of the Senate.*

D. E. R. I. C.   De ea re ita censuerunt.
I. N.   Intercessit nemo.
S. C.   Senatus consultum.

Scr. arf.   Scribendo adfuerunt.
V. F.   Verba fecit.

(7) *Miscellaneous.*

A. U. C.	Anno urbis conditæ.	F. F. F.	Felix, faustum, for-
D. D.	Dono dedit.		tunatum.
DD.	Dederunt.	ITER.	Iterum.
D. D. D.	Dat, dicat, dedicat.	L.	Libertas.
D. M.	Dis manibus.	M. P.	Mille Passuum.
Q. B. F. F. Q. S.	Quod bonum felix faustumque sit.		

(8) *Modern Latin.*

A. C. Anno Christi.
A. D. Anno Domini.
a. C. n. } ante } Christum natum.
p. C. n. } post }
C. P. P. C. Collatis pecuniis ponendum curaverunt.
cet. cetera.
cf. confer, or, conferatur.
coll. collato, or, collatis.
Cod. Codd. Codex, Codices.
del. dele, or deleatur.
D. O. M. Deo optimo maximo.
ed. edd. editio, editiones.
etc. et cetera.
h. e. hoc est.
I. C. Jesus Christus.
Ictus. Juris consultus.
ibid. ibidem.
id. idem.
i. e. id est.

i. q. id quod.
L. or Lib. Libb. Liber, Libri.
L. B. Lectori Benevolo.
l. c. loco citato.
l. l. loco laudato.
leg. lege, or, legatur.
L. S. Locus Sigilli.
MS. MSS. Manuscriptum, Manuscripta.
N. B. Nota bene.
N. T. Novum Testamentum.
obs. observa, or, observetur.
P. S. Postscriptum.
sc. scilicet.
sq. sqq. sequenti, sequentibus.
vid. vide.
viz. videlicet.
V. cel. Vir celeberrimus.
V. cl. Vir clarissimus.
V. T. Vetus Testamentum.

For EU product safety concerns, contact us at Calle de José Abascal, 56–1°,
28003 Madrid, Spain or eugpsr@cambridge.org.

www.ingramcontent.com/pod-product-compliance
Ingram Content Group UK Ltd.
Pitfield, Milton Keynes, MK11 3LW, UK
UKHW010335140625
459647UK00010B/623